The Sāṃkhya System

SUNY series in Hindu Studies

Wendy Doniger, editor

The Sāṃkhya System

Accounting for the Real

Edited by
Christopher Key Chapple

SUNY
PRESS

Cover art: Gayatri Sehgal

Published by State University of New York Press, Albany

Printed in the United States of America

For information, contact State University of New York Press, Albany, NY
www.sunypress.edu

Library of Congress Cataloging-in-Publication Data

Name: Chapple, Christopher Key, 1954– editor.
Title: The sāṃkhya system : accounting for the real / edited by Christopher Key Chapple.
Description: Albany : State University of New York Press, [2024]. | Series: SUNY series in Hindu studies | Includes bibliographical references and index.
Identifiers: LCCN 2023050587 | ISBN 9781438498362 (hardcover : alk. paper) | ISBN 9781438498386 (ebook)
Subjects: LCSH: Sankhya. | Īśvarakṛṣṇa. Sāṅkhyakārikā—Criticism and interpretation. | Prakṛti (Sankhya) | Reality—Religious aspects—Hinduism.
Classification: LCC B132.S3 S165 2024 | DDC 181/.41—dc23/eng/20240305
LC record available at https://lccn.loc.gov/2023050587

Dedicated to Gerald James Larson

Contents

Regarding Ardhanārīśvara ix
Gayatri Sehgal

Preface xi

Introduction 1
Christopher Key Chapple

Sāṃkhya Kārikā of Īśvarakṛṣṇa 11

Part I
Philosophical and Textual Approaches to the *Sāṃkhya Kārikā*

Chapter 1
What Is the Ground of Manifest Reality in the *Sāṃkhya Kārikā*? An Existential Phenomenological Theory of *Vyaktaprakṛti* as the Self-Manifesting of *Saṃyoga* 25
Geoff Ashton

Chapter 2
The Role of Vitality (*Prāṇa*) in the Sāṃkhya Quest for Freedom 41
Ana Laura Funes Maderey

Chapter 3
The Place of Meditative Soteriological Practice in Sāṃkhya Philosophy 77
Mikel Burley

Chapter 4
The Determinative Nature of the Guṇas and Bhāvas in the *Sāṃkhya Karikā* 93
Christopher Key Chapple

Chapter 5
प्रत्यय Pratyaya: State of Mind in Yoga and Sāṃkhya 115
Srivatsa Ramaswami

Part II
Living Expressions of Sāṁkhya

Chapter 6
Kāpil Maṭh: A Contemporary Living Tradition of Sāṃkhyayoga 123
Marzenna Jakubczak

Chapter 7
Observing Sāṃkhya Categories in a Mid-Twentieth-Century Village 149
McKim Marriott

Chapter 8
Sāṃkhya/Yoga as Culture and Release 187
Alfred Collins

Appendix: *Sāṃkhya Kārikā* Grammatical Analysis 213
Rob Zabel

Bibliography 269

Contributors 279

Index 281

Regarding Ardhanārīśvara

The painting on the cover of this book refers directly to the Vedic deity Ardhanārīśvara, often used to depict the Sāṃkhya concept of Puruṣa and Prakṛti. A translation of Ardhanārīśvara is "the half-female Lord," referring to the masculine half as the base from which the half-feminine has emerged. The dominant right side is typically the masculine. This painting reinterprets the common depiction, with a mirror-like intent. With ecofeminist intentionality, this depiction of Ardhanārīśvara fuses Kālī Mātā, a form of Pārvatī who embodies the destructive masculinity of Lord Śiva, with a *hijra* individual, a traditional gender identity adopted commonly by assigned-male-at-birth or intersex people in South Asia. One may choose to view the Kālī Mātā half as Lord Śiva's depiction and the human half as Pārvatī's depiction.

The imagery invites viewers to question current conceptions around philosophy and gender. Whereas, in Sāṃkhya, Puruṣa is mapped out as masculine with Prakṛti as the feminine, each individual one of us contains and occupies both these entities. Therefore, associations implying woman/feminine/female as the same, or man/masculine/male as the same, rob us from our full expression and self-understanding.

Within Nature, non-human animals such as clownfish and seahorses can transition between male and female, and species such as crustaceans, snakes, and some songbirds can be gyandromorphic, meaning they have both male and female characteristics at one time. That is just the tip of the ecological iceberg. Today, more than ever, Earth's expressions yearn to be protected and seen for Their sacred value.

And the Earth, too, is within us. Many cultures have acknowledged the existence of humans outside the gender binary, such as two-spirit, trans, gender expansive, and *hijra* people, amongst many others. Regardless of our present identity, as we read this translation of the *Sāṃkhya Kārikā,* we have an opportunity to contemplate our true Nature. With this painting, I invite us to reimagine our cultural expectations to include all forms of all sentient beings.

Gayatri Sehgal
they / them / fae / faer
artivist & founder of bodhisattvism
M.A. Yoga Studies, LMU

Preface

Gerald Larson advanced the study of Sāṃkhya within academic discourse in the 1960s. The field of religious studies as a discipline separate from seminary training emerged during the tumult of the countercultural movement in America. People were searching for the alternative worldviews offered by Asian and shamanic systems of thought and practice. Influenced by the philosophy of Friedrich Nietzsche, a "death of God" movement emerged, paving the way for what is now referred to as the spiritual-not-religious movement. As a student of Sanskrit at Columbia, Larson landed upon Sāṃkhya as an important non-theistic voice. The publication of *Classical Sāṃkhya* in 1969 inspired an entire generation of young scholars, eager to understand this paradoxical worldview, conceptually adjacent to the perspectival phenomenology of Husserl, Heidegger, Heisenberg, and Ortega y Gasset.

Larson responded positively to an invitation from me, a newly minted PhD, to participate in a conference on Sāṃkhya and Yoga in 1981 at The Institute for Advanced Studies of World Religions at the State University of New York at Stony Brook where I served as Assistant Director. He suggested that we also invite Professor Usharbudh Arya of the University of Minnesota, who later took the name Swami Veda Bharati. We were joined at the conference by Frank Podgorski, who did his doctoral dissertation at Fordham on Sāṃkhya; John B. Chettimathan, author of several well-regarded books on Indian thought; John Borelli, who had studied Carl Jung's fraught and freighted relationship with Yoga; as well as Gerald Turchetto (heremeneutics) and Ernest McClain (musicality and number usage). My own paper focused on the three "languages" of the *Yoga Sūtra*: emergence, retreat, and freedom. We all listened intently to Larson as he held forth on various aspects of the Sāṃkhya tradition, including the bridge it makes to then-new ideas regarding consciousness.

Gerry and I became Southern California colleagues for a number of years after I arrived at Loyola Marymount University in 1985, before he left to found the India Studies Center at Indiana University. We were both regular participants at the Southern California Seminar on South Asia and collaborated on various projects with Ninian Smart and Dr. Pratapaditya Pal, Curator of Indian Art at the Los Angeles County Museum of Art. We also met up at the Muktananda Ashram in South Fallsburg at the invitation of Swami Chidvilasananda, who hosted many scholars of Indian philosophy there. I taught the *Bhagavad Gītā* and the *Yoga Sūtra*. Gerry taught Sāṃkhya. After retiring from Indiana, Gerry lectured on Sāṃkhya at LMU to the first class of Yoga Studies graduate students. Three years after his unexpected passing, his wife Claire invited me, at Dr. Pal's urging, to peruse Gerry's library. Many important and rare materials have now been integrated into the LMU collection, to be used by future students and scholars.

Honoring the ancestors has long been part of the human narrative. By dedicating this book to Gerald James Larson, we hope to acknowledge, explain, and perhaps improve upon his pioneering studies of what he and many others considered to be the original philosophy of India.

Introduction

CHRISTOPHER KEY CHAPPLE

This book seeks to elucidate the *Sāṃkhya Kārikā* and its view of self and world. The late Gerald Larson hailed Sāṃkhya as the foundation for all aspects of Indian philosophy. Sāṃkhya spans the fields of physics, metaphysics, psychology, and ethics. Its intent is soteriological: Sāṃkhya charts a pathway to freedom. Notably not theological, its key premises and observations overlap with virtually all religious traditions that originate from India.

Sāṃkhya espouses a reciprocity between Prakṛti, the realm of activity, and Puruṣa, the silent witness. It also delineates the phenomenal experiences that arise from Prakṛti, including the operations of the human body, the five great elements, and mental states. Its foundational ideas can be found in *Ṛg Veda* 1.164.20, also quoted in the *Maṇḍuka* and *Śvetāśvatara* Upaniṣads: "Two birds associated together, and mutual friends, take refuge in the same tree; one of them eats the sweet fig; the other abstaining from food, merely looks on." The active bird symbolizes Prakṛti and the bird looking on serves as a metaphor for Puruṣa.

The legacy of Sāṃkhya studies is vast, stretching back at least 1500 years. Gauḍapāda's commentary or Bhāṣya (sixth century) was brought into English translation by T. G. Mainkar, who acknowledges the works of "Colebrooke, Wilson, S. Sastri, N. A. Sastri, Har Dutt Sharma, Sovani . . . Keith, Takakusu, Jacobi, Dasgupta, [and] Radhakrishnan" as important resources for his own work. He also consulted the unattributed *Yuktidīpikā* as he prepared the second edition of his translation.[1] Gerald James Larson opened a new chapter on Sāṃkhya studies with *Classical Sāṃkhya: An Interpretation of Its History and Meaning* (Motilal Banarsidass, 1969, 1979), his volume on Sāṃkhya in the Encyclopedia of Indian Philosophies (1987), and his final work, *Classical Yoga Philosophy and the Legacy of Sāṃkhya* (2018).

The appeal of Sāṃkhya can be summarized in comments made by two late scholars, Bhagwan B. Singh (Philosophy, University of Nevada, Las Vegas) and Frank Podgorski (Religious Studies, Seton Hall). Bhagwan Singh saw Sāṃkhya as a perfect fit for those inclined toward existentialism. For him, Sāṃkhya avoids the pitfall of religious belief. Its arguments rest upon empirical evidence, starting with the Buddhist-like acknowledgement of human suffering. In his commentary on the Īśvara section of the *Yoga Sūtra* (I:23–29), Singh notes that "the highest freedom is to be attained only by the highest knowledge and its cause, highest non-attachment, which includes non-attachment to the divine objects also. Further, God is not conceived here as a creator of controller of the world."[2] Singh asserts that Īśvara serves as an object for meditation, not as an external power to be worshipped. Singh writes that Yoga itself, due its grounding in Sāṃkya, "is opposed to any kind of metaphysical and epistemological idealism."[3]

For Podgorski, Sāṃkhya provided a blueprint for a universal spirituality. Its call for dispositional improvement bridges the gap between a life without purpose and one driven by dogma or blind religious belief. Like Singh, Podgorski applauds Sāṃkhya's empiricism, likening it to the thought of Hegel: "Somewhat like the *aufhebung* of which Hegel speaks, life's very experience itself may be regarded as an enriching revelation."[4] Podgorski, alluding to Prakṛti, defines "matter" as "our natural environment, our foundational habitat" noting that "matter" concerned Jean Paul Sarte, Maurice Merleau-Ponty, and Claude Levi-Strauss. He asserts that Teilhard de Chardin, Martin Heidegger, and Paul Ricoeur "all testify that matter, particularly that matter which embraces each person, both reveals and yet conceals our real nature and authentic identity."[5] Affirming its psychological emphasis, he writes "Sāṃkhyan analysis has sharpened our understanding of the depths of individuality . . . suggests that each individual is far more than body, Ego, mind, or even the entire psyche . . . [it] points to a spiritual core or center as our deepest human dimension."[6] For Podgorski, Sāṃkhya dealt not with abstractions but the very stuff of human emotions, including suffering and the possibility of freedom.

Sāṃkhya provides a Zen-like paradox that denies fixed identity. At the moment of freedom, the liberated person proclaims: Nothing to do! Nothing to be! Nothing to own! When the dancer (the ego) ceases to dance, a moment of awareness dawns, along with a catharsis that unburdens attachment. After carefully delineating the relationship between ontology and psychology in the first five dozen verses, the *Sāṃkhya Kārikā* reaches up into the realm of metaphor by evoking the delicate interplay between the dancer and the one who watches the dance in the last dozen verses. However, the text does not hypothesize about the people who actually experience freedom or what happens in the afterlife, other than to cite yet another metaphor: the spinning of the potter's wheel.

Perhaps because of its perceived ambivalence concerning the relationship between consciousness and reality and its somewhat perplexing use of metaphor, Buddhists, Jains, and Vedāntins point out inconsistencies in Sāṃkhya. Like the Buddhists, Sāṃkya calls for the extirpation of ego. Like the Jains, Sāṃkhya proclaims the reality of things in the world and the existence of multiple points of consciousness. Like the Vedāntins, Sāṃkhya seeks to reverse suffering. However, Sāṃkhya does not assent to the idea of no-self as found in Buddhism, though it includes the dramatic proclamation of being freed from ego: *nāham, nāsmi, na me*. Unlike the Jainism, it does not profess or promote an ethical code. It contradicts Vedānta by eschewing all language that would point toward a non-dual experience. Prakṛti is real, not illusory. Prakṛti does not join with Puruṣa, nor does Puruṣa join with Prakṛti. Sāṃkhya remains a tradition of difference. It does not proclaim union. Although it holds much in common with other philosophies of India, Sāṃkhya remains distinct, not unlike the pure points of consciousness that it lauds.

Christopher P. Miller emphasizes soteriology in summarizing Sāṃkhya:

> The *Sāṃkhya-Kārikā* begins with the assertion that to be alive is to suffer (*duḥkha*) (verse 1). The text asserts that Sāṃkhya has been passed down with compassion as a lasting means to assist aspirants in their quest to coun-

> teract this suffering through the cultivation of spiritual knowledge that dispels ignorance (*ajñāna*) and eventually leads to the realization of the inherent freedom of one's consciousness (*puruṣa*) (see verses 1, 62, and 70). Sāṃkhya provides the prescription for attaining this knowledge via the disciplined analysis (*tattva-abhyāsa)* of twenty-five fundamental and irreducible categories of reality known as *tattvas* (verse 64). Taken together, the twenty-five *tattvas* (literally "thatnesses"), which are the basic building blocks of all experience, provide a comprehensive schema to help one understand the ongoing, indissoluble link between the physical world, the body, and emotional and mental experience. By realizing the way in which this schema repeatedly unfolds, one gains knowledge (*jñāna*) of the ontological difference between one's pure, indwelling consciousness (*puruṣa*) and the entire emotional-mental-physical matrix (*prakṛti*). To possess such knowledge is tantamount to the experience of liberation (*kaivalya*) from suffering existence.[7]

Sāṃkhya's core principles have come to suffuse virtually all aspects of Indian thought, from its careful assessment of physical realities to its call for emotional refinement. Its influence has been taken up in numerous works in the above-mentioned books by Gerald Larson.

The importance of Sāṃkhya can be gleaned in two key texts: the *Yoga Sūtra* and the *Bhagavad Gītā*. The *Yoga Sūtra* embeds a summary of Sāṃkhya in its second book, 15–26. It asserts the reality of suffering caused by fluctuations of the *guṇas* and proclaims that discernment through the *jñāna bhāva* is essential for freedom:

> II.15. For the discriminating one, all is suffering due to the conflict of the fluctuations of the *guṇas* and by the sufferings due to *pariṇāma* (outward flow of the senses), sorrow, and *saṃskāra* (past conditioning).
>
> II.16. The suffering yet to come is to be avoided.
>
> II.17. The cause of what is to be avoided is the confusion of the Seer with the Seen.

II.18. The Seen has the qualities of light, activity, and inertia, consists for the elements and the senses, and has the purposes of experience and liberation.

II.19. The distinct, the indistinct, the designator, and the unmanifest are the divisions of the *guṇas*.

II.20. The Seer only sees; though pure, it appears intentional.

II.21. The nature of the Seen is only for the purpose of that (Puruṣa).

II.22. When [its] purpose is done, [the Seen] disappears; otherwise it does not disappear due to being common to others.

II.23. Confusion (*saṃyoga*) results when one perceives two powers of owner [Puruṣa] and owned [Prakṛti] as (one) self-form.

II.24. The cause of it is ignorance.

II.25. From the absence [of ignorance], confusion ceases; [this is] the escape, the isolation from Seen.[8]

Īśvarakṛṣṇa's *Sāṃkhya Kārikā* is quite succinct, yet Patañjali manages to further condense its core ideas into these eleven short statements. Specifically, the first two statements encapsulate the first Kārikā and its concern to overcome sufferings. The definition of ignorance in YS II:17 points to verses 59–68 of the *Sāṃkhya Kārikā*. The discussion of the *guṇas* in YS II:18–19 summarizes several verses in the SK, including 11–16, 22–36, 38, 46, and 60. The allusion to the Seer and the Seen in YS 20–22 can be found explicitly taken up in more than 40 SK verses (3–11 17–21, 51–69).

Similarly, Sāṃkhya pervades the *Bhagavad Gītā* of the *Mahābhārata*.[9] Chapter II of the *Gītā* equates knowledge of the undying self with the wisdom of Sāṃkhya (II:39). Starting with verse II:45 Krishna repeatedly urges Arjuna to rid himself of identification with the three *guṇas*. Paraphrasing the no-ego proclamation of *Sāṃkhya Kārikā* 63 (*nāham, nāsmi, na me*), Krishna urges Arjuna to adopt the attitude of "I am not doing anything at all" (*naiva kiṃcit karomīti*) in BG V:8. Krishna describes his own being as possessing the eightfold Prakṛti: the five great elements (*bhūmi, āp, anala, vāyu, kha*), the mind (*manas*), the "intellect" (*buddhi*) and ego (*ahaṃkāra*, BG VII:4) as well as a higher nature (*parām-jīvabhūtāṃ*, VII:5). Krishna again invokes the *guṇas*, reminding Arjuna not to identify with any of them (VII:12–14). Chapter XIII starts with a concise summary of the principles of Sāṃkhya: Puruṣa, Prakṛti, and the various states (*tattvas*). Chapter XIV describes each of the *guṇas* vividly, giving examples of how goodness (*sattva*), passion (*rajas*) and dullness (*tamas*) pervade things and attitudes. Chapter XVII characterizes forms of religious practice according to varying degrees of *sattva, rajas,* and *tamas*. The *Bhagavad Gītā* concludes with an assessment of renunciation, actions, knowledge, and happiness through the prism of the three *guṇas* in chapter XVIII. In a certain sense, Arjuna moves from profound sadness and an inability to act (*tamas*) in the first chapter to, by the end of the Gītā, a place of engaged action (*rajas*) informed by a sense of the higher good (*sattva*). Krishna systematically instructs Arjuna to see all aspects of reality through the Sāṃkhya prism of the three *guṇas*, allowing him to become a Seer and not a victim of identifying with what is seen.

This volume revisits the *Sāṃkhya Kārikā* in three primary ways: translation, meaning of its content, and various ways of reception and interpretation. The intent is to make the text more accessible, shedding light on its internal complexity as well as its philosophical, ethical, and cultural implications.

First, this book presents a new and readable translation of this text, which finds itself in a genre unto its own. Though seen primarily as philosophical text, it also passes as a work of literature, replete with metaphors and a tinge of mystery. Composed in a complex rhythmic meter, it invites a read-aloud experience. The Āryā meter, a bit like a sonnet or haiku, requires enunciation and counting, and defies ready translation. Rather than attempting anything nearly as clever as Edgerton's brilliant translation of the *Bhagavad Gītā* which replicates both word order and syllabification as best possible, we have chosen to render the text in blank verse, the American-English modality that also invites reading aloud in a punctuated manner. More on the technical aspects of the translation can be found at the start of chapter 5.

Second, the *Sāṃkhya Kārikā* holds tremendous metaphysical, physical, and soteriological import. Its six dozen verses describe the human experience of suffering, lay out its logical methods and premises, articulate consciousness in relationship with material realities, probe the depths of human psychology, and chart a pathway to freedom. Its principles and practices have been absorbed into the fabric of virtually all systems of Indian thought. Like Buddhism, it acknowledges the difficulties inherent in life. Its delineation of the five elements, the five senses, the five action organs, and the five rudiments of experience draws from the Vedas and the Upaniṣads as well as Buddhist and Jaina canonical literature. The building blocks of reality (*tattvas*) enunciated in Sāṃkhya are found in all Indic speculative cosmological traditions. Its articulation of the complex relationship between the unmanifest and the manifest world presages the Vedānta heralding of the two forms of Brahman: with form (*saguṇa*) and without form (*nirguṇa*). Sāṃkhya's itemization of states of existence (*bhāvas*) parallels the enumerations found in the various Buddhist Abhidharma texts and the lists of forms of karma (*prakṛtis*) delineated in Jaina literature.[10]

Sāṃkhya's core principles of Puruṣa and Prakṛti signal consciousness and activity respectively. They find gendered expressions both in narratives of gods (*devas*) and goddesses (*devīs*) and in the dynamics of human relationships. The dance of Prakṛti serves to entertain and liberate the conscious awareness of the Puruṣa. Just as the wrinkle of the Moebius strip frees the mind of binary thinking, so also, the quelling of the dance frees awareness from the shackles of attachment, powerlessness, and duty. By applying a single twist to a strip of paper and joining it end to end, the downside of the paper becomes the upside of the paper. Similarly, by applying the focus of attentive knowledge to all karmic circumstances, one can repeatedly untie the knots that confine human behavior. The platform of human impulse (*buddhi*), the constantly self-referential ego (*ahaṃkāra*), and the wandering mind (*manas*) become transparent in such moments of release. Lethargy and passion (*tamas* and *rajas*) give way to enlightenment (*sattva*).

Third, this volume includes an array of interpretive voices. As Gerald Larson once famously proclaimed, Sāṃkhya is not merely one of the six traditional schools of Indian thought (*ṣad-darśana*). The principles and inherent call to action embedded in Sāṃkhya inform all schools of Indian thought, even beyond its five companions that describe logic (Nyāya), ritual (Mīmāṃsa), physicality (Vaiśeṣika), theology (Vedānta), and spiritual practice (Yoga). As noted above, elements of the Buddhist and Jaina traditions exist in dynamic conversation with Sāṃkhya. Sāṃkhya categories find expression in the literature of the Mahābhārata and the practices of Yoga. Furthermore, to the extent that the three *guṇas* undergird social organization and dietary and by extension health practices, Sāṃkhya informs the day to life of South Asia regardless of religious ideology.

Five scholars weigh in on various philosophical and psychological aspects of the tradition following the translation. Geoffrey Ashton takes up the great mystery of Sāṃkya: how does the stuff of circumstance serve to inform and liberate awareness? Ashton articulates the bridge between the two in a new way. He renders the all-important term *saṃyoga* as compresence. When Prakṛti comes into proximity of awareness or Puruṣa she vibrates and performs. When she fulfills this functionality and ends her dance, Puruṣa enters a state of repose, a moment of fulfilment and peace. Ashton explores the chief premise of this reciprocal exchange: without experience, there can be no freedom. Ana Funes turns to the *Yuktidīpikā*, a text designated as a commentary yet complete within itself, interpreting its account of the five breaths (*prāṇas*) that enliven experience. Without breath, there can be no life. How does breath take expression? What role can knowledge play? Mikel Burley chooses a philosophical path: given that freedom stands as the primary motivating factor for taking up a life guided by Sāṃkhya, what ethical imperatives must be followed? Chapple provides a close textual reading to suggest how the general patterning of the *guṇas* yields a complex analysis of states of being (*bhāvas*) that must be understood and mastered to advance to the goal of freedom. Srivatsa Ramaswami explores the centrality of one's state of mind (*pratyaya*) in the study and practice of Sāṃkhya and Yoga.

The next section of the text explores concrete forms and applications of Sāṃkhya. More than a hundred years ago, Hariharānanda Āraṇya created a community that seeks to live by the Sāṃkhya code. Marzenna Jakubczak describes visits to the Kapil Math community in West Bengal, which continues this tradition through following a monastic form of Sāṃkhya. She notes that the Sāṃkhya practitioners there employ a practice similar to modern adaptations of Buddhist mindful awareness practice. McKim Marriott revisits his original field notes from the 1950s, mapping village life onto the Sāṃkhya schematic, noting the ubiquity and universality of the Sāṃkya architectonic. The last paper in this section, by Alfred Collins, gives a nuts-and-bolts applied interpretation of Sāṃkhya from a psychotherapeutic perspective.

The book ends with a grammatical analysis of the text by Robert Zabel. By exploring the vocabulary of the text through its roots and possible translation terms, and by pointing out the vagaries of breaking apart compound words, a toolbox is given for readers to construct their own approach to the text, and to more fully discern the choices made by earlier translators.

This book arose from a conference of the same name convened under the auspices of the Master of Arts in Yoga Studies program at Loyola Marymount University in 2015. The presentations may be viewed on the LMU Yoga Studies YouTube channel. The preparation of this book entailed the hard work of all the participants in the conference and those who have contributed to this volume. Special appreciation goes to the staff of SUNY Press, to Gayatri Sehgal for preparing the beautiful cover, and to Gabrielle Sigrist, graduate assistant and student in LMU's Yoga Studies MA program.

Notes

1. T. G. Mainkar, *Sāṃkhyakārikā of Īśvarakṛṣṇa with the Commentary of Gauḍapāda* (Delhi: Chaukhamba Sanskrit Pratishthan, 1964, 1972).

2. Bhagwan B. Singh, *Yoga Siddhi: Yoga Sutras of Patanjali with Commentary* (Las Vegas, NV: International Institute of American and Indian Studies, 1997), 11.

3. Ibid., 82.

4. Frank R. Podgorski, *Ego Revealer-Concealer, A Key to Yoga* (Lanham, MD: University Press of America, 1984), 64.

5. Ibid., xii.

6. Ibid., 156.

7. Christopher P. Miller, "Sāṃkhya" in Pankaj Jain et al. (eds.), *Hinduism and Tribal Religions, Encyclopedia of Indian Religions,* Springer 2018, online resource consulted January 21, 2023 https://link.springer.com/referenceworkentry/10.1007/978-94-024-1188-1_45

8. Christopher Key Chapple, *Yoga and the Luminous* (Albany, NY: SUNY Press, 2008), 123–124.

9. Extensive analysis of Sāṃkhya can also be found in the *Mokṣadharma Parvan* of the *Mahābhārata* as studied by Jayadeva Yogendra, James Fitzgerald, Angelika Malinar, Knut Jacobsen, and John Brockington.

10. See Th. Schterbatsky, *The Central Conception of Buddhism and the Meaning of the Word "Dharma"* (London: Royal Asiatic Society, 1923) and Helmuth von Glasenapp, *The Doctrine of Karman in Jain Philosophy* (Varanasi: Parshvanath Research Institute, 1942).

Sāṃkhya Kārikā of Īśvarakṛṣṇa

1. What is the cause of the torment
   of the threefold suffering?
Would you like to know?
The apparent ways of dealing with it do not work.
They are insufficient.

2. Vedic rituals are impure, destructive, and excessive.
They are wrong.
The better way arises from the discernment of
the manifest, the unmanifest, and the knower.

3. *Mūlaprakṛti* is not derivative.
Seven aspects derive from *Prakṛti,*
starting with the *Mahat* (*buddhi*)
[and the *ahaṃkāra* and earth, water, fire, air, space].
Sixteen aspects further emerge
[mind, sense organs, action organs, rudimentary elements].
The *Puruṣa* is neither *Prakṛti* nor a derivative of *Prakṛti.*

4. Indeed, from the perfection of all means of knowledge,
it can be agreed upon that they are threefold:
that which is apparent, inferred, or declared authoritatively.
Success in obtaining knowledge arises from inference.

5. Evident is the apprehension of sense objects.
Inference is declared to be threefold:
From a clear mark (*tal liṅga*),
from a prior mark (*liṅga-pūrvakaṃ*),
and from reliable authority.
Authoritative declaration arises
   from an authoritative source.

6. From appearance, one can know
what is common to all.
From inference one can know
what is beyond the reach of the senses.
From authoritative declarations,
one can establish successfully
something that cannot be established otherwise.

7. [Why are we not able to see the unmanifest and the knower, *Prakṛti* and *Puruṣa*? Why must we rely upon inference to gain knowledge?]

(1) Some things are too far away.
(2) Some things are too close.
(3) Sometimes our faculties fail.
(4) The mind can be unstable.
(5) Some things are too subtle.
(6) Obstructions arise.
(7) [The evidence] can be overpowered.
(8) Intermixture of similar qualities [can obscure distinctions].

8. Due to her subtlety, she cannot be apprehended.
This does not mean she does not exist.
She is apprehended through her effects.
These effects begin with the *Mahat*.
They are similar to and different from *Prakṛti*.

9. (1) No action arises from non-existence.
(2) Anything that can be grasped arises from perception.
(3) There is no existence that arises from all things.
(4) The efficacy of an action arises from its power.
(5) Existence arises from a material cause.
Hence, each occurrence (*karaṇa*) is real.

10. The manifest is
(1) caused
(2) finite
(3) non-pervasive
(4) active

(5) multifold
(6) supported
(7) marked with personality (*liṅgam*)
(8) composed of parts
(9) dependent on another.
The unmanifest is the opposite.

11. An object is discerned due to the three *guṇas*.
It is held in common and is not conscious.
It proceeds according to its constitution (*dharma*).
The manifest is therefore linked to the *pradhāna*.
The *pumān* (*Puruṣa*) stands apart from it.

12. In regard to the *guṇas*,
their nature is delight, dis-rest, and despair.
Their purpose is luminosity, activity, and restraint.
Their fluctuations combine as one overpowers the others.
One predominates while the others support.

13. *Sattva* is light and luminous.
Rajas stimulates and moves.
Tamas is heavy and concealing.
A fluctuation is like a lamp.
Its purpose is to make a thing apparent.

14. The humble jumble of nondiscernment
arises from the three *guṇas*.
The absence of that results in the contrary (the *pumān*).
The material cause be found in the nature of the *guṇas*.
The unmanifest is thus established in the effect.

15 and 16. The unmanifest is the cause
(1) Because of the number of distinctions.
(2) Because all things hold a common origin.
(3) Because activity follows its own power.
(4) Because there is a distinction
between cause and effect.
(5) Because all distinctions disappear
back into a universal form.

(6) All things arise from the three *guṇas,*
like the emergence of water as steam, liquid, and ice.
(7) All specificity relies
upon the distinctness of the *guṇas.*

17. *Puruṣa* exists
(1) Because combinations exist
for the sake of another.
(2) Because there must be something distinct
from the *guṇas.*
(3) Because there must be a superintendent.
(4) Because there must be an enjoyer.
(5) Because both activity and freedom exist
for its sake.

18. It is established that there are many *Puruṣas.*
(1) Because of the diversity of births, deaths and
faculties.
(2) Because activities take place at different times.
(3) Because the distinctions of the proportions
of the three *guṇas* vary.

19. Hence it is established that *Puruṣa*
is the opposite of the three *guṇas.*
It is the witness.
It is solitary (*kaivalyaṃ*) and neutral (*madhyastha*).
It is the seer. It does nothing.

20. Furthermore, due to compresence (*saṃyoga*),
the unconscious personality appears as if it were conscious.
Because of the fluctuations of the *guṇas,*
the indifferent one appears as if active.

21. The *pradhāna* provides the twin purposes
of experience and freedom for the *Puruṣa,*
like a blind person who teams up with a lame person.
Creation occurs due to compresence (*saṃyoga*).
Puruṣa needs *pradhāna* for experience and freedom.
Pradhāna needs *Puruṣa* in order to see.
When the two connect, creation emerges.

22. From *Prakṛti* come the *Mahat* and then the *ahaṃkāra,*
after which the group of sixteen arises (see verse three).
Then, from the midst of the sixteen,
one group of five (the rudiments or *tanmātras*)
produces the five elements.

23. Mental effort in its elevated state (*sattvika*)
leads to *dharma,* knowledge, freedom from attachment,
and power.
From *tamas,* the reverse arises.

24. Pride characterizes ego and yields a twofold creation:
the eleven (mind, sense organs, and action organs)
and the battalion of the five rudiments (the *tanmātras*).

25. From the energization of the ego
arises the illuminating (*sattvika*) eleven
(the mind and the ten organs)
and the heavier (*tamasika*) elements, rudimentary and gross.
Both are suffused with *tejas* (*rajasika*).

26. The sense organs (*indriya*) are
eyes, ears, nose, taste buds, and skin.
The action organs are speech, hands, feet, anus, and genitals.

27. The mind is of the nature of both
(the sense organs and action organs).
The organs follow its creative intention.
From the distinctions of its constitutive *guṇas,*
the various aspects of the external world arise correspondingly.

28. A fluctuation correlates to the awareness-only
of the five (rudimentary elements) starting with sound
or the five operations of speaking, holding, walking,
excreting, or sexual pleasure.

29. In regard to the special characteristic of each
fluctuation of the three (*buddhi, ahaṃkāra,* and
manas), each functions differently.

The five winds, expressed through the breath,
form a fluctuation that is common in every operation.

30. A fluctuation, it is said,
arises in steps and simultaneously
due to four [functions of *buddhi, ahaṃkāra, manas,* and
an *indriya*].
Furthermore, it can be seen that every action
has an unseen precedent [governed] by the three (*guṇas*).

31. Each fluctuation arises
due to its mutuality of cause and resulting condition.
Each occurrence (*karaṇa*) is created
for nothing other than for the purpose of *Puruṣa.*

32. Occurrences happen through a thirteen-fold process
resulting in holding, sustaining, and revealing.
The result of this is tenfold,
allowing all that is to be held, sustained, and revealed
[through the ten sensory and action organs].

33. The inner occurrence is threefold
(*buddhi, ahaṃkāra, manas*)
The external is tenfold [involving sense and action organs].
The context for experiencing an object is predicated by
the three (*guṇas*).
The external always exists in the present.
The internal occurrence (*karaṇam*)
resides at all three times
(past, present, and future).

34. The sense organs take five forms.
Their objects can be distinct (*mahābhūtas*)
or indistinct (*tanmātras*).
Speech (an action organ) finds its object in sound.
The remaining (action organs) include all five objects.
[holding, walking, passing of water, and moving of
the bowels entail all five elements, with degrees
of breath, heat, water, and earth involved in each
occurrence]

35. The *buddhi*, as part of the inner occurrence,
comprehends all objects.
Therefore, the threefold occurrence
(*buddhi, ahaṃkāra, manas*)
holds the door for all remaining doors.

36. These [experiences], like a lamp, are distinct, one
from another, determined by the *guṇas*.
They are brought to light in the *buddhi*,
utterly for the purpose of *Puruṣa*.

37. Hence, the *buddhi* delivers all experience to *Puruṣa*.
Furthermore, it alone distinguishes
the subtle boundary between the *pradhāna* and *Puruṣa*.

38. The rudimentary elements are indistinct.
From them the five gross elements arise.
These are seen to be distinct:
peaceful, turbulent, and stultified.

39. Three distinct factors can be postulated
[in regard to the human]:
(1) the subtle [factors],
(2) [the body] born of a mother and father,
(3) and acts of will.
The subtle influences and restraints endure
[from life to life]
while those [bodies] born of mother and father pass away.

40. The personality, which is cloaked with the *bhāvas*,
has already arisen but is not yet empowered.
It endures within the *Mahat* to the edge of the subtle.
Because it has not experienced enjoyment,
it transmigrates.

41. Just as art requires color,
just as without pillars there can be no shadow,
similarly, the personality cannot exist without the
specifics [of the *bhāvas*].

42. The personality performs like an actor
due to its connection (*yoga*) with the allurement of *Prakṛti*.
This is the cause of human exertion:
yearning for both the secular (*nimitta*, experience)
and the transcendent (*naimittika*, freedom).

43. The *bhāvas*, *dharma* and the others, are primary.
They are seen in the way life occurrences unfold,
and in the unfolding growth of an embryo.

44. With *dharma* there is movement upward.
Without *dharma*, things move downward.
With knowledge freedom arises.
From its opposite, bondage.

45. From nonattachment,
things resolve themselves back into *Prakṛti*.
From passionate attachment, *saṃsāra* arises.
From power, obstacles dissolve.
From its opposite, they persist.

46. The mental drama can also be described as
ignorance, incapacity, complacency, and perfection.
Due to the diversity of disturbances of the *guṇas*,
there are fifty varieties.

47. There are five varieties of ignorance.
There are twenty-eight incapacities
due to defects in occurrences (*karaṇa*),
nine contentments, and eight perfections.

48. There are eight varieties of darkness (*tamas*),
ten varieties of delusion [extending] to great delusion,
eighteen forms of darkness [down] into the abyss.

49. There are eleven injuries to the senses.
There are also injuries to the *buddhi*.
The injuries to the *buddhi* are seventeen:
These are opposite to the nine contentments
and the eight perfections.

50. The contentments are imagined as nine.
There are four inherent contentments that arise:
nature (*Prakṛti*); material goods (*upādāna*);
time (*kāla*); and luck (*bhāgya*).
There are five external contentments,
derived from overcoming the objects of the senses.

51. Thoughtfulness, [attentiveness to] sound,
introspection, overcoming threefold suffering,
obtaining a good heart,
and generosity are the eight successes (*siddhis*).
From success, one tames the threefold (suffering).

52. Without the *bhāvas*, there is no personality.
Through the personality,
there is the quelling of the *bhāvas*.
Therefore, the created world (*sarga*) that results
emerges in a twofold manner, subtle and gross.

53. The heavenly realm is eightfold.
Animals are fivefold
(domestic, wild, birds, reptiles, and plants).
Humans are all of one kind.
In short, this is the threefold world (*sarga*).

54. In the upper realm, there is an abundance of *sattva*,
at the lower side of creation, an abundance of *tamas*,
and in the middle, an abundance of *rajas*.
This extends from Brahmā to a blade of grass.

55. Therein, the conscious *Puruṣa*
meets with the suffering of old age and death.
Due to the *svabhāva*s of the personality
not being turned back,
there is suffering.

56. This is created by *Prakṛti*,
from the *Mahat* down to the distinct elements.
Its purpose is to liberate each *Puruṣa*.

This is undertaken for the purpose of the other,
but as if it were for the purpose of itself.

57. Just as milk spontaneously flows forth for the growth of the calf,
the flow from the *Pradhāna* occurs
for the liberation of *Puruṣa.*

58. Just as actions in the world proceed
for the purpose of quelling anxiety,
likewise, the *avyaktam* proceeds
for the purpose of liberating *Puruṣa.*

59. Just as a dancer stops dancing when the charade ends,
so too, *Prakṛti* ceases once the nature of *Puruṣa* is revealed.

60. She is helpful in various ways.
He is not helpful.
She possesses the *guṇas.*
He has no *guṇas.*
She moves for the sake of him.
He has no purpose.

61. It is my thought that there is nothing more exquisite
than *Prakṛti,* who exclaims "I have been seen!"
and retreats from the view of *Puruṣa.*

62. Therefore, no one is bound.
Indeed, no one is released.
It is only *Prakṛti*
in her various costumes
that transmigrates, is bound, and is free.

63. By seven forms, Prakṛti binds herself through her own self.
She does this for the purpose of Puruṣa.
One form (*eka rūpeṇa*) causes freedom.

64. Thus from the practice of the *tattvas*
comes the knowledge:
"I am not, nothing is mine, there is no I."
From this certainty, knowledge (*jñāna*) arises,
pure and singular, without remainder.

65. Through that, *Puruṣa,* like a spectator
standing established in himself,
sees *Prakṛti* who, from completing her purpose,
has ceased her outflows
and no longer manifests the seven forms.

66. He who is indifferent says, "The dancer stands still!"
She who stands still says, "I have been seen!"
The confusion of the two comes to an end,
There is no more incentive for further creation.

67. From the advent of this perfect knowledge,
dharma and the six others no longer hold sway.
Yet, due to the force of *saṃskāras,*
the body holds on, standing like a spinning potter's wheel.

68. From this purpose having been told and fulfilled,
the body is cast off and the *pradhāna* ceases.
Kaivalyam is attained, both enduring and singular.

69. This mystery, this knowledge
regarding all things serving the purpose of *Puruṣa*
has been explained by the Supreme Sage.
The origin, development, and dissolution
of the elements (*bhūta*)
is thus brought to consciousness.

70. The sage imparted this excellent and pure knowledge
to Āsuri with compassion.
Āsuri in turn passed it to Pañcaśikha,
who expanded it into a complete philosophy.

71. Through guru–disciple transmission,
it was rendered into verse by Īśvarakṛṣṇa,
who compiled this with noble thoughts,
arguing the case for correct knowledge.

72. Verily, in these seventy verses are contained
all the purposes found
in the complete sixtyfold philosophy,
though the illustrative stories are not told,
nor the objections of others.

73. Therefore, this summary *śāstra* leaves out nothing.
The vast form of philosophy is here,
like the reflection of the moon in a mirror.

If you understand this small text, you understand the universe.

I

Philosophical and Textual Approaches to the *Sāṃkhya Kārikā*

Chapter 1

What Is the Ground of Manifest Reality in the *Sāṃkhya Kārikā*?

An Existential Phenomenological Theory of *Vyaktaprakṛti* as the Self-Manifesting of *Saṃyoga*

GEOFF ASHTON

Introduction

As Mikel Burley rightly demonstrates in his 2007 monograph, *Classical Sāṃkhya and Yoga: An Indian Metaphysics of Experience*, standard renditions of the *Sāṃkhya Kārikā* (SK) misconstrue the nature of *vyaktaprakṛti* (manifest reality) by imputing an external realist metaphysics. This critique applies especially to Gerald Larson's widely influential 1979 study, *Classical Sāṃkhya: An Interpretation of Its History and Meaning*, which takes *vyaktaprakṛti* to exist independent of consciousness (*Puruṣa*) and to represent the self-manifestation of *mūlaprakṛti* ("fundamental matter"). However, Burley's interpretation wrongly imposes an idealist framework on the Sāṃkhya system.[1] Certainly, manifest reality (*vyaktaprakṛti*) is not a set of mental appearances constructed by the *Puruṣa* qua transcendental ego, and the *satkāryavāda* doctrine unambiguously takes *mūlaprakṛti* to be a productive cause of manifest reality—something that Burley's model does not accommodate. If neither co-fundamental duad—*mūlaprakṛti* or *Puruṣa*—can stand as the ground of manifest reality (*vyaktaprakṛti*), then what can? In order to respond to this puzzle, this chapter aims to liberate the SK from the confines of the realism–idealism debate, and in its place turns to the existential phenomenology of Jose Ortega y Gasset. Not unlike Heidegger, Ortega investigates the aboriginal nature of our being in the world. But he does so in order to spotlight the theme of life or lived reality, not that of being. Approaching Sāṃkhya metaphysics through Ortega's phenomenology of life helps to reveal that the SK is not so concerned with the cosmological origins of a world-in-itself or the abstract structure of mental experience. Rather, it is fundamentally interested in the question, "What does it mean to live?" and seeks to establish a radical perspective—a standpoint primordial to "the world," the ego, and the interrelation between the two—from which to explore the meaning of manifest reality (*vyaktaprakṛti*) as lived reality. Having reframed Sāṃkhya metaphysics as an inquiry into life and its vital ground, this chapter argues that manifest reality (*vyaktaprakṛti*) exhibits a dynamic interplay or dialectical compresence (*saṃyoga*) between *Puruṣa* and *mūlaprakṛti*, not an intention, design, or telos that proceeds from either relata.

Neither Mūlaprakṛti nor Puruṣa Is the Ground of Vyaktaprakṛti: A Critique of Realist and Idealist Interpretations

In the midst of developing their reconstructions of Sāṃkhya metaphysics, Larson and Burley exaggerate the role played by *mūlaprakṛti* and *Puruṣa*, respectively, in the creation of manifest reality (*vyaktaprakṛti*). Contrary to realist and idealist models, neither *mūlaprakṛti* nor *Puruṣa* can suffice as the ground of manifest reality (*vyaktaprakṛti*).

According to Larson's external realist account, the *Puruṣa* stands juxtaposed against an aboriginally unified *Prakṛti*. *Prakṛti* exists as a cosmos or world of objects, a manifest reality (*vyaktaprakṛti*) that persists external to and independent of the knowing subject, *Puruṣa*, and simply waits to emerge from its unmanifest, material root, the fundamental matter known as *mūlaprakṛti*. What brings manifest reality (*vyaktaprakṛti*) to light is *Puruṣa*. Thereafter,

Prakṛti evolves once *Puruṣa* illuminates *mūlaprakṛti,* which stirs the three *guṇas* into action and reveals an order of *tattvas* already latent within *mūlaprakṛti.*[2]

As valuable as this interpretation has been for making sense of Sāṃkhya metaphysics, it misconstrues the doctrine in some considerable ways.[3] For one, *Puruṣa* is a pure, detached witness consciousness (SK 19). It is not a cognizing, world-experiencing mind, ego, or proto-rational "soul" that gets wrapped up in empirical affairs. It is not even an illuminating light that reveals the order of manifest reality (*vyaktaprakṛti*). Mind, ego, cognition, and illumination (*prakāśa-karam*) are accounted for by the *tattvas* of the *antaḥkaraṇa* (inner instrument of the *buddhi, ahaṃkāra,* and *manas*) (SK 12, 32).

Meanwhile, *mūlaprakṛti* is not "fundamental matter," "unconscious thing-ness," or "an undifferentiated plenitude of being" that naturally evolves into a spatio-temporal field of objects (Larson 1979: 201, 242). For one, *mūlaprakṛti* is uncreated (*avikṛti*), uncaused, atemporal, and nonspatial (SK 3, 10). It thus never gets objectified or made manifest. This is not to deny that it has a causal role in bringing *vyaktaprakṛti* into being, but the relation between the two cannot be one of material causation. This is especially unlike the cause–effect relation invoked through the example of clay and pot, wherein both the cause (clay) and the effect (pot) can be located in space and time. *Pradhāna* (*mūlaprakṛti*) in-itself cannot be so identified; we see only manifest reality (*vyaktaprakṛti*), not *mūlaprakṛti,* precisely because *mūlaprakṛti* exceeds spatio-temporal conditions.[4] Thus, the causality of *mūlaprakṛti* qua "fundamental matter" cannot be ascertained. A second reason *pradhāna* cannot produce manifest reality (*vyaktaprakṛti*) is because it is blind ("*andha,*" as SK 21 indicates) both cognitively and teleologically. *Mūlaprakṛti* does not bear within itself a design, direction, or telos for manifest creation. (Consider that the *karmans,* which infuse *vyaktaprakṛti* with its intentionality, reside in the *mahat-buddhi,* not in *mūlaprakṛti.*) The blueprint for *vyaktaprakṛti* is not already formed within *mūlaprakṛti,* as if it simply waits to be revealed, awakened, or approved for construction. Indeed, a creative potency is causally necessary for the existence of *vyaktaprakṛti,* yet *mūlaprakṛti* is not that creative intention.

Finally, Larson and other realist interpreters wrongly construe the relation between *vyaktaprakṛti* and consciousness. If by "consciousness" Larson means the *Puruṣa,* then he distorts the nature of *vyaktaprakṛti*'s ontological dependence. Manifest reality requires causal conditions besides just *mūlaprakṛti.* It also requires the presence of a *Puruṣa,* since any given *vyaktaprakṛti* emerges from (or as) the *samyoga* of *mūlaprakṛti* and a numerically distinct *Puruṣa.* In other words, while *mūlaprakṛti* exists necessarily and is autonomous of the *Puruṣa* (as pure consciousness), the being of *vyaktaprakṛti* is contingent upon the nearness of the *Puruṣa* to *mūlaprakṛti.* However, where Larson takes "consciousness" to denote the *antaḥkaraṇa* (recall that the most basic tattvas of manifest reality—*buddhi, ahaṃkāra,* etc.—have psychical or epistemological qualities), then this too cannot hold. For how could *vyaktaprakṛti* refer to a "world-in-itself"—that is, a world independent of a cognizing subject—when "the world" (which is comprised of more derivative empirical tattvas: the *tanmātras* and *mahābhūtas*) does not arise prior to the manifestation of the *buddhi, ahaṃkāra,* etc.

Burley offers a compelling alternative reading. He argues that the Sāṃkhya metaphysical schema presents a synchronic analysis of those conditions that are necessary for the experience of phenomenal appearances. Instead of describing the structure of a world that exists "out there" and evolves diachronically independent of the knower, he contends that Sāṃkhya examines just the nature of our subjective experience, wherein all of the *tattvas* manifest simultaneously, not consecutively (2007: 6–7). Supplementing his Kantian analysis with Husserlian phenomenology, Burley enacts an idealist turn that helps to disclose hidden nuances of Sāṃkhya metaphysics.

But the idealist hypothesis leads to problems of its own, starting with its inability to clearly explain who or what the *Puruṣa* is. Burley exaggerates the role of *Puruṣa* in giving rise to manifest reality (*vyaktaprakṛti*) by correlating it to Kantian and Husserlian notions of a transcendental ego. However, the *Puruṣa* is so thoroughly indifferent (*mādhyasthya*) and withdrawn (*kaivalya*) from experience that it is empty of not just objectual content but the very impetus to fashion a "world" or field of experience, such as through some sort of intentional action (*karma*). *Puruṣa* is marked by sheer inactivity or non-agency (*akārtṛbhāva*) (SK 19).

Burley takes a step forward by translating *mūlaprakṛti* as "fundamental productivity" (2007: 183). But his interpretive model fails to preserve this insight. The Husserlian approach ignores *mūlaprakṛti,* leaving it empty (Husserl's system includes no correlative "other" that transcends the transcendental ego). Burley's Kantian interpretation better accommodates *mūlaprakṛti*: it at least maintains an ontology of consciousness-independent *things-in-themselves*. But this understates the continuity of *mūlaprakṛti* and manifest reality (*vyaktaprakṛti*). *Mūlaprakṛti* bequeaths to *vyaktaprakṛti* its essential *guṇa*-constitution and its causal-creative power or "*Prakṛti,*" which *Puruṣa* lacks (SK 3, 11–16). As the sum of Kant's *things-in-themselves, mūlaprakṛti* gets assigned only passive, lifeless involvement in the constitution of phenomena—as if *mūlaprakṛti* were a storehouse of unlimited, material standing reserves that submissively await an "I" who can fashion them into objects of value. But in fact, the SK defines *mūlaprakṛti* by its potency to generate, and less so by a potential to be passively revealed.

With respect to manifest reality (*vyaktaprakṛti*), Burley's idealist reading denies its alterity and ontological meaning by reducing it to something wholly contained within the bounds of mental experience—that is, within the "field or domain" of *Puruṣa*-consciousness.[5] But *Puruṣa* cannot serve as the creative ground, source, or agent of the purposiveness of manifest reality because, as a structureless, nonintentional, lame (*paṅgu,* per SK 21) non-agent (*akārtṛ*), it can neither produce, organize, nor hold mental representations—quite unlike Kantian and Husserlian versions of a transcendental ego. Moreover, the SK's doctrine of effect somehow preexisting within its cause (*satkāryavāda*) explicitly recognizes that manifest reality (*vyaktaprakṛti*) has *another* side, namely its rootedness in *mūlaprakṛti* (SK 9).[6] That manifest reality (*vyaktaprakṛti*) actually exists as reflected in the SK's formulation of the inner instrument (*antaḥkaraṇa*), which is not strictly psychological. The *buddhi,* for example, is *mahat,* which has deeply ontological connotations, and the *mahat-buddhi* contains the *bhāvas* and *karmans,* which are vital to generating manifest reality (*vyaktaprakṛti*).[7] On the whole, Burley provides a compelling critique that manifest reality cannot entail externality and independence with respect to consciousness. However, his idealist rendition swings too far toward the other extreme of the realism–idealism spectrum. The SK gives little to no indication that manifest reality (*vyaktaprakṛti*) marks a domain of mental appearances—an alternative that would have been well-known to Īśvarakṛṣṇa (in the form of Vedānta and Yogācāra, among others) but which he makes no effort to accommodate in his metaphysical framework.[8]

Manifest Reality (*Vyaktaprakṛti*) as the "Turning Forward" (*Pravṛtti*) of Dialectical Compresence (*Saṃyoga*)

If neither *mūlaprakṛti* (per realism) nor the *Puruṣa* (per idealism) can stand as the singular ground of manifest reality, then upon what does *vyaktaprakṛti* rest? In preparation for an existential phenomenological response to this question, let us first consider how the ontological ground of manifest reality (*vyaktaprakṛti*) is the compresence (*saṃyoga*) of *mūlaprakṛti* and *Puruṣa*, with *samyoga* understood as a dialectical compresence between these duads.

SK 20–21 are key to understanding the relationship between *mūlaprakṛti, Puruṣa,* and *saṃyoga*. I render these passages as follows: "The non-conscious subtle body (*liṅgam*), as if conscious, comes to life (*bhavati*) owing to the compresence (*saṃyogāt*) of those two [i.e., *Puruṣa* and *mūlaprakṛti*] . . . Like the coming together (*saṃyogaḥ*) of the lame and the blind (*paṅgu-andha-vad*), creation (*sargaḥ*) takes place (*kṛtaḥ*) thusly as the compresence (*saṃyogaḥ*) of the two [*mūlaprakṛti* and *Puruṣa*] for the purpose of seeing *pradhāna* [*mūlaprakṛti*] and isolating *Puruṣa*." Situated in its larger context, these two *kārikā*-s imply an equivalence between manifest reality (*vyaktaprakṛti*) and the creation (*sarga*) that takes place (*kṛta*) in this relatively early part of the text. Significantly, it also highlights that "creation (*sargaḥ*) takes place (*kṛtaḥ*)" thusly as "the compresence (*saṃyogaḥ*) of *mūlaprakṛti* and *Puruṣa*." This indicates that manifest reality (*vyaktaprakṛti*) emerges as *saṃyoga*, not from *samyoga*. Below I will examine the implications of rendering *saṃyogaḥ* in the nominative case ("*as* the compresence") instead of the ablative ("*from* the compresence"). For now, I call attention to how the order of manifest creation (*vyaktaprakṛti/sarga*) cannot emerge from *mūlaprakṛti* or *Puruṣa*, since it does not even emerge from *samyoga* (again, it manifests as *saṃyoga*). Moreover, neither *mūlaprakṛti* nor *Puruṣa* can stand as the sole basis for actual creation because *mūlaprakṛti* is blind (*andha*), and hence cannot *intend* or procreate anything on its own (not even teleologically), while *Puruṣa* is lame (*paṅgu*), and hence cannot generate anything—not a thought, feeling, desire, or volition, and certainly not an object or event. The order of creation (*sarga*), then, derives from neither *mūlaprakṛti* (as its self-manifestation) nor *Puruṣa* (as its constructed mental appearances).

In addition to providing textual support for the philosophical arguments made in the previous section, this translation of *kārikā*-s 20–21 helps to avoid reading Sāṃkhya metaphysics in terms of the realist and idealist questions, "What is the nature of the world-in-itself?" and "What are the necessary conditions for mental experience?," respectively. Instead, I propose interpreting Sāṃkhya's most basic categories through existential phenomenological themes, namely, "What does it mean to exist?" and "What does it mean to live?" Sāṃkhya is engaged in a kind of fundamental ontology from which it can better understand the nature of our being in the world. But it couches this within a phenomenology of life which, in the case of Sāṃkhya, involves an inquiry into the meaning of procreativity (cognate with *Prakṛti*), consciousness (*Puruṣa*), and the showing or manifesting (*vyañjana*) of procreativity.[9] These concerns inform my translation of *mūlaprakṛti*, which I render in terms of its etymological constitution. *Mūla* connotes "root, basis, foundation, origin, the bottom of anything." The prefix *pra-* (cognate with the English "pro-") conveys the sense of "forward," "forth," "in front," "onward," "away," and the present participle *kṛti* ("doing, manufacturing, making, creating") derives from the verbal root, √*kṛ* (Monier-Williams 1960, 654). This is similarly expressed in the cognate Latin term, *procreatrix*, except in the absence of a preceding *mūla*. From this, I take "root-procreativity" to be a safe but also provocative translation of *mūla-prakṛti* that opens new conceptual space for thinking through Sāṃkhya metaphysics. In contrast with *Puruṣa* (which tends toward absence), "root-procreativity" perpetually leans toward presence but never itself arrives—since *mūlaprakṛti* does not itself take empirical form.

In keeping with its usage of the language of procreation, the SK explains what I now propose to be translated as "manifest procreativity" (*vyakta-prakṛti*) in terms of sexual reproduction and life-begetting alchemy. This has implications for understanding *satkāryavāda* in Sāṃkhya metaphysics. Any cause requires an effect in order to properly become a cause. This holds in the case of a woman becoming a mother. Biologically speaking, she requires a child to be born of her own body in order to become a cause of life—in order to become a mother. Likewise, *mūlaprakṛti* requires the manifestation of manifest reality/procreativity (*vyaktaprakṛti*) (as *kārya*) in order to become a cause (*karaṇa*). Further, *mūlaprakṛti* requires a partner. Just as a mother cannot birth a child of her own procreative potency, and hence requires the compresence or "*saṃyoga*" of a male partner or the essence thereof, so too is *mūlaprakṛti* not the only parent in the procreative process. She requires *Puruṣa* (lit., "man") to be "present-with," or "*saṃ-yoga*." Indeed, *mūlaprakṛti* is a cause of manifest reality/procreativity (*vyaktaprakṛti*). But the will, intention, or capacity to produce *this particular manifest reality* (e.g., *vyaktaprakṛti* "A"), not that one (*vyaktaprakṛti* "B"), does not lie within *mūlaprakṛti* (which is *andha*).[10] It resides in the *saṃyoga*, or compresence of *mūlaprakṛti* with *this numerically distinct Puruṣa* (respectively, *Puruṣa* "A"), *not that one* (*Puruṣa* "B").

SK 21 indicates this when it strips *mūlaprakṛti* down to its unseeing, blind "root." *Mūlaprakṛti* is simply the "natural," unprocessed drive to beget, but itself lacks direction.[11] Since *mūlaprakṛti* is not compelled *by* or *toward* anything in particular, then from where does actual creation spring? The procreative directedness that gets shown or made manifest (*vyakta*) must be *born of* and proceed *as* compresence (*saṃyoga*). Neither the self-evolution of *mūlaprakṛti* (the realist model) nor a field of *Puruṣa*-constructed appearances (the idealist model), manifest reality/procreativity (*vyaktaprakṛti*) represents the self-manifestation of a given compresence event (*saṃyoga*). As the *kṛta-sarga* (or "creation which takes place") of SK 21, manifest reality/procreativity (*vyaktaprakṛti*) is co-terminus and co-extensive with compresence (*saṃyoga*). *Puruṣa* and *mūlaprakṛti* are equi-primordial, mutually transcending categories that preexist any and all *vyaktaprakṛti*-s, and hence persist upon the respective cessations of these *vyaktaprakṛti*-s. *Puruṣa* endures by virtue of its utter solitude (*kaivalya*), and *mūlaprakṛti* continues by virtue of its infinite creative potency. But this is not the case with respect to the *saṃyoga* of *mūlaprakṛti* and a given *Puruṣa*. Just as the approximation of this witness consciousness (let us say, *Puruṣa* "A") to *mūlaprakṛti* is a necessary condition for the emergence of this manifest reality (let us say, *vyaktaprakṛti* "A"), but not that one (*vyaktaprakṛti* "B"), so too is the *a-samyoga* (disjoining) of this *Puruṣa* (*Puruṣa* "A") apart from *mūlaprakṛti* consonant with the passing away of just this *vyaktaprakṛti* (*vyaktaprakṛti* "A"), but not that one (*vyaktaprakṛti* "B," which persists even while *vyaktaprakṛti* "A" dissolves). There is nothing to suggest that a given *saṃyoga* temporally precedes or survives its corresponding *vyaktaprakṛti*.

SK 16 lends support to this interpretation. It links together *Prakṛti* and *pravṛtti* (as *pravartate*) in order to convey *Prakṛti* as an actualized creative potency that proceeds (*pravartate* [SK 16]) as a turning outward (*pravṛtti*). *Pravṛtti* shares the same prefix ("*pra-*") as *Prakṛti*, while *vṛtti* derives from the verbal root, "√*vṛt*," "to take place," "to happen," "to turn" (Monier-Williams 1960, 1055). When *Prakṛti* takes the mode of *pravṛtti*—not just the crude generativity of an unprocessed source (*mūla*) that cannot actually produce anything in and of itself—*Prakṛti* becomes the actual "happening," "taking place," or "turning forward" (*pra-vṛtti*) of a compresence that, unlike either of its foundational duads, has a design or directedness to it, and hence exhibits an actual "going forward," "proceeding," turning forward," "arising," "springing," or even a "striving," "self-exerting," or "acting toward" (Monier-Williams 1960: 693–694). Commencing from a spontaneous point-instant, the intention, telos, or *artha* of manifest reality/procreativity (*vyaktaprakṛti*) intensifies and exceeds itself by turning outward and toward a certain "completion," "perfectedness," or "satisfaction" due to a sense of its "being without" or enduring a lack—a lack that could not be known to blind (*andha*), non-conscious *mūlaprakṛti* or lame (*paṅgu*), utterly passive *Puruṣa*.[12]

But in what sense are *Puruṣa* and *mūlaprakṛti* present to each other in their togetherness? Besides recognizing *samyoga* as the creative intentional ground of manifest reality/procreativity (*vyaktaprakṛti*) that births itself through worlds of striving and self-exertion, what more can we say about this togetherness? And can any Western philosophical paradigms help us with these questions, having demonstrated the limitations of realist and idealist paradigms?

Toward an Existential Phenomenological Interpretation of Sāṃkhya Metaphysics: The Ground of Manifest Reality/Procreativity (*Vyaktaprakṛti*) is *Saṃyoga* (Dialectical Compresence)

This final section responds to these questions by way of Ortega's existential phenomenology. Bearing a number of similarities to

Heidegger's fundamental ontology, Ortega's philosophy of lived reality helps to illustrate how the question of procreativity and a dialectical understanding of life *as lived* are central to Sāṃkhya metaphysics.

Later in his career, Ortega viewed his existential phenomenology as encapsulated in his early dictum: "I am I and my circumstance. If I cannot save [my circumstance], then I cannot save myself" (1914, 45). Ortega saw himself presenting a middle path between two ends. At one end, we find the epistemology of the natural sciences. In particular, biology reduces "life" to an external phenomenon that proceeds according to fixed patterns seemingly beyond our control (circumstances). At the other end, the subjective idealist views of Neo-Kantianism and Husserlian phenomenology subordinate life to the mental activities of the individual subject. In lieu of either extreme, he develops a phenomenology that envisions the ultimate "I" as life or lived reality—as expressed by the first "I" in the dictum "I am I and my circumstance." I qua life consist in an alternation between the two poles of the I as the empirical ego and the ego's circumstance. Circumstance is understood as "world." But this is not a merely external world. It is rather a kind of Heideggerian world of social others. Here, the ego finds itself in reciprocal interrelation. However, the ego and the alter-ego or circumstance retain their mutual transcendence. "Life" or "lived reality" thereby becomes defined by one's feeling pulled in two directions: falling inward into the solitude of the ego and reaching out into the horizons of the other.

On the surface, Sāṃkhya metaphysics bears a similar framework to that of Ortega, particularly when their fundamental relata are considered in relation to each other. Both Ortega and Sāṃkhya acknowledge multiple conscious subjects (Ortega's second "I" and Sāṃkhya's *Puruṣa*) who abide in compresence with another (circumstance, *mūlaprakṛti*) that transcends and, in some sense, stands opposed to the subject.[13] Ortega's empirical ego exists in relation with and yet juxtaposed against *alter*-egos (other I's), and typically encounters circumstances (which is populated by alter egos) as limiting its freedom, power, and desires. According to Sāṃkhya, meanwhile, *Puruṣa* is characterized by its simultaneous compresence with (*saṃyoga*) and ontological distinction from *mūlaprakṛti*, whose overflowing power is often represented as pulling the self into suffering (*duḥkha*).[14] Consequently, the self, as identified with Ortega's second "I" or Sāṃkhya's *Puruṣa,* tends toward retreat from the other and self-enclosure as its essential condition ("I am only I, and not my circumstance," as it were). Ortega declares "man does not *appear* in solitude—although his ultimate truth is solitude (*soledad*)," while the SK tells us that "it is as if the indifferent one (*udāsīnaḥ,* i.e., *Puruṣa*) is an engaged agent," though in actuality the *Puruṣa* eternally abides in *kaivalya* (1932, 148; SK 20).[15]

Of course, important differences lie beneath these similarities. Certainly, the *Puruṣa* is not an experiencing ego or a being-in-the-world; it is non-intentional, and thus does not participate in a world or make meaning of its circumstance. And *mūlaprakṛti* is not equivalent to a "circumstance" or "world"; circumstance offers a range of discrete existential possibilities that implicate the ego in the world (and *hence* frame the ego's interpretations of its world). In contrast, *mūlaprakṛti* is a non-empirical, undirected urge for productivity. Ortega (and perhaps all of Western Philosophy) has no clear match for Sāṃkhya's *Puruṣa* and *mūlaprakṛti.* Moreover, the link between Ortega's intentionally active subject and its world precedes their manifestation as individual relata; their relation is internal to a more primordial reality. Sāṃkhya's seeming duality, however, is itself "radical reality" (to borrow Ortega's term).[16] Indeed, the *saṃyoga* relation of *Puruṣa* and *mūlaprakṛti* is real (unlike Advaita Vedānta's *māyā,* for example), but *samyoga* itself is nonetheless contingent upon some other conditions, namely, the preexistence of a given *Puruṣa* and *mūlaprakṛti.*

In spite of these incongruities, however, these correlated terms display enough association that imputing Ortega's "empirical I-circumstance" dualism upon Sāṃkhya metaphysics merits further exploration. Accordingly, let us shift the focus away from the equivalencies and incongruities between individual terms and toward the relation between the respective pairs of duads. In a literal sense, the term *saṃyoga* means "with" (*sam*) and "union" or "joining" (*Yoga*). Translations such as "contact" and "conjunction" (often deployed by Larson and Burley, respectively) capture this. However, they violate the basic dualism of the system: the *Puruṣa* and *mūlaprakṛti* never come into actual connection. Translating *saṃyoga* as "compresence" captures not only the peculiar togetherness of the *Puruṣa* and *mūlaprakṛti* to each other but the insurmountable separateness between the two; though in close proximity to each other, the two never meet. Meanwhile, in order to accommodate *saṃyoga's* fundamental role in begetting manifest reality/procreativity (*vyaktaprakṛti*), I take "compresence" to mean a "dialectical compresence." The *saṃyoga* of *Puruṣa* and *mūlaprakṛti* involves a series of reversals and interchanges that unfold throughout *saṃyoga's* self-manifestation across the manifest *tattvas*. Transcending time, space, and *teloi*, neither *Puruṣa* nor *mūlaprakṛti* can be directly presented. However, through a dialectical exchange involving the reluctant presence of *Puruṣa* and the overflowing productivity of *mūlaprakṛti*, a dynamic interplay of passive receptivity and creative potency unwinds.

Larson appears to hint at something like this when he notes that "Sāṃkhya might be described as a kind of '*logos*' of that which appears to consciousness" (1979, 207). But by reading external realism into Sāṃkhya metaphysics, Larson distorts the nature of *Puruṣa* and *mūlaprakṛti* coming together *as* interplay. This is unfortunate, since the term *logos* could open new conceptual terrain if articulated from the hermeneutic phenomenology of Heidegger. In Heidegger's system, *logos* implies "discourse," "a making manifest," "unconcealment" (*aletheia*), or "letting something be seen" in its togetherness with something else. Instead, Larson's usage of *logos* appears to invoke the rational order of a cosmos-in-itself, independent of the witnessing *Puruṣa*, and more along the lines of some ancient Greek usages of *logos*. I argue that the SK anticipates something more like this Heideggerian insight. Manifest reality/procreativity (*vyaktaprakṛti*) uncovers itself out of hiddenness by way of the logos or primordial synthesis structure of *saṃyoga*. Instead of turning to Heidegger's phenomenology, though, I approach *saṃyoga* and Sāṃkhya through the dialectical compresence underlying Ortega's existential phenomenology. In this interpretation, manifest reality/procreativity (*vyaktaprakṛti*) gets understood as "life" or "lived reality" (the first "I" in his dictum). "Life" is reducible to neither a world of mind-independent entities that lie in waiting for our observation and analysis, nor the mental activity of a transcendental ego. Not unlike the SK, Ortega was concerned to pave a middle path between the subject–object duality of realisms and the subjectivism of idealisms. What paved this middle path was the alchemical reaction of two gendered principles that birth a lived reality only through their compresence. Life unfolds as the *logos*, as it were, of the dialogical interchange between a discrete, passive, male consciousness and an immensely potent, female other whose roots lie external to the given center of consciousness.

Conclusion

Through this existential phenomenological reading, manifest reality (*vyaktaprakṛti*) comes to life, as it were, upon the simultaneous presence and sustained interplay between *Puruṣa* and *mūlaprakṛti*. In keeping with this line of reasoning, manifest reality or life itself exhibits the design of the encounter between the two relata, not the *telos* or intentionality of either gendered parent as already given prior to their compresence. Interpreting Sāṃkhya through Ortega's phenomenology of life helps to portray this. It highlights the questions of being (namely, "what does it mean *to exist*?") and procreativity ("what does it mean to live reality, and hence generate life?"). These questions are central to Sāṃkhya metaphysics. Sāṃkhya articulates the perspective of reality as lived firsthand, and thus as including the empirical, cognizing subject as always already in relation with a world of experienced objects. Of course, there are differences between these two systems. But Ortega's analysis is akin to that of Sāṃkhya nonetheless. For both Ortega and the SK, manifest reality is an ongoing, dialectical, procreative interplay between two co-fundamental duads. One direction of this interchange orients the discrete subject toward the other in terms of a basic openness. A countermovement pulls the subject away from the other into self-containedness or solitude (*soledad, kaivalya*). Life contains this bidirectional movement of extroversion (openness to the other, or *pravṛtti*) and introversion (withdrawal into the inwardness of the I, or *nivṛtti*). Emerging in the betweenness of *Puruṣa* and *mūlaprakṛti* and their two-way pull, life (*vyaktaprakṛti*) exhibits this interplay as a vital clash that engenders lived reality. In these respects, the dualisms of these two systems are homologous: as with Ortegan life, the structure of Sāṃkhya is relational, dialectical, and procreative.

Notes

1. In this chapter, I will use the term "Sāṃkhya" to refer just to the Sāṃkhya doctrine of the *Sāṃkhya Kārikā*, and I will abbreviate this text as "SK." However, I am well aware of the long history and rich diversity of *sāṃkhya* texts, theories, and contexts for existential *praxes*.

2. Larson explains that "the world in and of itself is simply 'unmanifest' (*avyakta*) apart from the presence of the *Puruṣa* . . . the world in and of itself, although containing potentially everything in the manifest world, is simply an undifferentiated, unmanifest plenitude of being . . . The Sāṃkhya dualism is not a dualism of mind and body, or a dualism of thought and extension. All such dualisms are included or comprehended on the side of the unconscious world" (1979, 197–198).

3. Much of my analysis here is informed by Burley's critical commentary (2007).

4. Īśvarakṛṣṇa makes this clear at SK 8: "The non-perception of that [i.e., *mūlaprakṛti*] is due to its subtlety, not its non-existence; the understanding of that [*mūlaprakṛti*] is by way of its effects" (all translations of the SK are my own unless noted otherwise).

5. Burley explains: "The reorientation that I have in mind here is that which takes place when one ceases to conceive of empirical reality—that is, the world as we experience it—as something that exists outside and independently of our consciousness [*Puruṣa*], and instead conceives of consciousness [*Puruṣa*] as being, in some sense, the field or domain within which empirical reality exists. It is this reorientation that constitutes the first step towards idealism and away from metaphysical realism" (2007, 12–13).

6. Burley's interpretation cannot adequately explain the most important doctrine of *satkāryavāda*. According to Burley, *satkārya* points to nothing more than a theory of transcendental analysis. He writes: "Indeed, in the Sāṃkhya-Yoga doctrine of *Prakṛti* I think we can now observe the result of a two-tier transcendental reflection upon experience: at one level the manifest categories are inferred to be the necessary constitutive elements of the complex repertoire of our experiential possibilities, while at a deeper level, the *guṇas* are inferred to be the irreducible conditions for manifestation, and hence of experience in general" (2007, 104).

7. The term "*bhāva*" derives from the verbal root, "*√bhū*," which means "to be, become, or make be." "*Bhāva*," then, can be taken in such a manner that expresses the causal force of "making be." (This interpretation borrows from conversations with Arindam Chakrabarti, who argues that "*bhāva*" connotes "manner of making be.")

In addition to the *mahat-buddhi*, the *ahaṃkāra* shows dual ontological and epistemological meanings. Consider that it produces from itself a "double-barreled creation": at one end, the intentional subject (as demarcated by the *sattvic ahaṃkāra*, comprised of "the group of eleven," including *manas* and the ten *indriyas*), and at the other end, the empirical world (as demarcated by the *tamasic ahaṃkāra*, from which emerges the putatively external world). SK 24–25 explain: "A double-barreled creation (*dvividhaḥ sargaḥ*) proceeds from the *ahaṃkāra* as the feeling of self (*abhimānaḥ*): namely, the group of eleven and the five *tanmātras*. The eleven, which are characterized by lucidity (*sattvikaḥ*), proceed from the modified *ahaṃkāra*, while the *tanmātras* proceed from [the *ahaṃkāra* as] a dark (*tāmasaḥ*) elemental source (*bhūtades*). But both [the group of eleven and the five *tanmātras*] proceed from splendor (*taijasāt*)."

8. For an alternative perspective, see Chapple's perspective in this volume.

9. Both "*vyañjana*" and "*vyakta*" derive from the verbal root, "*√vyañj*," "to appear, manifest, display" (Monier-Williams 1960, 1029).

10. Recall that the SK holds to a doctrine of multiple *puruṣas* (SK 18). This, conjoined with *saṃyoga* as the ontological ground of each *vyaktaprakṛti*, implies the existence of multiple *samyoga-s*, with each *saṃyoga* denoting the compresence of *mūlaprakṛti* and a numerically distinct *Puruṣa*. There is a one-to-one correlation between a given *Puruṣa* (e.g., *Puruṣa* "A") and a given *vyaktaprakṛti* (*vyaktaprakṛti* "A"). The presence of just this *Puruṣa* (*Puruṣa* "A," not *Puruṣa* "B") to *mūlaprakṛti* helps to bring about just this *vyaktaprakṛti* (*vyaktaprakṛti* "A") and not that one (*vyaktaprakṛti* "B," whose existence would depend upon the *samyoga* of *mūlaprakṛti* and *Puruṣa* "B"). In a moment, I will argue that each *vyaktaprakṛti* is a given life or lived reality. Accordingly, we can take *Puruṣa* "A" in compresence with *mūlaprakṛti* to be the ontological ground just for the lived reality that is Aaron (*vyaktaprakṛti* "A") but not for the life that is Bob (*vyaktaprakṛti* "B"). Moreover, the dissolution of this *saṃyoga* of *Puruṣa* "A" and *mūlaprakṛti* would only bring about the cessation of the lived reality of Aaron (but it would not entail the termination of Bob's life).

The Sāṃkhya doctrine of the *saṃskāra-s* (karmic traces or impressions) lends further support to this explanation. These residual traces are what generate and give the particular character to a specific lived reality. Importantly, the SK takes these to reside in the *mahat-buddhi* (the first empirical tattva of *vyaktaprakṛti*), not in *mūlaprakṛti* or the *Puruṣa* (SK 67).

11. In some respects, *mūlaprakṛti* is similar to Schopenhauer's notion of the will as extra-mental, causally active, singular, and teleologically blind. I explore parallels between Sāṃkhya's *mūlaprakṛti* and Schopenhauer's will in a larger study of the *Sāṃkhya Karika*.

12. The terms in quotations are taken from Apte's notes on "*pravṛtti*" (see 1998, 1052).

13. I use these terms "self" and "other" rather loosely as correlates to *Puruṣa* and *mūlaprakṛti*, respectively.

14. For Ortega, the ego is "a *nativitate* open to the other, to the alien being," and in the case of Sāṃkhya the *Puruṣa* is susceptible to being drawn toward *mūlaprakṛti* (1932, 149–150).

15. Ortega y Gasset, José (1932), *Obras Completas*, Vols. I–XI. Madrid: Revista de Occidente, 1965.

16. Ortega eschewed any philosophy (including Husserlian phenomenology and Cartesianism) that pulled one into abstractions and away from the concrete reality of one's life. He writes: "[I] abandoned Phenomenology at the very moment of accepting it. Instead of withdrawing from consciousness, as has been done since Descartes, we become firm in the radical reality which is for every one his [or her life]" (1932, 273).

References

Apte, Prin. Vaman Shivaram. 1998. *The Practical Sanskrit-English Dictionary*, revised edition. Kyoto, Japan: Rinsen Book Company.

Burley, Mikel. 2007. *Classical Sāṃkhya and Yoga: An Indian Metaphysics of Experience*. New York: Routledge.

Larson, Gerald. 1979. *Classical Sāṃkhya: An Interpretation of its History and Meaning*, 2nd edition. Delhi: Motilal Banarsidass.

Monier-Williams, Sir Monier. 1960. *A Sanskrit-English Dictionary*, 3rd edition. Oxford: Oxford University Press.

Ortega y Gasset, José. 1914 [1961]. *Meditations on Quixote* (*Meditaciones del Quijote*), trans. by Evelyn Rugg and Diego Marin, Introd. by Julián Marías. New York: W. W. Norton.

Ortega y Gasset, José. 1932. *Obras Completas*, Vols. I–XI. Madrid: Revista de Occidente, 1965.

Chapter 2

The Role of Vitality (Prāṇa) in the Sāṃkhya Quest for Freedom

ANA LAURA FUNES MADEREY

Introduction

Classical Sāṃkhya has usually been interpreted as an intellectualist school. Its presumed method for the attainment of liberation is essentially characterized by rational inquiry into reality, which involves the intellectual understanding of the distinction between two principles: the conscious and the material. Some have argued that this liberating process is not only theoretical, but that it entails yogic practice, or that it is the natural outcome of existential forces that tend toward freedom. However, recent studies in Sāṃkhya involving detailed analysis of an anonymous commentary of the *Sāṃkhyakārikā*, the *Yuktidīpikā*, suggest a more complex picture. The external functions of the five vital winds (*prāṇas*) in relation to the sources of action (*karmayonis*) and dispositions of being (*bhāvas*) seem to play an important role in the liberating path. In this chapter, I review the relation between *bhāvas*, *karmayonis*, and the five *prāṇas* by considering the social, moral, and interpersonal aspects of the five vital winds as described in the *Yuktidīpikā*. It will be shown how the external functions of *prāṇa* are related to the moral cultivation of vitality, leading to the enactment and manifestation of dispositions of being (*bhāvas)* that bring about the realization of oneself as a knower in the ethical engagement with others. It is this unique way of understanding *prāṇa* in the *Yuktidīpikā* that makes the Sāṃkhya path for liberation something more than a theoretical cognitive method or a spontaneous and predetermined realization of one's Self.

Is There a Sāṃkhya Discipline that Brings Freedom?

Sāṃkhya is defined in the *Sāṃkhyakārikā* (*SK* 1) as an inquiry into the real means of terminating suffering. It distinguishes this inquiry (literally, the "desire to know" or *jijñāsā*) from other means of getting rid of pain such as medicine, morality, sciences, arts, and religion in that its effect promises to be definitive and final, not just partial and temporary like the others. The Sāṃkhya inquiry which, according to K. C. Bhattacharyya's analysis (1956, 135) entails knowing how to be free from the very desire to be free from pain, requires seeing the distinction between the material and conscious principles of reality, that is, *prakṛti* and *puruṣa.* This knowledge would then provide the means to transcend suffering once and for all. How exactly this knowledge is attained has been the subject of some debate among scholars.

The *Kārikā* says that these principles are indeed not perceivable with the senses. Nevertheless, it argues, what cannot be empirically perceived can be known through inference or trustworthy testimony (*SK* 8). This is why many have taken the inquiry into the distinction between *puruṣa* and *prakṛti* to be a theoretical investigation that emphasizes the rational understanding of the constituents of reality. Others have insisted that mere rational inquiry and intellectual effort are not enough to produce a liberating state of existence; a transformational intuitive discernment of these principles is also necessary (Larson, 156).[1] In this sense, some think that Sāṃkhya's liberating knowledge (*jñāna)* should be understood as a liberating wisdom (*vijñāna)*, a type of internal knowledge (*SK* 23) that yields a direct experience by means of which one's own intellect realizes its difference from the self. But can this direct experience be attained by the intellect alone? Some scholars such as Mikel Burley (2007, 47–48) think that the Sāṃkhya inquiry also entails the cultivation of a yogic practice, such as the one outlined in the *Yogasūtra* of Patañjali. However, since the *Sāṃkhyakārikā* does not contain any explicit prescription for a specific practice, there is some debate as to whether it is the Yoga of Patañjali that is to be paired up with the Sāṃkhya rational inquiry or whether Sāṃkhya proposes a contemplative practice or "soteric methodology" of its own (Oberhammer 1977, 16).

Some indication that Sāṃkhya considers a contemplative practice as part of this inquiry can be found in *SK* 64 where repeated contemplation of the constituents of reality (*tattvābhyāsa)* is mentioned as necessary to attain liberating knowledge. Both the commentaries by Vācaspati Miśra, the *Tattvakaumudī* (ninth or tenth century), and the anonymous commentary on the *SK*, the *Yuktidīpikā* (between seventh and ninth centuries), interpret *abhyāsa* as continuous, repeated, and one-pointed focus of the mind on an element of reality (Shevchenko 2017, 873–874), bringing it very close to the practice of one-pointed focus (*ekatattvābhyāsa* or *ekāgratā)* in the *Yogasūtra* (1.32 and 3.12). Dimitry Shevchenko points out that the *Sāṃkhyakārikā* also mentions in *kārikā*s 23 and 45 another important concept for the Yoga practice in the *Yogasūtra,* that of *virāga/vairāgya* or dispassion, that is, the "practice of disengaging the mind from the objects of desire" (Shevchenko 2017, 874–875). However, he argues that the practices of *vairāgya* and *abhyāsa* as understood by the classical Sāṃkhya tradition presented in the *Sāṃkhyakārikā* and the *Yuktidīpikā*[2] do not fully coincide with the ones described in the *Yogasūtra,* mainly because they are not considered to be the result of the will or personal effort as within the Yoga tradition. According to Shevchenko (2017, 888), "liberating praxis in the *Sāṃkhyakārikā* should be seen as manifestation of liberating knowledge predetermined by the material forces of *prakṛti,* rather than an independent act of will." Shevchenko supports K. C. Bhattacharyya who states that: "there is apparently in Sāṃkhya no sādhana or discipline for freedom . . . The spiritual process of freeing from mind or the general potentiality of pain is nothing but reflection and is already above the egoistic attitude that conditions willing" (1956, 141). Yogic efforts are certainly accepted as one of the many possible forms that the process of liberation might require. These processes may be guided by nature's unconscious drives toward freedom, but they are not seen as the cause of the process nor as its result, liberating knowledge (Shevchenko 2017, 888). Means of liberation other than yogic practice within Sāṃkhya include listening to teachings of the sages, study of treatises, and even spontaneous realization by independent reflection (*idem*, 878).

In my reading of the classical Sāṃkhya tradition, I do find that the *Yuktidīpikā* outlines a unique yogic discipline that contradicts K. C. Bhattacharyya's statement above and Shevchenko's defense of the "natural liberation approach." Shevchenko suggests that liberation in Sāṃkhya happens on its own and without the intervention of human effort or will. While it is true that the desire to seek freedom from existential pain may be determined by one's own natural processes, circumstances, level of understanding, psychological predispositions, and the unconscious drive of *prakṛti* toward liberation, a further step is needed to maintain our attention and actions in that direction. This also seems to be the position found in the *Suvarṇasaptati*[3] where the commentator opens with the story of Kapila, foremost sage and legendary founder of the Sāṃkhya tradition, who pays repeated visits to brahmin Āsuri in various spans of thousands of years. Āsuri is not interested in nor ready to commit to the path of liberation because he enjoys the life of a householder. One day, after some time, Kapila visits him once again to remind him of the path to freedom and to see if he is ready for it. Without any reason or explanation for Āsuri's change of attitude other than the passage of time, he responds that he can now become a "brahmacārin," one who renounces all pleasures in the pursuit of freedom. "Thenceward he renounced the way of his family and commenced the ascetic observances, as a disciple of Kapila."[4]

Āsuri's decision to leave his previous life in the pursuit of liberation could indeed be seen as a natural outcome of *saṃsāra*. Life in *saṃsāra* includes the natural consequences of constantly experiencing desire, attainment, loss, frustration, and existential pain. These painful experiences may be caused by any of these three factors: oneself, others, and the natural environment. However, Āsuri's commitment to the "observances" in the pursuit of freedom is not explained just by the "natural outcome of any activity of *prakṛti*," as Shevchenko suggests (2017, 886). Tara Chatterjea's critical comment in regard to Sāṃkhya is on point here: "the desire to get rid of sorrow cannot solely motivate a person to realize the pure self" (2003, 99). Indeed, as Oberhammer has shown in his exposition of Sāṃkhya meditation, the aspirant, even after having spontaneously felt the desire for ultimate liberation, must transcend several states of complacency, including the very idea that liberation is a result of nature's processes: time, luck, or fate (SK 50). To this I would add that the Sāṃkhya path also includes the right use of one's vitality or *prāṇa* in order to modify the ways in which we undertake actions. This cannot be understood merely by leaving behavior up to nature's unconscious drives. In the next sections, I proceed to argue for this position, first by reviewing Oberhammer's description of the Sāṃkhya meditation, and then by showing how the *Yuktidīpikā* describes a Sāṃkhya practice that involves the conscious and ethical cultivation of the external aspect of vitality *(prāṇa)*. Finally, it will be seen how the conscious and moral cultivation of *prāṇa* produces a change in the use of our capacities of knowing and, with this, develops the will to freedom.

The Internal and External Functions of *Prāṇa*

According to Oberhammer (1977, 17–57), following the *Yuktidīpikā* (on *SK* 50–51), the meditative path proper to Sāṃkhya is based on a progressive striving towards the total arrest of passions through the transcendence of nine types of complacencies (*tuṣṭi*s). The nine types of complacencies are divided into internal and external. The external refer to (1) the satisfaction that people feel when they have detached from certain types of objective reality such as detachment from sensory enjoyment, or (2) from things that are difficult to preserve, or (3) from things that are ephemeral, or (4) difficult to obtain, or (5) from the very impulse of fulfilling one's own desires, or (6) from activities that harm others. The internal complacencies are those that refer to (7) the satisfaction that someone feels when attaining the knowledge of nature and its processes, or (8) to the satisfaction felt when one discovers that material existence has as its natural purpose both enjoyment and liberation, and (9) the consequent state of contentment in thinking that final liberation may be a matter of time, luck, or the result of ascetic practices. The Sāṃkhya path, according to the author of the *Yuktidīpikā,* would thus entail detaching from all feelings of contentment in regard to one's achievements.

Oberhammer notices that the motivation to pursue this path of progressive detachments arises from a profound feeling of dissatisfaction due to the recognition of the painful structure of existence (1977, 49). Perhaps we could understand this motivation as an "ontological" disillusionment that naturally arises from the unfulfilled expectation that happiness can be found in objects, whether these are concrete, material and external, or abstract, internal realities. However, the process of moving toward freedom and away from suffering is a difficult one because natural tendencies are constantly pulling a person to remain in the present state of seeming satisfaction. It is easy to forget that real contentment cannot be found in any object of knowledge or desire. It cannot be found even in the accomplishment of a certain level of dispassion or virtue. In Sāṃkhya, true contentment is found in the understanding that self-realization is different from the obtainment of objects in general, whether they are physical or mental.

Oberhammer (1977, 29) explains that Sāṃkhya practice starts with the purification of the *karmayoni*s—literally "sources of action"—that is, the subconscious processes that motivate action. This is done by directing all actions towards righteousness or *dharma,* which prepares the mind to contemplate (*dhyāna*) the basic constituents of reality (*tattva*s), to distinguish them from the conscious principle, and to eventually realize the self. The repeated practice of knowing the *tattvas* as different from *puruṣa* prevents the practitioner from deriving satisfaction from lesser objects of contemplation, which tend to stop one's search for true knowledge and freedom. Yet it is not dispassion itself, which is the cause of liberation, but the dispassion that arises from the correct knowledge (*vijñāna*), that is, the discerning knowledge that recognizes the Self as the conscious principle distinct from the rest of the objects constitutive of material reality. Oberhammer (1977, 54) states that it is the lack of passion *as* reflective knowledge in the form "This is not me, this is not mine" that liberates a person from suffering. He characterizes meditation on the different levels of complacencies leading to a lack of passion as extremely theoretical, albeit a theory that becomes a way of life (*idem,* 49–50). But how can such an abstract theory become a way of life? In other words, how can the understanding of a metaphysical distinction between matter and consciousness cause someone's mind to make one particular set of choices rather than another?

I believe this can be answered by understanding the role of *prāṇa* in Sāṃkhya. *Prāṇa* or vitality is mentioned only once in the *Sāṃkhyakārikā.* It refers to the "common activity of the instruments of knowledge" (*SK* 29): intellect (*buddhi),* sense of individuality (*ahaṃkāra),* and the operative mind (*manas).*[5] While each of the elements of our cognitive system has a separate and distinct function,[6] as a whole they all have the ability to "grasp" (*grahaṇa),* that is, to perceive and experience the world.[7] In more accurate terms, the instruments of knowledge share a common activity of "grasping" or taking the world in, as it were, to present it to the "eye" of *puruṣa,* so that through its awareness, experience becomes manifest (*SK* 36 and 37). *Prāṇa* and its five different modalities: *prāṇa, apāna, samāna, udāna,* and *vyāna,* refer to the very performance of this "grasping" function that is set in motion by the instruments of knowledge (*antaḥkaraṇa).*

The modalities of *prāṇa* are usually known in the commentarial tradition of Patañjali's Yoga[8] for their function in relation to different parts of the anatomical body and the movements inherent in its physiology. Sāṃkhya follows Yoga in this but it also adds functions that it calls "external." These external functions of *prāṇa* refer to moral and psychosocial dispositions. The following chart shows this original view of *prāṇa* as it appears in the *Yuktidīpikā* (*YD*) divided in four categories: modality of *prāṇa,* internal functions, external functions, and manifest activity. The chart is based on the *YD*'s commentary on *SK* 29.[9]

As can be seen in table 2.1, both the internal and external functions of *prāṇa* refer to an "anatomy" of motions that sustain life: inclination, descent, balance, elevation, circulation. These "motions" of vitality encompass the physiological as well as the mental functions of the living body. The internal functions manifest as physiology through interoceptive and proprioceptive awareness. The external functions of *prāṇa,* while also based on bodily directions, are essentially moral in character; they manifest through our interactions with others and the environment. The prāṇic internal movement is an automatic, unconscious dynamism. The external movement entails intentionality, the performance of an action, and the recognition of a moral value. As "motion," *prāṇa* is visible in the activities of living beings, both humans and non-human animals, in their bodies and interactions with other bodies. *Prāṇa* is the felt movement of manifested nature (*vyakta),* that is, *prakṛti* as being observed by *puruṣa.*

Table 2.1. The Internal and External Functions of the Five Modalities of *Prāṇa*

Modality of	**Internal Functions (*antarvṛtti*)**	**External Functions or Objective Sphere (*viṣaya*)**	**Activity Manifests in: (*abhivyakta*)**
Prāṇa[1]	It is *prāṇa* because it moves outward from mouth or nostrils and because it is inclined forward (in the exhalation). Breath that flows through the mouth or the nostrils.	That inclination is also found, for example, in an army moving forward, or in a bent tree, or in a person inclined toward virtue, or toward wealth, or toward desire, or toward wisdom, or in the inclination toward objects opposite to these [i.e., vice, ignorance, etc.]	A person afflicted by a great pain, or in someone who has been separated from important relatives, or in the motion of a buffalo that accompanies a herd of cattle to drink water from a tank.
Apāna[2]	It is called *apāna* because it is a descending motion and because it moves away from something. Descending and pulling down motion involved in the fluids of the body: sweating, ejaculating, urinating, excreting, flatulence, menstruation, giving birth. Restrains *prāṇa* from below.	Descending motion of those beings who depart from virtue, knowledge, etc. or who depart from objects opposite to them.	Manifests in someone who goes around a well or a hole without falling into it, or in someone who jumps over a centipede [avoids stepping over it].

Samāna[3]	Located in the heart, between *prāṇa* and *apāna*. Restrains and restricts the *prāṇa* above and the *apāna* below.	Related to community (being together, companionship, etc.). This vital breath exists in association with others [enjoying being with one another], for example serving with others; worshiping with others; practicing discipline with others; being in relation with one's partner, children, relatives, and friends.	Manifests in the panting (or salivating) of a dog [literally, the giving forth of the essence of a dog]; the bull who bears the load [on his back]; the fast shaking tail of a female sheep (ewe) in heat.
Udāna[4]	It brings itself (or the self) upward, ascending up to the head. Takes up with it the bodily essential fluid [semen]; it ascends to the head and then due to particular emissions of air striking different locations in the vocal chords, *udāna* becomes the cause of manifested sounds such as syllables, words, sentences, verses, and texts. ——— Existing above prāṇa, apāna, and samāna, it draws them upwards, whether they are in the bottom, middle or above.	It brings the self above other beings such as [when we have the thoughts]: "I am better than the faulty one," or "I am similarly [good] to the proper ones," or "I am better than the good ones," or "I am similar to the best," or "I am better than the best," or "Being the best, I am proud, one who has attained knowledge," or "being one without qualities, I possess unique fewer qualities than the one who possesses many other qualities."	As when someone is sprinkled with cold water [wakes up], or when a sword becomes visible after being unsheathed [by sliding it up its sheath].

continued on next page

Table 2.1. Continued.

Modality of *prāṇa*	**Internal Functions (*antarvṛtti*)**	**External Functions or Objective Sphere (*viṣaya*)**	**Activity Manifests in: (*abhivyakta*)**
Vyāna[5]	Pervades the whole body and is present in intimate association. Pervading from "head to toes," it moves around vital points, physical elements, essential bodily substances, and abides in all the vital winds. Pervading the whole body, vyāna controls the rest of the vital winds, keeping them balanced (or steady) as a staff [does to the body].	Found in the intimate association among beings such as in the case of a wife who follows her husband even after dead and hopes that "may only this person be my husband in the next life." In this way, vyāna appears with [the way someone follows] the virtues, etc. and also their opposites.	It becomes manifest at the end of life, when the ankles, legs, thighs, hips, buttocks, belly, chest, and throat become cold, just as they do [when] shivering at the touch of the two feet on cold snow.

1. *tatra mukhanāsikābhyāṃ pragamanāt prāṇateś ca prāṇaḥ / yo'yaṃ mukhanāsikābhyāṃ saṃcarati so'ntarvṛttir vāyuḥ prāṇa ity abhidhīyate / yā kacit praṇatir nāma bhūteṣu tadyathā praṇateyaṃ senā, praṇato'yam vṛkṣaḥ, praṇato'yam dharme, praṇato'yam arthe, praṇato'yam kāme, praṇato'yam vidyāyām, tadviparīteṣu vā bāhyaprāṇavṛttir eṣā / prāṇaviṣaya evaiṣā bhavati | sa khalv ayam atrābhivyakto bhavati tadyathā mahatā vā duḥkhenābhiplutasya mahatā vā bandhunā viyuktasya sahitasya vā saurabheyasya nipānāvatīrṇasya vā mahiṣasya/* (*YD* 1998, 206, 35-207, 5, on *SK* 29).

2. *avagater apakramanāc cāpānaḥ / yo'yaṃ rasaṃ dhātūn śukraṃ mūtraṃ purīṣaṃ vātārtavagarbhāṃś cākarṣann adhogacchann ayam antarvṛttir vāyur apāna ity abhidhīyate / yac cāpi kiṃcid apakramaṇaṃ nāma bhūteṣu tadyathāpakrānto'yaṃ dharmādibhyas tadviparītebhyo veti bāhyā khalv apāna vṛttir eṣā / apānaviṣaya evaiṣa bhavati / balavattaraś cāyaṃ prāṇād vāyoḥ / kasmāt / eṣā hy etaṃ prāṇam ūrdhvaṃ vartamānam arvāg eva sanniyacchati arvāg eva sannirūṇaddhi / eṣa atrābhivyakto bhavati / tadyatho'pakūpam upaśvabhraṃ vā parivartamānasyāpakrāntiḥ śatapadīṃ laṅghayataḥ /* (*YD* 1988, 207, 5-15, on *SK* 29).

3. *hṛdy avasthānāt sahabhāvāc ca samānaḥ/ yas tv ayaṃ prāṇāpānayor madhye hṛdy avatiṣṭhate sa samāno vāyur antarvṛttiḥ / yaś cāpi kaścit sahabhāvo nāma bhūteṣu [dvandvārāmatā] tadyathā saha dāsye, saha yakṣye, saha tapaś cariṣyāmi, saha bhāryāputrair bandhubhiḥ suhṛdbhiś ca vartiṣya iti bāhyā samānavṛttir eṣā / samānaviṣaya evaiṣa bhavati / balavattaraḥ khalv ayaṃ prāṇāpānābhyām / eṣa hy etau prāṇāpānāv ūrdhvam avāk ca vartamānau madhya eva sanniyacchati, madhya eva sanniruṇaddhi / sa caiṣo'trābhivyakto bhavati / tadyathā srutasārasya vā sārameyasya anaḍuho voḍhabhārasya gharmābhitaptāyā vaiḍakāyāḥ ardhārdhakāyam śakaśaketi prāṇānte sarvaprāṇinām prāṇāpānāv utsṛjyordhvam adhaś ca muktayoktrau hayāv iva viṣamaṃ saṃcārayan śarīraṃ sa parāsyati /* (*YD* 1988, 207, 15-25, on *SK* 29).

4. *Mūrdhārohaṇād ātmotkarṣaṇāc codānaḥ / yas tv ayaṃ prāṇāpānasamānānāṃ sthānāny atikramya rasaṃ dhātūṃś cādāya mūrdhānam ārohati tataś ca pratihato nivṛttaḥ sthānakaraṇānupradānaviśeṣād varṇapadavākyaślokagranthalakṣaṇasya śabdasyābhivyaktinimittam bhavaty ayam antarvṛttir vāyur udāna ity ucyate / yaś cāpi kaścid ātmotkarṣo nāma bhūteṣu tadyathā hīnād asmi śreyān, sadṛśena vā sadṛśaḥ, sadṛśād asmi śreyān, śreyasā vā sadṛśaḥ, śreyaso vā śreyān | etasmiṃs tathārūpābhimāno vā prāptavidyasya tadyathā bahvantaraviśeṣād alpāntaraviśeṣo 'smi, aguṇavato vā guṇavān asmīti bāhyodānavṛttir eṣā / udānaviṣaya evaiṣa bhavati / balavattaraḥ khalv ayaṃ pūrvebhyaḥ / katham / eṣa hy etān prāṇādīn ūrdhvam avāṇ madhye ca vartamānān ūrdhvam evonnayati, ūrdhvam evotkarṣati / sa caiṣo 'trābhivyakto bhavati śītodakena vā paryukṣitasya prāsam asiṃ vikośaṃ codyatam abhipaśyataḥ /* (*YD* 1998, 207, 25-208, 10, on *SK* 20).

5. *śarīravyāpter atyantāvinābhāvāc ca vyānaḥ / yas tv ayam ā lomanakhāc charīraṃ vyāpya rasādināṃ dhātūnāṃ pṛthivyādīnāṃ vyūhaṃ marmanāṃ ca praspandanaṃ prāṇādīnāṃ ca sthitiṃ karoti so 'ntarvṛttir vyānaḥ / yaś cāpi kaścid atyantāvinābhāvo nāma bhūteṣu tadyathā pativratā bhartāraṃ mṛtam apy anugacchati bhavāntare 'py ayam eva bhartā syāt tathā dharmādibhis tadviparītaiś ceti bāhyā vyānavṛttir eṣā/ vyānaviṣaya evaiṣa bhavati/ balavattamaś cāyam sarvebhyaḥ / katham/ anena hi vyāpte śarīradaṇḍake tadvaśīkṛtānāṃ prāṇādīnāṃ samāsthitir bhavati / sa eṣo 'ntakāle prāṇabhṛtām avinābhāvena vartamāno 'bhivyajyate tadyathā hā tarhi pādau hemau śītībhūtau gulphe jaṅghe ūrū kaṭir udaram uraḥ kaṇṭhe 'sya khuraghuro vartate hū ity evaiṣo bāhyo vyāna iti /* (*YD* 1998, 208, 10-20, on *SK* 29).

Unlike other philosophical systems in India, *prāṇa* does not seem to have a metaphysical status in classical Sāṃkhya. It is not one of the twenty-five elements of reality (*tattva),* nor is it considered the material substrate of reality (as it is for Kashmir Śaivism or for the *Yogavāsiṣtha),* nor a layer of embodiment (as within the *Taittirīya Upaniṣad*), nor is it identified with the conscious Self (*ātman,* as it is sometimes done in Advaita Vedānta). Instead, classical Sāṃkhya gives the vital energy a functionalist role. In contrast to other commentarial traditions, the *YD* explains why this is the case.[10] The activity of *prāṇa* is itself the performance of an action. However, such an action is not intrinsically caused or determined, otherwise it would never stop or change its course. It is also not caused just by the determination of external elements such as the wind, water, or environmental factors, for their effect is always mediated by the embodiment of a person, just as the movement of the bellows requires the arms of a person to push the air through it. Neither is it an action caused by the Self (*puruṣa*), since the Self is inactive by definition. And yet action is not causeless, since its activity is caused by something other than itself. The performance of an action, that is, the activity of *prāṇa,* is instead caused by the conjoint activity of the instruments of knowledge (intellect, ego, mind).

Thus, *prāṇa* is an intentional, directed motion or activity; it is the movement of life itself, manifested in judging, feeling, thinking, perceiving, acting, eating, digesting, breathing, etc. It is neither reducible to material unconscious activity nor to conscious pure intentionality. It is both a biological and moral activity, unconscious and conscious. The *Yuktidīpikā* refers to this living energy as an "effort" (*prayatna*),[11] one that is both, as we will see, in one sense effortless and in another, effortful.

The External Functions of *Prāṇa* and the "Ways of Being" (*Bhāvas*)

In one sense, *prāṇa* is the unrestrained course of life, a ceaseless "becoming" (*bhāvana*) determined by predispositions (*bhāva*s) such as memories, habits, and other impressions from past experiences (*saṃskāra*s).[12] In another sense, it is a vital energy that can be guided, restricted, modified, cultivated. "The internal function of the instruments of knowledge collectively is like that of a lamp without light [of its own], the nature of which is to act as a sustainer (pillar) of the living body. As long as that activity is unobstructed, abundant in *rajas*, striking the vital wind due to the incessant power of the virtues, etc., the human being lives."[13]

The capacity to think and determine reality cognitively and affectively (*buddhi*), the sense of being an individual (*ahaṃkāra*), and the attentive mind (*manas*) are called "pillars" because they are, according to Sāṃkhya, the basis of experience, the basis of the individual embodied self. The activity of the three pillars (the three functions constitutive of *antaḥkaraṇa*) exerts an influence on the embodied self according to the internal predispositions or *bhāva*s active at the moment. These *bhāva*s, which could also be understood as "ways of being," are eight: righteousness (*dharma*), knowledge (*jñāna*), detachment (*virāga*), power (*aiśvarya*), and their opposites: vice, ignorance, attachment, and powerlessness. I am calling these *bhāva*s "ways of being" because they shape the way someone thinks and chooses to act. One's predisposition toward virtue, knowledge, passion, power, or any mixture of them and/or their contraries, becomes evident in the use of the intellect, sense of individuality, attention, and senses. Since the activity of the instruments is called *prāṇa*, it could be said that the *bhāva*s influence the prāṇic motion of the embodied self. *Prāṇa* will continue to move in a certain direction as long as the *bhāva*s continue to flow in that way, the consequence of which will be a particular experience and the way someone relates to existence and suffering. The *SK* calls this manifesting or projective power of the *bhāva*s an intellective, intentional creation or *pratyayasarga*, and categorizes it in four types of experiential realms according to the way in which the embodied self is positioned before the world through the determinative function of the intellect (*buddhi*) (See Yamaguchi 1967, 977). The four states are delusion (*avidyā*), incapacity (*aśakti*), complacency (*tuṣṭi*), and accomplishment (*siddhi*), each with their respective varieties. These give rise to fifty different categories of experience or *pratyaya*s (*SK* 46–51). See table 2.2 below.

The relation between the *bhāva*s and the *pratyayasarga* is not fully developed by Īśvarakṛṣṇa, who provides much more detail on the *bhāva*s in his *Sāṃkhyakārikā* than on the process of intellective, intentional creation or *pratyayasarga*. Frauwallner (1973, 268) thought this was because the *bhāva*s represented a more advanced "doctrine of feelings" in Sāṃkhya than the more ancient theory of the *pratyayasarga*. He considered that the group of "fifty ideas" (*pratyaya*s) had little to add to Sāṃkhya psychology (*idem*, 258). Unlike Frauwallner, I do not read the relation between *bhāva*s and the *pratyaya*s only as the historical development of two paradigms of evolution in Sāṃkhya, but as a phenomenological description of the dynamic relationship between affective predispositions of the individual and the phenomenal realm of experience. As James Kimball (2016, 554–555) shows in his discussion on this topic, the *bhāva*s determine the phenomenal categories of experience (*pratyaya*s), which in turn affect the attainment or obstruction of the development of future dispositions of being (*bhāva*s). The intellective, intentional creation (*pratyayasarga)* is thus the process by which the affective predispositions of being (*bhāva*s) cause an individual to have a particular existential position within the world of experience. At the same time, this existential position gives rise to new predispositions or ways of being (*bhāva*s). Kimball, however, does not take into consideration the role that *prāṇa* has in such a process. Frauwallner takes the theory of the five bodily winds as a third stage of development in the theory of Sāṃkhya evolution and acknowledges its importance for the Sāṃkhya path towards liberation (1973, 263), just as much as the *bhāva*s and the *pratyaya*s. However, he also does not articulate the precise way in which the five bodily winds relate to the affective predispositions and the varieties of experience in the path toward liberation.

To establish this relationship, let us first show, in a schematic way, and drawing from the relevant passages in the *Yuktidīpikā*, how these *bhāva*s or ways of being produce a certain consequence in the realm of experience which is expressed in the existential positioning of the embodied self within the world. This existential positioning encompasses several "varieties of experience" each of which is guided or governed by the predominant activity of one of the three functions of the instruments of knowledge.

The existential position of the embodied self within the world relates to the varieties of experience in the way a person directs herself both morally and epistemically. A person "grasps" the world through one's faculties of perception and action. If a person is in a state of delusion (*avidyā*), for example, one might have the *inclination toward*—a movement related to *prāṇa* (see "External functions of the vital winds" in table 2.2)—certain vices, constantly ignoring

Table 2.2. Relation between the *Bhāvas* and the *Pratyayasarga*

Bhāvas[1] **Ways of Being:**	**Consequence in the Realm of Experience: (*gamanaviśeṣa*)**[2]	***Pratyayasarga***[3] **Position of the Embodied Self within the World:**	**The 50 *Pratyayas* Varieties of Experience:**	**Governed by the Activity of:**
Virtue (*dharma*)	Elevation	Accomplishment[4] (*siddhi*)	Gifts (*dānam*) Good friendship (*suhṛt prāptiḥ*) Personal sorrow (*ādhyatmika*) Sorrow caused by others (*ādhibhāutika*) Sorrow caused by natural elements (*ādhidaivikam*) Study of scriptures (*adhyāya*) Lessons from trustworthy teacher (*śabda*) One's own reasoning (*ūha*)	*buddhi* *sattva*
Knowledge (*jñāna*)	Liberation			
Detachment (*virāga*)	Absorption			
Mastery (*aiśvarya*)	Absence of obstacle			

continued on next page

Table 2.2. Continued.

Bhāvas[1] **Ways of Being:**	**Consequence in the Realm of Experience: (*gamanaviśeṣa*)**[2]	***Pratyayasarga***[3] **Position of the Embodied Self within the World:**	**The 50 *Pratyayas* Varieties of Experience:**	**Governed by the Activity of:**
Vice (*adharma*)	Degradation	Delusion[5] (*avidyā*)	8 varieties of ignorance (*tamas*) 8 varieties of delusion in the form of attachment to body and the sense of I (*moha*) 10 varieties of supreme delusion due to attachment to things in the world and belongings (*mahāmoha*) 18 varieties of profound darkness such as anger (*tāmiśra*) 18 varieties of blind darkness including fear of death (*andhatamiśra*)	*indriyas* *tamas*
Ignorance (*ajñāna*)	Bondage			

Attachment (*rāga*)	Transmigration	Complacency[6] (*tuṣṭi*)	4 internal: natural processes (*prakṛti*) means (*upādānam*) time (*kāla*) fate (*bhāgyam*) 5 external (*bāhyā*): abandonment of objects of the senses.	*ahaṃkāra* *rajas*
Lack of Mastery (*anaiśvarya*)	Obstacles	Incapacity[7] (*aśakti*)	injury of the 11 sense faculties (*indriyavadhāḥ*) injury of the faculty of knowledge (17 varieties: 9 opposites of the complacencies and of the perfections) (*buddhivadāh*)	*manas* *rajas+tamas*

1. *ucyate: dharmādyā bhāvāḥ / dharmo jñānam vairāgyam aiśvaryam adharmo'jñānam avairāgyam anaiśvaryam ity ete bhāvāḥ /* (*YD*, 233, 5, SK on 43).
2. *dharmeṇa gamanam ūrdhvaṃ gamanam adhastād bhavaty adharmeṇa/ jñānena cā 'pavargo viparyayād iṣyate bandhaḥ* (*SK* 44).
3. *eṣa pratyayasargo viparyayā'-śakti-tuṣṭi-siddhy-ākhyaḥ /guṇavaiṣamyavimardāt tasya ca bhedās tu pañcāśat* (*SK* 46)
4. *ūhaḥ śabdo'dhyayanaṃ duḥkhavighātās trayaḥ suhṛtprāptiḥ/ dānaṃ ca siddhayo'ṣṭau siddheḥ pūrvo'ṅkuśas tri-vidhaḥ* (*SK* 51)
5. *bhedas tamaso'aṣṭavidho mohasya ca daśavidho mahāmohaḥ/ tāmisro'aṣṭādaśadhā tathā bhavaty andhatāmisraḥ* (*SK* 48).
6. *ādhyātmikāś catasraḥ prakṛtyupādānakālabhāgyākhyāḥ bāhyā viṣayoparamāc ca pañca nava tuṣṭayo'bhimatāḥ* (*SK* 50).
7. *ekādaś' endriyavadhāḥ saha buddhivadhair aśaktir uddiṣṭā/ saptadaśa vadhā buddher viparyayāt tuṣṭisiddhīnām* (*SK* 49).

(*ajñāna*) what is good. An existential position of incapacity (*aśakti*) might make it impossible for a person to avoid *falling down into* or *moving away from*—movements related to *apāna*—unforeseen and undesirable situations due to one's lack of mastery (*anaiśvarya*) over one's senses and cognitive capacities. In an existential position of accomplishment (*siddhi*) of virtue (*dharma*), for example, a person would choose to *be together with*—a movement associated with *samāna*—other virtuous people. Someone in the position of accomplishment of mastery (*aiśvarya*) might *compare themselves to others in a lower position*—an attitude associated with *udāna*—and become proud of themselves for having attained important knowledge. And someone in the existential position of complacency (*tuṣṭi*) might experience attachment (*rāga*) due to *intimate and all-encompassing association*—a function related to *vyāna*—with activities, objects, people, and environments that nurture the desired way of life.

An existential position within the world might be equally influenced by a combination of ways of being (*bhāva*s). Virtue, knowledge, detachment, and capability are present in the existential position of accomplishment (*siddhi*). These ways of being are evident in a generous person who is inclined toward (*prāṇa*) the experience of giving (*dānam*), or in a friendly person who enjoys the company (*samāna*) of good friends (*suhṛt prāptiḥ*), or in someone who has achieved detachment (*apāna*) from experiences of sorrow, or in someone who improves themselves (*udāna*) through the study of scriptures (*adhyāya*), hearing from teachers (*śabda*), or cultivating reasoning (*ūha*).

When table 2.1 is read in association with table 2.2, we find that there is a correlation of the external functions of *prāṇa* with certain "movements" that are implied in the performance of moral and intersubjective actions determined by the *bhāva*s. Giving, the cultivation of good friends, and learning are examples of how those *prāṇic* movements—"moving away from" in the case of *āpana*, "being together with others" in the case of *samāna*, "comparing oneself to others from a position of superiority" in the case of *udāna*—manifest into moral actions. I am not suggesting that the external functions of the *prāna*s are uniquely correlated with specific moral actions. Rather, moral actions such as the ones related to the different varieties of experience (*pratyaya*s) imply certain vital motions that are directly determined by the *bhāvas*. However, it will be shown later that only some actions manifest the right cultivation of *prāṇa.*

The relation between *bhāvas*, *pratyayasarga*, *pratyayas*, and the five *prāṇas* become evident when the phenomenal experiences that they encompass are seen in connection with the cognitive and moral activities that are implied in each of the *pratyayas*. The activity of the five senses of cognition, together with the five faculties of action, and the conscious state of being "I" are also called *prāṇa* in the *YD*: "Thus, it is said that *prāṇa, apāna,* etc. are five vital winds due to their ability of grasping which is the activity common to the instruments of knowledge. [In this way,] the cognitive senses are the sixth vital wind; the agentive senses are the seventh; *pūr* is the eighth. By '"*pūr*'" it is meant the conscious state of being '"I.'"[14] Here "*pūr*" refers to the "body" configured by the instruments of knowledge (*antaḥkaraṇa)* reflecting the pure consciousness of *puruṣa* within their own self-referential activity which is "colored" by the *bhāvas. Puruṣa* does not act, since the ones doing the reflection of consciousness are the instruments of knowledge. The *Yuktidīpikā* is not committing here to any sense of "direction" coming from an activity of the *puruṣa.* Instead, it will become clear later in this essay how *puruṣa* "guides" an action by its presence alone.

It is interesting, however, to note that K. C. Bhattacharyya refers to the *bhāvas* as "modes of freedom" (1956, 186), since their influence in our experience of the world and behavior determines everything, from the very embodiment we get at birth, to the circumstances we experience in the present and even in the future, depending on the predispositions that remain active at the subtle level, after the physical body has stopped functioning. Indeed, the *bhāvas* determine the transmigratory path that leads one toward a state of bondage or freedom (*SK* 44). Thus, it is exactly these elements that the Sāṃkhya discipline attempts to modify, not by willing one way of being (*bhāva*) over another—which is impossible as those who have dealt with addiction, depression, and powerlessness may attest—but by understanding the relation between the sources of action (*karmayonis*) and our capacities to perceive and act (*indriyas*).

The External Functions of *Prāṇa* and the Sources of Action (*Karmayoni*s)

K. C. Bhattacharyya (1956, 135) understands the Sāṃkhya notion of liberation (*mokṣa*) as freedom from the wish to be free from pain. According to him, all felt pain already presupposes the wish to be free from pain. Otherwise the experience would not be felt as painful. But freedom from all pain requires that one have "the wish for freedom from the reflective wish to be free from pain . . . It is the necessary wish for absolute freedom, freedom not only from pain, but from the potentiality of pain, and implies the belief not only that it can be attained but also *that it has already begun to be attained* (*ibidem*)."[15] It is in this sense that the impulse towards freedom is naturally embedded in existence, and the reason why Shevchenko says that for Sāṃkhya, existence is a "disease that heals itself by itself" (2017, 886). This is certainly in line with the Sāṃkhya theory of *satkāryavāda,* that the effect already exists in the cause. However, *the desire to be free from the wish to be free from pain* does not by itself explain how one can naturally get established in such desire, for one would also need to want to modify the tendencies that make us fall back into the wish to be free from pain. This is where volition and knowledge come together in Sāṃkhya. To desire to know how best to get rid of such tendencies requires *wanting to act according to the* method for their modification. This wanting-to-know (*jijñāsa*) requires also the *will* to remain receptive to the teachings of the liberated ones. This *will* then allows the seeker to remain firm in that liberating knowledge and practice without doubting the path. Engrained in the system, however, is also the lack of will to know. One is free not to want to be liberated, that is, not to want to be free from the wish to be free from pain. It is true that the desire to know how to attain ultimate liberation might appear spontaneously, as Shevchenko has argued in 2017 and 2023. However, my position is that the natural wish to pursue a path of liberation in Sāṃkhya does not account for the wish to remain committed to the process such a path involves. In other words, the natural arising of *jijñāsa* accounts for Āsuri spontaneously becoming Kapila's disciple, but not for the sustained commitment to the observances that he is then taught to practice. With the exception of Kapila, who was born liberated, in the majority of cases the wish for absolute liberation requires an effort to engage in the practices involved to realize the liberating state.[16]

The connection between *prāṇa*—understood as the moral and cognitive activities encompassed by the different vital winds—and volition is made in the *Yuktidīpikā*'s commentary to *SK* 29 when the unknown author of the *YD* responds to the question regarding the origin of the functions of *prāṇa*s and the five *karmayoni*s or sources of action. "There are five sources of action: steadiness (*dhṛtiḥ*) to remain in the pursuit of a resolution, trust (*śraddhā*) in the teachings of those who know, the inclination toward delightful experiences (*sukhā*), desire to know (*vividiṣā*), and the desire not to know (*avividiṣā*). They remain [in the mind] like an embryo, that develops as a dynamic modification that is streamed forth from the cosmic mind."[17] The five sources of action (*karmayoni*s) are volitional forces that possess particular characteristics based on the fundamental qualities (*guṇa*s) that lie in potency within the mind. Table 2.3 shows the general definition of the sources of action, the qualitative aspects of their natural activity, their purified nature, and their sphere of action as described in the *YD*.

The sources of action manifest and develop in the very performance of actions. These actions can strengthen, weaken, or guide one's volitional forces towards a particular way of being. For example, through the performance of virtuous actions such as the constant study of texts, one develops and strengthens the desire to know and the trust in those who know. One could develop the same sources of action, that is, desire to know and trust, by performing vicious actions. For example, a person could develop the desire to know how to harm others, or have faith in untrustworthy people, or steadiness and firmness in false beliefs, but the result of the experience would be quite different. Whether one develops a purified source of trust, steadiness, and delight in the state of absolute freedom from pain (i.e., that is, in being free from the wish to be free from pain) will depend on whether a person has the desire to know how to discern between that which liberates and that which does not. The question is, then, what determines the desire to know that which needs to be known—that is, that which liberates? "When the living being leaves the body, it attains the sources of action according to whether those actions were virtu-

Table 2.3. The Sources of Action (*Karmayonis*) and Their Objective Spheres of Action

Sources of Action	Definition[1]	Particular Sequence of Elemental Qualities or Guṇas	Attainment of Purified Sources of Action[2]	Objective Sphere[3]
Steadiness or determination (*dhṛtiḥ*)	Non-deviation from a resolution.	*tamas* and *rajas*	The one who keeps a promise in intention, words, and actions; who firmly holds a stance and vow; these are the characteristics of determination or steadiness.	All worldly objects.
Trust (*śraddhā*)	Seminal state of what is to be done according to the scriptures without aiming for the fruit of actions.	*rajas* and *sattva*	Absence of envy, practice of chastity, performance of a sacrifice (for oneself), performance of a sacrifice for others, discipline, giving or receiving gifts, purity of body and mind (integrity) are considered as characteristics of trust.	Four stages of life: infancy, adolescence, youth, and old age
Delight (*sukhā*)	Enjoyment through the intellect caused by the desire for the fruit of things [that must be] heard and seen.	*sattva* and *tamas*	One who is content delights in knowledge, in disinterested action, or in discipline. The one who looks for atonement always remains happy.	Objects that are seen and heard [as being delightful].

Desire to know (*vividiṣā*)	Having the desire to know.	*Rajas*	Those who have the desire to know, and know that which is desired to be known: duality, oneness, plurality; the eternal consciousness, non-consciousness; the subtle and minute; the existence of an effect, and the non-existence of an effect.	The manifested realm (*vyakta*)
Lack of desire to know (*avividiṣā*)	The cessation of that desire [to know].	*Tamas*	The one without the desire to know, like one who has drunk poison or is sleeping or intoxicated, is always absorbed in the source (*pradhāna*). It is said to be similar to the ones who become merged with *prakṛti*, where there is the dissolution of causes and effects. (Ed. Note: See *YS* I:19 on *prakṛti-laya*)	The unmanifested realm of pure potentiality (*avyakta*)

1. *tāsāṃ lakṣaṇaviṣayasatattvaguṇasamanvayā bhavanti / tatra lakṣaṇam tāvad vyavasāyād apracyavanaṃ dhṛtiḥ / phalam anabhisandhāya śāstrokteṣu kāryeṣv avaśyakartavyatābījabhāvaḥ śraddhā / dṛṣṭānuśravikaphalābhilāṣadvārako hi buddher ābhogaḥ sukhā / vettum icchā vividiṣā / tannivṛttir avividiṣā* / (*YD*, 209, 25-30, on *SK* 29).

2. *vāci karmaṇi saṃkalpe pratijñāṃ yo'nurakṣati / tanniṣṭhas tatpratijñaś ca dhṛter etad dhi lakṣaṇam / / anasūyā brahmacaryaṃ yajanaṃ yājanaṃ tapaḥ / dānam pratigrahaḥ śaucaṃ śraddhāyā lakṣaṇaṃ smṛtam / / sukhārthī yas tu seveta vidyāṃ karma tapāṃsi vā / prāyaścittaparo nityaṃ sukhāyāṃ sa tu vartate / / dvitvaikatvapṛthaktvaṃ nityaṃ cetanaṃ acetanaṃ sūkṣmam / satkāryam asatkāryaṃ vividiṣitavyaṃ vividiṣāyāḥ / / viṣapītasuptamattavad avividiṣā dhyāninām sadā yoniḥ / kāryakaraṇakṣayakarī prākṛtikā gatiḥ samākhyātā / /* (*YD*, 210, 30-15, on *SK* 29).

3. *viṣayasatattvaṃ punaḥ sarvaviṣayiṇī dhṛtiḥ | āśramaviṣayiṇī śraddhā | dṛṣṭānuśravikaviṣayiṇī sukhā | vyaktaviṣayiṇī vividiṣā | avyaktaviṣayiṇy avividiṣā / guṇasamanvayas tu rajastamobahulā dhṛtiḥ | sattvarajobahulā śraddhā | sattvatamobahulā sukhā | rajobahulā vividiṣā | tamobahulāvividiṣeti* / (*YD*, 210, 15, on *SK* 29).

ous or not virtuous, desirous of knowledge or not. The attainment of the sources of action produces certain actions according to the essential characteristics of the source."[18] The *Yuktidīpikā* makes it clear that the desire to know is not determined by fate nor by natural impulse, but by actions. The performance of actions determines and modifies volition. It is through actions that specific ways of being (*bhāva*s) are preserved or transformed. The performance of actions depends upon the way the individual puts *prāṇa* into motion. Without any discipline, these motions are determined to reproduce the same pattern following the unconscious sources of action. However, it is through the conscious use of one's own effort that one can change the tendency of those volitional forces.

The postulation of these sources of action (*karmayoni*s) can explain why someone engages in certain actions and not in others. If someone does not have the desire to know, then that person will not read the texts, nor listen to teachers, nor have any discipline to practice what was learnt. Yet, the volition to know what has to be done for one's liberation is something that can be developed through study and other means. It is not enough to desire absolute freedom from pain. One must know the proper way of becoming established in such freedom, and then one must want to act in that direction. This "wanting" is not a mere subjective willing, nor a natural impulse, nor the effect of an externally determined circumstance. There must be a concerted effort to engage the sources of action in the right way. This effort presupposes a certain awareness that is not given by the natural forces of *prakṛti* alone.

The Right Way of Cultivating *Prāṇa*

The *YD* states: "The wise one, once established in the right path through the development of the external activity of the vital winds, stops the [influence] of the turbid and dense [aspects of reality] and attains the place of eternality and immortality. Having succeeded in assuming the form of *dharma,* etc. as causes of the sources of action, the accomplished one does not ever descend into the lower states again."[19] Unlike the traditional view that takes the Sāṃkhya method of liberation to consist only in the rational inquiry of the constituents of reality or in the cultivation of a gnostic insight of those principles, the *YD* shows that the path includes—it actually starts with—the development of the performance of proper actions. Without guiding one's own capacities to act towards virtue (*dharma*), there cannot be attainment of knowledge (*jñāna*) of *puruṣa*. Without knowledge, there cannot be proper transcendence of satisfaction in material objects (*virāga*), and without detachment, there is no mastery (*aiśvarya*) to guide the sensory-motor faculties toward freedom.

> Having studied these two [the sources of action and the internal and external functions of *prāṇa*], what follows is the practice of the right path. The internal activity of the *prāṇa*s remains unceasing due to its being unconditioned by the cessation of the accomplishment of the states of *tamas*, *rajas*, virtue, vice, etc. Indeed, it is the external function of the *prāṇa*s which are employed in relation to the virtuous or non-virtuous paths. How is this? It is said: As long as the objective sphere of *prāṇa* is inclined towards virtue, etc., it should be concentrated in that realm. In this way, there is an increase of *sattva* in it [in the activity of the vital wind]. Due to the increase of *sattva*, the intellect attains higher and higher forms. The descending activity, which is the sphere of *apāna*, is to be restricted in relation to vices, etc. In this way, the tamasic quality in relation to that which is non-acting [i.e., *puruṣa*] which is the object of discrimination, diminishes. Thus, the intellect attains higher and higher forms. Then companionship, the objective sphere of *samāna*, is to be practiced according to the sattvic quality of virtue, because, as the scriptures have said: "May one always delight in *sattva* and be associated with those who are sattvic." The objective sphere of *udāna* is the upliftment of the self. After having abandoned the last form of the stages of ignorance, their effects vanish, due to the practice of the opposite (*pratipakṣa*). Finally, the objective sphere of *vyāna*, which is the necessary connection of one thing with another, is to be experienced as the object of knowledge. One must make the dharmic way of being the seed of the four sources of action [steadiness,

> trust, purity of delight, and desire to know]. Even in the absence of the desire to know, the undesirable may happen in relation to those who are motivated by the results. The person who is directed towards virtue and to the other accomplishments of the Self, rejects their opposites, delights in *sattva,* is devoid of ego, is devoted to knowledge, has purified the sources [of action], and attains quickly the supreme *brahman.*[20]

As can be understood from the passage above, the modification of the external functions of *prāṇa* entails the modification of the performance of one's own actions. Cultivating a *dharmic* way of being requires repeated performance of virtuous actions which changes the quality of one's capacities to know and to act. Developing the capacity to act virtuously creates new dispositions or "ways of being." Reinforced by one's own actions and the help of others on the same path, these new dispositions make it possible for one to become firmly established on a trajectory toward freedom. The performance of virtuous actions manifests existential, intentional states (*pratyaya*s) that are required to attain discerning knowledge.

The act of giving (*dāna*), for example, considered an existential expression of accomplishment (see table 2.2 above), could be understood as involving the right cultivation of *apāna*, since the action of giving expresses the external movement of releasing a particular object. In the performance of giving, one establishes a habit of perceiving the gift as that which is "not mine."[21] This is precisely the knowledge that Sāṃkhya deems liberating and from which a purified sense of delight (*sukhā*) is strengthened.

Another accomplishment is expressed in cultivating the company of good-hearted friends (*suhṛt prāptiḥ*). This type of friendship involves the right cultivation of *samāna*. In the act of sharing and delighting in the company of others, one learns to step out of one's own egocentricity by keeping one`s word, avoiding jealousy, being helpful, etc. This establishes a purified sense of determination (*dhṛtiḥ*).

The right cultivation of *udāna* is fostered in learning from scriptures or teachers. This sets the habit of receptivity towards those who know more than oneself. There is upliftment into knowledge of the Self in the act of learning from others who have realized it themselves. This diminishes the lack of desire to know (*avividiṣā*) what does not help towards the liberating path. Learning also happens when one is affected by disease, or when suffering is caused by others, or by the environment.

Overcoming undesired and painful circumstances allows one to realize the intimate connection (*vyāna*) between the false sense of self and suffering. A renewed and purified sense of contentment, atonement, and delight in objects may emerge out of overcoming these painful experiences. Finally, the existential position of accomplishment where someone is inclined toward knowledge—an example of right cultivation of *prāṇa*—through one's own reasoning (*ūhaḥ*) increases the *sattvic* quality of the intellect. This makes the mind better dispositioned to acquire higher levels of understanding, strengthening the desire to know (*vividiṣā*) that which must be known to experience ultimate freedom.

If the right cultivation of the five *vāyu*s is read in relation to the existential positions (*pratyaya*s) that are derived from the ways of being (*bhāva*s) of accomplishment (*siddhi*) and guided by the purified sources of action (*karmayoni*s), then it is easier to see that without the right effort, the sources of action would continue to influence our behavior in an unconscious, deterministic way. The external action of *prāṇa* can be modified by conscious activity, as Oberhammer states in his study of Sāṃkhya meditation (1977, 22). The right cultivation of *prāṇa,* however, should not be confused with a mere contemplative practice on the vital winds. For instance, it is not enough to concentrate on the movements associated with *apāna* in the hopes of becoming more generous. One must take action. The idea of "cultivation" must not be taken only as the practice of certain techniques to modify the flows of *prāṇa,* as it is done in the *haṭhayoga* tradition with the practice of *prāṇāyāma.*[22] Changing the breath changes action. Changing action changes the world.

Right cultivation, in the context of Sāṃkhya, refers to the practice of making a conscious choice at the moment of performing an action. Contemplating the different motions of the vital winds in relation to their moral possibilities, as well as performing certain breathing exercises to modify the flows of *prāṇa* within one's own body can contribute to gaining more awareness of the relation between *prāṇa,* our ways of being, and that which determines our actions. But it is the actual conscious effort of modifying those vital motions in our actions that create the transformation toward freedom. If one understands the relation between the sources of action (*karmayonis*) and the way vitality (*prāṇa*) moves in our capacities to perceive and act, then one can notice the way our actions move *prāṇa* and thus foster our capacity to modify it by choosing to act otherwise.

There are certainly many factors that cause an individual to act virtuously, and one could see those factors as the product of fate, time, or the natural development of *prakṛti*. Yet, whether one has had the good fortune of finding or having good friends, teachers, and an intellect of good disposition, it is still up to the individual person to modify the performance of actions and persist with the chosen way of behavior. If everything in our actions were mere impulse and dictated by natural processes then, as philosopher Luce Irigaray (2008) holds, we would never become a real person. Indeed, we find that in Sāṃkhya, it is precisely the awareness at the level of our capacity to act which can modify the performance of an action. Through *dharmic* action, one learns to stop the influence of the turbid and dense aspects of nature. In other words, it is through the conscious and effortful enactment of virtuous behavior and ethical engagement with others that one can transform the volitional forces that function as the sources of action. In Sāṃkhya, it is through conscious actions that one develops a "will to freedom." Through the ethical enactment of the will, one becomes and realizes the person (*puruṣa*) discerned as one's own real Self. A person's ethical becoming establishes the conditions for the direct liberating experience of the self. The right cultivation of *prāṇa* produces new predispositions that re-shape the form of one's intellect (*buddhi*). Only then, a *dharmic* way of being can naturally guide how to know and act. As seen above, the right cultivation of *apāna* produces the disposition of detachment in actions such as giving; *samāna* produces dispositions of firmness in actions such as keeping one's promise; *udāna* reduces ignorance in actions such as learning from others and studying by oneself.

As Oberhammer (1977, 29) explains, the processes of striving towards liberating knowledge need to become effortless before one can advance onto the next stage. Subconscious forces determine that striving itself. These forces cannot be changed just by thinking or by having an abstract understanding of how they work. It is only through the external functions of *prāṇa* that one can alter action.

Prāṇa and the Possibility of Freedom and Free Will in Sāṃkhya

It has been argued in this essay that neither the natural unconscious processes that drive our actions and experiences nor the mere rational or gnostic inquiry into the self can account for the transformative process that moves toward liberation involved in Sāṃkhya. Instead, it has been proposed here that the liberating process requires the conscious and initially effortful cultivation of the external aspects of *prāṇa* and the ethical involvement of the way we use our capacities of knowing and acting. Through the sustained and repeated practice of virtuous ways of using our intellect, sense of ego, mind, and sensory-motor faculties, one can modify the sources of action that unconsciously determine our way of being. In other words, the external functions of *prāṇa* directly influence and modify our *bhāvas*, and it is through their enactment in our ethical actions that the *karmayonis* can be transformed. The sources of action are modified indirectly through intentional actions rather than directly through a willful act of mere thinking. This means that the modifying influence in our volition and behavior is not a matter of luck, fate, or impulse from predeterminate forces intrinsic in nature.

The idea that there is a certain determinism running through the veins of Sāṃkhya is common among scholars. Edwin Bryant (2014, 20) clearly formulates the problem: To be an agent means to be able to "produce" an action. To produce an action requires a change of qualities. But according to Sāṃkhya, only the material embodied nature (*prakṛti*) is subject to change; *Puruṣa* is by definition changeless and eternal. Thus, only *prakṛti* (the embodied self) can be an agent within Sāṃkhya philosophy (*idem*, 21). However the agent, i.e., the body with all its intellectual and sensorimotor constituents (*buddhi, ahaṃkāra, manas, indriyas*), is regulated by existential predispositions (*bhāvas*) and other unconscious factors such as memories, habits, past lives, present circumstance, etc. How then can an unconscious entity that is determined mechanistically can be called an agent (*idem,* 27)?

To make sense of this problem, Bryant quotes some of the classical commentaries where it is "solved" by appealing to *prakṛti's* inherent intentionality. Whether *prakṛti* knows it or not, she is always acting for the purpose of bringing experience to the self, both the experience of bondage and liberation. Commentaries usually add, quoting *SK* 62,[23] that *puruṣa* is in reality neither bound nor liberated. If the agent binds itself with its own dispositions and releases itself through them, one does not have to presuppose a "will" that does the liberation. The Self does literally nothing except being aware of this natural process. These passages have also been used to support the natural liberation approach proposed by Shevchenko and K. C. Bhattacharyya, which seems to be in agreement with the core Sāṃkhyan principle of *satkāryavāda,* the view that the effect pre-exists in the cause. Liberation happens because it is already embedded in the structure of existence and in the natural dynamics of material reality.

However, an implication from the argument developed in this essay is that there are two types of actions an agent (i.e., the embodied Self) can undertake: the ones determined by the unceasing becoming of the unconscious sources of action and the ones developed by a conscious effort to modify our capacities to act. This effort is neither intrinsically material, nor completely caused by external factors, nor a pure act of a conscious will, nor causeless or random. Instead, it is a *prāṇic* effort produced by the conjoint activity of our capacities of knowing. The mind, intellect, and sense of individuality that, together with the senses, the organs of action and *puruṣa's* implicit awareness, determine the way we have a "grasp" on the world. Fate, luck, or nature gives us several opportunities to learn to detach from worldly objects and relate to the world virtuously via friends, family, teachers, experiences of sorrow, one's own reasoning. Yet it is through conscious effort that one chooses to persevere in the enactment of *dharmic* acts. Without the presence of such consciousness (*puruṣa*), the possibility of choosing to act otherwise and change habits would never arise. With time, effortful cultivation of our ethical relation with the world, that is, of our external *prāṇa,* becomes an effortless way of being, that is, a *bhāva.* For Sāṃkhya, it is the *dharmic* way of being which paves the path towards knowledge. Thus, it is through the conscious cultivation of *prāṇa* in the enactment of *dharmic* actions that the liberating knowledge of the Self as distinct from matter is brought about.[24]

Acknowledgments

I am very grateful to Meenal Kulkarni for reading with me the *Yuktidīpikā* in Sanskrit, to Arindam Chakrabarti for encouraging me to write about this topic, and to the Sanskrit translation group at Loyola Marymount University directed by Chris Chapple for their motivation to continue with this project. I would also like to thank the anonymous reviewer whose comments helped improve this chapter.

Notes

1. For a thorough exposition of interpretations on the Sāṃkhyan inquiry as means of liberation see Shevchenko (2017). This part draws substantially from his extended discussion on the topic in that paper.

2. The *Yuktidīpikā* is considered the most extensive and comprehensive philosophical commentary on the *Sāṃkhyakārikā*. It focuses on responding to objections against Sāṃkhya coming mainly from Buddhists, Vedāntins, and Naiyāyika opponents. The text has seen renewed interest by scholars since the second half of the twentieth century (see Honda 1977; Motegi 1978; Harzer 2006). In 1998 a critical edition was produced by Wezler and Motegi. My translation of the passages of the *Yuktidīpikā* referred to in this chapter are based on this edition.

3. The *Suvarṇasaptati* or the "Golden Seventy" is the Chinese translation attributed to Paramārtha in the sixth century of a commentary to the *Sāṃkhyakārikā* that closely resembles the *Māṭharavṛtti*.

4. See the *Suvarṇasaptati* in Takakusu (1932, 1) and Larson (1987, 169–170).

5. *sāmānyakaraṇavṛttiḥ prāṇādyā vāyavaḥ pañca* (the translation of all *SK* verses quoted in this chapter is my own).

6. The intellect (*buddhi*) determines reality (*adhyavasāyo buddhiḥ . . .* , *SK* 23). The sense of individuality is self-assertion (*abhimāno'ahamkāraḥ . . .* , *SK* 24). The operative mind (*manas*) has a sensori-motor nature (*ubhayātmakamatra manas . . .* , *SK* 27). The faculties of sensing (hearing, seeing,

etc.) are bare awareness (*śabdādiṣu pañcānāmālocanamātram . . .* , *SK* 28). The faculties of action are speech, grasping, locomotion, excretion, and sexual enjoyment (*vacanādānaviharanotsargānanda . . .* , *SK* 28).

7. *atra ca sāmānyakaraṇavrttigrahaṇasāmarthyāt prāṇādyāḥ pañca vāyavaḥ*/ (*YD* 1998, 208, 25, on *SK* 29) "Thus, it is said that *prāṇa, apāna*, etc. are five vital winds due to their ability of grasping which is the activity common to the instruments of knowledge." (All translations from the *YD* in this essay are my own.)

8. See *Pātañjalayogaśāstra* (PYS) 3.39.

9. The translations of the relevant passages are my own.

10. The whole argument is given in *YD* 1998, 206, 10–30, *SK* on 29. Here I am only summarizing it.

11. *teṣāṃ prerikā sāmānyakaraṇavṛttiḥ*/ *eṣā ca tantrāntareṣu prayatna ity ucyate* / *sa ca dharmādisaṃskārabhāvanāvaśād anuparato jīvanam* / (*YD* 1998, 208, 20, on SK 29). "Their setting in motion [of the five winds] is the common function of the instruments of knowledge. And this is referred to as "effort" in other philosophical texts. Life is manifested continuously due to the unceasing becoming, arising from the impressions [produced by] virtues, wisdom, etc." In his commentary to the *Yogasūtra* (III.39), the *Tattvavaiśāradī* (TV), Vācaspatimiśra refers to two kinds of fluctuations (*vṛtti*) of the organs or sense faculties (*indriyas*): an inner (*antarī*) and an outer (*bahyā*). He associated such internal fluctuation with "life" (*jīvanam*). The outer fluctuation is distinguished by the awareness of sensations coming from the external environment: color, odors, textures, sounds, etc. The internal one is distinguished by a special effort (*prayatnabhedaḥ*), common to the instruments of knowledge and cause of the different functions of the vital winds that support the body.

12. *sa ca dharmādisaṃskārabhāvanāvaśād anuparato jīvanam* / (*YD* 1998, 208, 20–25, on *SK* 29).

13. *vṛttir antaḥ samastānāṃ karaṇānāṃ pradīpavat* / *aprakāśā kriyārūpā jīvanaṃ kāyadhārikā* / / *sā yāvad aniruddhā tu hanti vāyuṃ 'ajo'dhikā*/ *dharmādy-anāvṛttivaśāt tāvaj jīvati mānavaḥ* / (*YD* 1998, 208, 20–25, on *SK* 29).

14. *atra ca sāmānyakaraṇavṛttigrahaṇasāmarthyāt prāṇādyāḥ pañca vāyavaḥ* | *buddhīndriyāṇi ṣaṣṭham* | *karmendriyāṇi saptamam* | *pūr aṣṭamam* | *pūr ity ahaṃkārāvasthāsaṃvidam adhikurute* / (*YD* 1998, 208, 25–209, 25, on *SK* 29).

15. My emphasis.

16. This section has been rephrased to clarify my position in response to the critical remarks made to the original version of this paper by Shevchenko in 2023, footnotes 9 and 12, 163–164.

17. *āha: kutaḥ punar iyam prāṇādivṛttiḥ pravartata iti ?*/ *ucyate: sā karmayonibhyaḥ* / *mahataḥ pracyutam hi rajo vikṛtam aṇḍasthānīyāḥ pañca*

karmayonayo bhavanti—dhṛtiḥ śraddhā sukhā vividiṣāvividiṣeti / (*YD*, 209, 15–20, on SK 29).

18. *tatra yadāyaṃ jantuḥ śubhāśubheṣu kāryeṣu vṛttyanusārī jijñāsur ajijñāsur vā śarīraṃ parityajati tām eva karmayonim upapadyate / tasyām upapannas tām eva bhāvayati / etat tāval lakṣaṇasatattvam* / (*YD*, 209, 25–30, *SK* on 29).

19. *āha ca—bāhyāṃ prāṇavivṛttiṃ samyaṅmārge budhaḥ pratiṣṭhāpya / vinivṛttavikharakaluṣo dhruvam amṛtaṃ sthānam abhyeti / / pañcānāṃ yonīnāṃ dharmādinimittatāṃ ca saṃsthāpya/ paripakvam ity adhastān na punas tadbhāvito gacchet* / / (*YD*, 211, 5–10, *SK* on 29).

20. *etad dvayam adhigamya samyaṅmārgānugamanaṃ kuryāt | rajastamodharmādisādhanabhāvavinivṛttitas tu/ atra prāṇānām antarvṛttir anupādhikatvād anivartyā / bahirvṛttis tu mārgāmārgaviṣayatayā prayoktavyā / katham ity ucyate / prāṇaviṣayā tāvat praṇatir dharmādiviṣaya evāvaroddhavyā/ tato hy asya sattvavṛddhiḥ / sattvavṛddheś cottarottarabuddhirūpādhigamaḥ / apānaviṣayaṃ tv apakramaṇam adharmādiviṣaya evāvaroddhavyam/ evaṃ hy asya khyātiviṣayāvārakasya tamaso nirhrāsaḥ / tataś cottarottarabuddhirūpādhigamaḥ / tathā samānaviṣayaṃ sāhacaryaṃ sattvadharmānuguṇaṃ kuryāt / yasmācchāstram "ha "sattvārāmaḥ sattvamithunaś ca sadā "yāt" iti / ātmotkarṣaṃ tūdānaviṣayam avidyāparvaṇo'ntyam rūpaṃ vivarjya tatpratipakṣair nivartayet/ atyantāvinābhāvaṃ ca vyānaviṣayam jñānaviṣaya eva bhāvayet/ yonīnāṃ catasṛṇāṃ dharmabījatām evādadyāt/ avividiṣām apy aniṣṭa phalahetuṣu bhāvayet /'so'yaṃ dharmādiṣu pravaṇas tatpratipakṣāpakrāntaḥ sattvārāmo vinivṛttābhimāno jñānaniṣṭhaḥ saviśuddhayonir acireṇa paraṃbrahmopapadyata iti* / (*YD*, 210, 20–211, 25, *SK* on 29).

21. Cfr. with Shevchenko (2017, 879) who does not see in *dāna* any relation with developing discriminative knowledge.

22. Some texts in the Haṭhayoga tradition establish a relation between *prāṇāyāma* and morality when they state that through the breathing techniques the practitioner can purify their sins (see *Vivekamārtaṇḍa* 92; *Śivasvarodaya* 376cd–379ab). However, there does not seem to be further mention regarding a correlation between specific breathing techniques, the vital winds, and the types of sins those techniques purify. I thank Jason Birch for providing these references in his online workshop: "The Yogic Breath: *Prāṇāyāma* in Medieval Yoga," November 2020, and for clarifying some of my doubts on this topic.

23. *tasmān na badhyate addhā na mucyate nā 'pi saṃsarati kaścit/ saṃsarati badhyate mucyate ca nānāśrayā prakṛtiḥ//*

24. This chapter was originally published as: Funes Maderey, A. L. "The Role of Prāṇa in Sāṃkhya Discipline for Freedom," *Journal of Indian Philosophy* 49: 81–103 (2021). https://doi.org/10.1007/s10781-021-09460-7

References

Primary Sources

GBh Gauḍapādabhāṣya. 1972. *Sāṃkhyakārikā of Īśvarakṛṣṇa with the commentary of Gauḍapāda*. Trans. T. G. Mainkar. Poona: Oriental Book Agency.

PYS Pātañjalayogaśāstra. Kāśinātha Śāstrī Āgāśe, ed. *Vācaspatimiśraviracitaṭīkā saṃvalitavyāsabhāṣyasametāni pātañjalayogasūtrāṇi, tathā bhojadevaviracitarājamārtaṇḍābhidhavṛttisametāni pātañjalayogasūtrāṇi. sūtrapāṭhasūtravarṇānukramasūcībhyāṃ ca sanāthīkṛtāni*. Ānandāśrama Sanskrit Series, no. 47. Pune: Ānandāśramamudraṇālaye, 1904.

SK Sāṃkhyakārikā. 1979. "Sanskrit and English Translation." In G. J. Larson, *Classical Sāṃkhya*. Delhi: Motilal Banarsidass (2nd revised ed.), Appendix B.

SS Suvarṇasaptati. 1932. *The Sāṃkhya Karikā Studied in Light of its Chinese Version*. Trans. M. Takakusu. Madras: The Diocesan Press.

TV Tattvavaiśāradī. 1904. *The Yoga-Sūtra with Three Commentaries: Vyāsa, Vācaspatimiśra and Bhojadeva*. Edited by Kashinath Shastri Agashe. Pune: Ananda Ashram Press.

YD Yuktidīpikā. 1990–1992. Two volumes. Trans. Dr. Shiv Kumar and Dr. D. N. Bhargava. Delhi.

Yuktidīpikā. 1998. The most significant commentary on the *Sāṃkhyakārikā*. Critically edited by A. Wezler and S. Motegi. Stuttgart: Franz Steiner Verlag.

Secondary Sources

Bhattacharyya, K. C. 1956. *Studies in Philosophy*. Calcutta: Progressive Publishers.

Bryant, Edwin F. 2014. "Agency in Sāṃkhya and Yoga: The Unchangeability of the Eternal," in Matthew R. Dasti and Edwin F. Bryant (eds.), *Free Will, Agency, and Selfhood in Indian Philosophy*, 16–41. New York: Oxford University Press.

Burley, M. 2007. *Classical Sāṃkhya and Yoga*. New York: Routledge.

Chatterjea, T. 2003. *Knowledge and Freedom in Indian Philosophy*. Lanham, MD: Lexington Books.

Frauwallner, E. 1973. *History of Indian Philosophy*, Vol. 1. Delhi: Motilal Banarsidass.

Harzer, Edeltraud. 2006. *The Yuktidīpikā. A Reconstruction of Sāṅkhya Methods of Knowing*. Aachen: Shaker Verlag.

Honda, M. 1977. "Karma-yoni." *Journal of Indian and Buddhist Studies* 26(1): 506–511.

Irigaray, L. 2008. *Sharing the World.* New York: Continuum.

Kimball, J. 2016. "The Relationship between the 'bhāvas' and the 'pratyayasarga' in Classical Sāṃkhya." *Journal of Indian Philosophy* 44(3): 537–555.

Larson, G. J., and R. S. Bhattacharya. 1987. *Sāṃkhya: A Dualist Tradition in Indian Philosophy, Encyclopedia of Indian Philosophies.* Vol. 4. Delhi: Motilal Banarsidass.

Larson, G. J. 1979. *Classical Sāṃkhya: An Interpretation of Its History and Meaning.* Delhi: Motilal Banarsidass.

Motegi, S. 1978–1980. "Research on the Yuktidīpikā I–III." *Journal of Indian and Buddhist Studies* 28(2): 904–907.

Oberhammer, G. 1977. *Strukturen Yogischer Meditation.* Vienna: Verlag der Österreichischen Akademie der Wissenschaften.

Shevchenko, D. 2017. "Natural Liberation in the *Sāṃkhyakārikā* and its Commentaries." *Journal of Indian Philosophy* 45(5): 863–892.

Shevchenko, D. 2023. "K. C. Bhattacharyya and Spontaneous Liberation in Sāṃkhya," in Daniel Raveh and Elise Coquereau-Saoua (eds.), *The Making of Contemporary Indian Philosophy.* 151–166. Abingdon, Oxon & New York: Routledge.

Yamaguchi, E. 1967. "A Consideration to 'Pratyaya-Sarga." *JIBSt* 30: 972–979. www.jstage.jst.go.jp/article/ibk1952/15/2/15_2_979/_pdf/-char/ja

Chapter 3

The Place of Meditative Soteriological Practice in Sāṃkhya Philosophy

MIKEL BURLEY

Sāṃkhya has a legitimate claim to be among the most influential of Indian philosophies, having had a pervasive impact on not only the philosophical milieu but also the culture of India more generally, including the domains of religion, mythology, and art.[1] In the sphere of philosophy, Sāṃkhya has been both a source of inspiration that has been modified and supplemented—by traditions such as Śaiva Siddhānta and Kashmir Śaivism—and a target for critical appraisal by its philosophical rivals, including the various schools of Vedānta, Nyāya, and Buddhism, among others. Thus, there is a sense in which a failure to understand Sāṃkhya risks impeding any attempt to comprehend much of Indian philosophical and religious thought. However, there remains much about Sāṃkhya that is poorly understood, including its form of soteriological practice.

It is generally recognized that Sāṃkhya's starting point—like that of many other branches of Indian philosophy, most notably Buddhist traditions—is an acknowledgment of the pervasiveness of *duḥkha* ("discomfort," "distress," "dissatisfaction"), both in human life and in the world as a whole, combined with an aspiration to eradicate or transcend that dissatisfactory condition. Sāṃkhya is therefore a soteriological system in the sense that its expressed purpose is to foster spiritual liberation. This is made explicit in the primary textual sources of the Sāṃkhya tradition. The *Sāṃkhya Kārikā* of Īśvarakṛṣṇa (*c.* fourth, fifth, or possibly sixth century CE) opens with the declaration that it is on account of "the affliction of the threefold *duḥkha* that the inquiry into its removal [comes about]" (SK 1) and the later text commonly known as the *Sāṃkhya Sūtra* (*c.* fourteenth or fifteenth century) asserts, similarly, that the ultimate goal or end is "the complete cessation of the threefold *duḥkha*" (SS 1.1).[2] Traditional commentators interpret "threefold *duḥkha*" to mean the pain or suffering derived from (i) "internal" sources, whether bodily or mental; (ii) "external" sources, including other people, animals, and the surrounding environment; and (iii) "divine" or "supernatural" sources, such as demons.[3] Whether or not we accept that particular exposition, it is clear that *duḥkha* has a foundational place in Sāṃkhya's conception of lived experience. We also learn from the *Sāṃkhya Kārikā* that the means of achieving release from *duḥkha* is discriminative knowledge (*vijñāna*), which differentiates between the manifest (*vyakta*), the unmanifest (*avyakta*), and the "knower" (*jña*) (SK 2). Although much of the text is concerned with elaborating the nature of each of these three categories, little is said about the methods for cultivating the discriminative knowledge itself. A crucial verse on this matter is *Sāṃkhya Kārikā* 64, which affirms that it is "from *tattva-abhyāsa*" that "the knowledge arises that 'I am not,' 'not mine,' 'not I,'" and that this knowledge, "being free of delusion, is complete, pure, and singular."[4] But in what does *tattva-abhyāsa* consist? This is the question with which this chapter is principally concerned.

I begin, in the next section, by outlining the prevalent view among interpreters, according to which the soteriological method of Sāṃkhya is essentially "rationalistic," in contrast to the more meditative or "mystical" approach of Yoga. The remainder of the chapter then examines in detail the concepts of *tattva* and *tattva-abhyāsa*, arguing that the "rationalistic" interpretation is, at best, an oversimplification. Although there remain certain obstacles to the construction of any consistent account of Sāṃkhya philosophy, there are strong reasons for supposing Sāṃkhya's soteriological method—as distinct from the method of articulating its conceptual framework within its philosophical texts[5]—to be closely aligned with that of the Yoga system associated with Patañjali.

Sāṃkhya's Purported Rationalism

From the time of the first systematic studies of Sāṃkhya philosophy by European scholars from the nineteenth century onward, it has become commonplace to characterize Sāṃkhya as rationalistic. For example, Richard Garbe's pioneering work *Die Sâṃkhya-Philosophie,* first published in 1894, is subtitled *Eine Darstellung des indischen Rationalismus nach den Quellen,* which translates as "A presentation of Indian rationalism according to its sources."[6] Thirteen years earlier, John Davies, referring to Sāṃkhya as "[t]he system of Kapila"—Kapila being a legendary figure to whom the Sāṃkhya teachings are traditionally attributed—equates the terms "Sānkhya" and "Rationalistic" and adds that this system "contains nearly all that India has produced in the department of pure philosophy."[7] Although the latter contention is an exaggeration, the connecting of the term *sāṃkhya* with English terms such as "rationalistic" or "ratiocination" is not unwarranted, for it is normally assumed that *sāṃkhya* originally meant "enumeration" or "calculation" and that this meaning was subsequently extended to encompass reasoning in general.[8] Regardless of the etymology of the term, however, the description of Sāṃkhya philosophy as rationalistic is misleading if this is understood to mean that Sāṃkhya's specifically soteriological methods take the form exclusively of discursive reason. Yet this is precisely the way in which Sāṃkhya is portrayed by certain interpreters who wish to drive a wedge between Sāṃkhya and the Yoga of Patañjali.

In his book *The Philosophy of Classical Yoga,* Georg Feuerstein sought to reinterpret the statements that constitute the *Yoga Sūtra* of Patañjali without "the overpowering influence" of the commentary known as the *Yogabhāṣya,* which is traditionally ascribed to Vyāsa.[9] Thus, despite the fact that Vyāsa, along with the commentarial tradition that followed him, defines the Yoga system of Patañjali as a *sāṃkhya-pravacana,* "an explication or explanation of Sāṃkhya,"[10] Feuerstein sets out to draw a sharp distinction between Yoga and Sāṃkhya, principally in terms of soteriological methods. On Feuerstein's account, Yoga is a "meditation-oriented" school that deploys "mystical" methods whereas "Sāṃkhya relies heavily on the power of ratiocination and discernment."[11] Construing the *vijñāna* of Sāṃkhya as "conceptual discrimination," Feuerstein contrasts this with the "direct experience" aimed at by Yoga.[12] More recently, Ian Whicher, while rejecting Feuerstein's attempt to prise apart the teachings of the *Yoga Sūtra* from Vyāsa's commentary, nevertheless endorses the presumption that Sāṃkhya emphasizes "theoretical/ intellectual analysis" whereas the goal of Yoga "is realized through consistent practice and self-discipline, and is not something to be demonstrated through inference, analysis, and reasoning."[13]

Interpreting the Sāṃkhya of the *Sāṃkhya Kārikā* as favoring ratiocinative methods of inquiry to the exclusion of the kind of sustained meditation outlined in the *Yoga Sūtra* is, admittedly, encouraged by *Sāṃkhya Kārikā* 4, which asserts that "perception, inference, and the receiving of verbal testimony" constitute "all the means of achieving knowledge."[14] This assertion, combined with the absence of overt instruction on meditative discipline anywhere in the text, has generated the impression that Sāṃkhya eschews yogic meditation. Later in this chapter I shall argue that this is a mistaken impression, since there are strong grounds for regarding both discursive reasoning and meditative discipline as having a firm place within Sāṃkhya's methodological repertoire. Developing that argument will require examining the concept of *tattva-abhyāsa* as it occurs in *Sāṃkhya Kārikā* 64.

The Concept of *tattva-abhyāsa*

Notwithstanding its prevalence in commentarial and interpretive literature, the term *tattva* occurs only once in the *Sāṃkhya Kārikā* itself. As I noted above, the sixty-fourth verse of the text reads: "Thus, from *tattva-abhyāsa*, the knowledge arises that 'I am not,' 'not mine,' 'not I'; being free of delusion, [this knowledge] is complete, pure, and singular." The compound term *tattva-abhyāsa* is generally agreed to mean the *practice* or *practising* of *tattva*, but there is disagreement between traditional commentators over what *tattva* denotes. Hence, while Gauḍapāda (sixth century CE) is among those who construe *tattva-abhyāsa* to mean "*practising* the meditation of twenty-five principles"[15]—or, in Horace Wilson's translation, "the *study of the twenty-five principles*"[16]—the later (ninth- or tenth-century) commentator Vācaspatimiśra understands it to mean something more like simply the "practice of reality" or "practice of truth." As translated by Gangānātha Jhā, Vācaspati remarks that "The word 'truth' [*tattva*] indicates the knowledge thereof. By means of practice of truth . . . through a long course of repeated, uninterrupted and respectful exercise of true knowledge, the wisdom manifesting the distinction of Spirit from Matter, is attained."[17] The phrase that Jhā here translates as "distinction of Spirit from Matter" in fact reads *sattvapuruṣānyatā*, which is more accurately rendered as "difference between (or otherness of) *sattva* and *Puruṣa*." In this context, *sattva* is likely to be a synonym of *buddhi*, which is the most refined of the products or manifestations of *Prakṛti*, *Prakṛti* being the underlying source of all the constitutive conditions of possible experience. Since Jhā is using "Matter" as a translation of *Prakṛti*, it is not hard to see why he translates the phrase *sattvapuruṣānyatā* as he does. To differentiate *Puruṣa* from *buddhi* is, in effect, to dissociate the ultimate source of conscious subjectivity from the very capacity for differentiation or discrimination, for *buddhi* is identified in the *Sāṃkhya Kārikā* with *adhyavasāya* (SK 23), which can itself be rendered as "discernment" or "determination," in the sense of picking something out or distinguishing it from something else or from a mere background.

We might note in this connection that the same phrase, *sattvapuruṣānyatā*, also occurs in the third chapter of the *Yoga Sūtra*, where it is said that, "From discerning the difference between *sattva* and *Puruṣa* alone is there all-powerfulness over states of being and all-knowingness" (YS 3.49).[18] The immediately subsequent *sūtra* adds that, "From nonattachment (*vairāgya*) even to this, by the destruction of the seed of this imperfection, *kaivalya* [is achieved]" (YS 3.50).[19] This implies that the distinguishing of the ultimate source of consciousness, on the one hand, from the capacity for distinguishing anything at all, on the other, must itself be dissociated from. It must be dissociated from because, being in a contentful mental state (even if the "content" is merely the making of a rarefied distinction), it is not itself *Puruṣa*, which is characterized in terms that imply that it is, in itself, consciousness devoid of content.[20] Although this specific step of dissociation from the very act of differentiating *Puruṣa* from *buddhi* (and hence from *Prakṛti* as *buddhi*'s constitutive source) is not explicitly mentioned in the *Sāṃkhya Kārikā*, the soteriological importance of *vairāgya*—the withdrawal of attachment and desire—is fully acknowledged to be what precipitates the "dissolution of *Prakṛti*" (SK 45). So no support is provided for the claim that Sāṃkhya's methods are purely "theoretical" or "rationalistic" whereas those of Yoga involve sustained meditation. The most we can infer is that the *Yoga Sūtra* is more concerned with spelling out the details of meditative procedures—albeit still in very condensed terms—than is the *Sāṃkhya Kārikā*. The rhetoric of "direct experience" versus "intellectual analysis" is a distraction from coming to see how such factors as meditation, nonattachment, and analysis are combined in the forms of practice characteristic of both Sāṃkhya and Yoga.

One modern interpreter who favors Vācaspati's reading of *Sāṃkhya Kārikā* 64 over that of Gauḍapāda is Suryanarayana Sastri, who maintains that understanding *tattva* to mean "truth" "is preferable, since it is by repeated study not of the categories but of the difference between the Spirit [*Puruṣa*] and the categories of Nature [*Prakṛti*] that wisdom results."[21] The practical difference between Gauḍapāda's and Vācaspati's respective interpretations is, however, meagre, for it is implicit within the idea of studying or meditating upon the categories of *Prakṛti* that one is doing so for the purpose of distinguishing them from *Puruṣa*. It is by this means that there arises the knowledge of *Puruṣa*'s fundamental non-identity with anything constitutive of an ordinary conception of selfhood—the knowledge that consists in the realization that, from the perspective of *Puruṣa*, " 'I am not,' 'not mine,' 'not I.' " The *Sāṃkhya Sūtra* expresses the same point by invoking the phrase *neti neti*, which most famously occurs in the *Bṛhadāraṇyaka Upaniṣad*: "not this, nor this" or simply " 'not—,' 'not—.' "[22] If we were to follow a hermeneutical approach such as that of Feuerstein, we should read this invocation as an "intellectualistic refashioning of an originally introspective-meditative practice."[23] But to read it in this way is to risk filtering every self-description of Sāṃkhya's methods through the presupposition that those methods simply cannot be meditative. In fact, there is no reason to suppose that any refashioning is happening when Sāṃkhya texts speak of realizing *Puruṣa*'s non-identity with *Prakṛti*.

Of course, if *Puruṣa* is understood to consist in pure nonintentional consciousness, devoid of any content, then the very idea of knowledge arising in *Puruṣa* is problematic, prompting some interpreters to insist that it cannot strictly be in *Puruṣa* that the knowledge arises: it must instead be in *buddhi*—the intellectual or intentional faculty. Gerald Larson, for example, interprets *Sāṃkhya Kārikā* 64 to be a pronouncement of *buddhi*'s knowledge that "I am not (conscious); (consciousness) does not belong to me; the 'I' is not (conscious)."[24] But such a reading, replete with gratuitous parenthetical interpolations, places strain on the text, especially when considered in the light of the immediately succeeding two verses, which read in part: "Then *Puruṣa*, remaining fixed (*avasthita*) in himself like a spectator,[25] sees *Prakṛti*, who has returned to inactivity . . . 'I have seen her,' says the spectating one; 'I have been seen,' says the other, desisting; although the two remain in conjunction (*saṃyoga*), there is no initiation of [further] emergence" (SK 65–66).[26] The phrase *prekṣakavad avasthitaḥ svacchaḥ*,[27] meaning "abiding (or remaining fixed) in oneself like a spectator," echoes a passage from the *Maitrāyaṇīya* or *Maitrī Upaniṣad* (*c.* first century CE),[28] which states: "Verily, he is pure, steadfast, unswerving, stainless, unagitated, free from desire, remains fixed like a spectator and abiding in his own self."[29] The *Maitrāyaṇīya* passage proceeds to assert that he (the self, *ātman*) "exists below the covering of the cloth [or veil] that is made up by the *guṇa*s [*guṇamayena*]."[30] Although this vocabulary resembles that of the *Sāṃkhya Kārikā*, the image could, on a certain reading, be taken to imply that *Puruṣa* actively envelops himself in the deceptive veil of the *guṇa*s—the *guṇa*s being the three "strands" that constitute the structure of *Prakṛti*.[31] The *Sāṃkhya Kārikā* develops the notion of the spectator differently by depicting the self neither as existing beneath nor as enveloping himself in a cloth or veil, but rather as becoming, temporarily, a witness of the *guṇa*s through the performance of *Prakṛti*, who dances before *Puruṣa*'s gaze (SK 59).

Yet there remains an unresolved tension in the *Sāṃkhya Kārikā*, and within Sāṃkhya philosophy as a whole, concerning the question of *Puruṣa*'s activity. On the one hand, as David Burke remarks, "The *Kārikās* are quite clear on the point that *puruṣa* is *passive* consciousness unable to pursue anything actively. . . . activity, including transformation (*pariṇāma*) and transmigration (*saṃsāra*), is all on the side of *prakṛti*."[32] This passivity is emphasized in, among other places, *Sāṃkhya Kārikā* 19, which maintains that owing to its being "the opposite" of *Prakṛti*, *Puruṣa* can be characterized in terms of "witnessing, aloneness, equanimity, awareness, and inactivity."[33]

On the other hand, the soteriological dynamic of Sāṃkhya philosophy demands that some change must occur in or to *Puruṣa*—a movement from entrapment and immersion in *Prakṛti*'s display to release and awakening to *Puruṣa*'s own independence. Thus, we find statements such as those in *Sāṃkhya Kārikā* 66, in which it is unambiguously *Puruṣa, qua* "spectator" (*prekṣaka*), who declares that he has seen *Prakṛti*, thereby confirming, in case there were any doubt, that in verse 64 it is similarly *Puruṣa* who is the subject of the realization that "'I am not,' 'not mine,' 'not I.'"

Ultimately, if we approach the *Sāṃkhya Kārikā* expecting to find a thoroughly watertight and internally consistent metaphysical system, we are liable to be frustrated. The conception of the relationship between *Puruṣa* and *Prakṛti* is articulated largely in terms of pictorial analogies, each of which has its limitations. Among these analogies—in addition to the image of the spectator and the dancer, which we have seen above—is that of a blind but mobile person carrying someone who is sighted but unable to walk (SK 21). The blind person represents *Prakṛti*, active but "nonconscious" (*acetana*, SK 20), and the sighted person represents *Puruṣa*: inactive consciousness. The limitations of these analogies are various. For a start, they do not even begin to explain the sense in which *Puruṣa* is held to be multiple. This principle of the "multiplicity of *Puruṣa*s" (*Puruṣa-bahutva*) is affirmed briefly in *Sāṃkhya Kārikā* 18 but then, apparently, downplayed throughout the rest of the text.[34] The reason for affirming that there are many *Puruṣa*s—many centers of consciousness—is not hard to comprehend. As verse 18 itself observes, different people are born and die at different times and exhibit different capacities over the course of their lives; hence (the text seems to imply) the claim that everyone partakes of the same essential self is simply incompatible with what we know empirically about human life. In a similar spirit, Vyāsa's commentary on *Yoga Sūtra* 2.22 distinguishes between the *Puruṣa* who is "proficient" (*kuśala*) and those who are "non-proficient" (*akuśala*). He does so in order to account for the fact that, when one person achieves spiritual liberation and ceases to undergo further experience, it is not the case that empirical reality dissolves for everyone else as well. Empirical reality—the manifestation of *Prakṛti*—persists in relation to the non-proficient, for "its purpose has not yet been fulfilled."[35] For the most part, however, neither the *Yoga Sūtra* nor the *Sāṃkhya Kārikā* gives much emphasis to the multiplicity doctrine, and hence, in the *Sāṃkhya Kārikā*'s analogies, it is only one sighted person who is carried by the blind one, and the dancer is said to desist from performing once *Puruṣa* avows that he has seen her: there is no mention of her continuing to dance for all the other *Puruṣa*s.

According to the commentarial literature, *Puruṣa* and *Prakṛti* stand in a relation of "nearness" or "proximity" (*sannidhāna, saṃnidhi*),[36] though not in the sense of spatial proximity. They undergo a "conjunction" (*saṃyoga*), despite *Puruṣa*'s being entirely "non-engaged" (*udāsīna*). Rather than trying to smooth over these apparent tensions and expecting them to be readily reconcilable at a purely theoretical level, it is important to keep in view the fact that Sāṃkhya represents itself as soteriologically, or liberatively, oriented. I return briefly to the problem of how contentless consciousnesses can be a subject of knowledge in the concluding section. Before that, however, it is important to appreciate a distinction between two types of knowledge in Sāṃkhya philosophy.

Two Types of Knowledge

As we have seen, one of the ways in which it is sometimes argued that Sāṃkhya's methods are exclusively "rationalistic" is by interpreting the term *vijñāna* to denote a specifically "conceptual" form of discriminative knowledge, where "conceptual" is intended to imply something more discursive and less "direct" than the knowledge arrived at through yogic meditation.[37] In the light of this interpretation, the threefold discrimination between manifest *Prakṛti*, unmanifest *Prakṛti*, and the "knower" (*jña, Puruṣa*), which is advocated as the "superior" means of eliminating or transcending *duḥkha* in *Sāṃkhya Kārikā* 2, is regarded as a purely "theoretical" or "intellectual" act that falls short of Yoga's emphasis on "personal experimentation and practical meditational techniques."[38] But this diremption between a "meditation-oriented" Yoga and a "rationalistic" Sāṃkhya can be maintained only if the *vijñāna* of Sāṃkhya is conflated with the "means of knowing" (*pramāṇa*) that are concisely expounded in, for example, *Sāṃkhya Kārikā* 4–6 and *Yoga Sūtra* 1.7. As Rodney Parrott has argued, however, what is meant in this context by *pramāṇa* is only a limited epistemic category; it concerns the type of knowledge that consists in demonstrating or, as Parrott puts it, offering a "proof" of something.[39] This, Parrott points out, must be distinguished from another type of knowledge, which is precisely the sort for which the author of the *Sāṃkhya Kārikā* uses both the terms *vijñāna* and *jñāna*. Knowledge of this latter type consists not in demonstrating or proving anything, but in directly discerning a difference—most notably the difference between *Puruṣa* and *Prakṛti*.

Support for the distinction that Parrott makes between the two types of knowledge is derivable from the traditional commentaries. Especially pertinent is a passage in the *Yuktidīpikā* (*c.* 680–720 CE), a text dubbed by certain scholars as the most "significant" and "comprehensive" commentary on the *Sāṃkhya Kārikā*.[40] According to this commentary, "Knowledge is of two kinds: that which is characterized by the understanding of words, and so forth, and that which is characterized by understanding the otherness of *Puruṣa* and the *guṇas*."[41] The first kind is said to be "of the form of perception, inference, and verbal testimony," whereas the understanding of the difference between *Puruṣa* and the *guṇas* itself comes in two varieties, namely that which is "unpreceded" (*apūrva*) and that which is "generated through practice" (*abhyāsaja*).[42] The *Yuktidīpikā* associates the first of these with "reflection, oral instruction, and [scriptural] study,"[43] and describes the second as arising upon one's "conquering the height of the level of nonattachment (*vairāgya*)" and as being characterized by "peace, purity, constancy, and contrariety to all produced and unproduced entities."[44] It then equates the latter with precisely the type of knowledge referred to in *Sāṃkhya Kārikā* 64, namely that which consists in the recognition "that 'I am not,' 'not mine,' 'not I' (*nāsmi, na me, nāham*)."

So, in summary, the *Yuktidīpikā* first differentiates knowledge arrived at by means of ordinary perception or discursive reasoning from the liberative knowledge that discriminates between *Puruṣa* and *Prakṛti*. It then distinguishes different methods of achieving knowledge of the latter sort and identifies that which includes a sustained process of "dispassion" or "nonattachment" (*vairāgya*) with what, in *Sāṃkhya Kārikā* 64, is referred to as *tattva-abhyāsa*. Hence we have practice (*abhyāsa*) paired with nonattachment (*vairāgya*), which is precisely the pairing that the *Yoga Sūtra* recommends as the twofold means of expediting the cessation (*nirodha*) of the modifications of the mind.[45] There is thus good reason to suppose that the method of soteriological practice enjoined in the *Sāṃkhya Kārikā* and in the commentarial tradition arising from it is either identical to or, at any rate, closely aligned with the methods of cultivating nonattachment to sensory objects and to their fundamental constituents (*guṇa*s) that are adumbrated in the *Yoga Sūtra* and its commentaries.[46] Sāṃkhya's purported rationalism relates to the systematic articulation of its philosophical system. This articulation is, inevitably, technical and "rationalistic" because expounding a system that enumerates and concisely defines the different means of acquiring knowledge, the diverse categories of mental state, the multiple constitutive conditions of possible experience, and so on, necessarily involves considerable conceptual, intellectual, and theoretical reasoning. But the definitions and enumerations of principles that compose the philosophical system are not all that Sāṃkhya's *soteriological* practice amounts to, which culminates in the *nāsmi, na me, nāham* insight.

A final point of interest to be noted in connection with *tattva-abhyāsa* in the *Sāṃkhya Kārikā* is the fact that the same compound term occurs in *Yoga Sūtra* 1.32, though preceded by *eka,* meaning "one" or "single." In that context, *eka-tattva-abhyāsa* appears to denote the practice of concentrating single-pointedly on an object of meditation, ostensibly to eliminate the various disturbances and distractions that are listed in the immediately preceding two *sūtra*s. The cultivation of such single-pointed attention, culminating in states of prolonged "absorption" (*samādhi*), is central to Yoga's soteriological procedure. Again, in the absence of strong reasons for supposing that *tattva-abhyāsa* means something different in the *Sāṃkhya Kārikā* from what it means in the *Yoga Sūtra,* we may infer that the practice alluded to in *Sāṃkhya Kārikā* 64 involves forms of meditation that are not well described as exclusively discursive or "rationalistic" in nature.

Conclusion

My purpose in this chapter has not been to argue that there is no place for rationality, or "rationalistic" methods, in Sāṃkhya philosophy, nor that the philosophy presented in the *Sāṃkhya Kārikā* is straightforwardly identical to that of the *Yoga Sūtra*. My point, rather, is that the divergences between these texts, and between what have become popularly known as the Sāṃkhya and Yoga *darśana*s, have been exaggerated by certain interpreters. The exaggeration has taken place in order to assert that Yoga's soteriological methods are superior to those of Sāṃkhya on account of their involving a more "direct" kind of knowledge, attainable through sustained meditation as opposed to "mere" ratiocination. Without simplistically overlooking dissimilarities where they exist, my proposal is that we take seriously the conceptual and terminological convergences between the texts at issue, especially when it comes to trying to understand the soteriological practice that is designated in *Sāṃkhya Kārikā* 64 as *tattva-abhyāsa*. By taking this approach, we find that the meditative soteriological methods of Sāṃkhya have much in common with those of Yoga, and that these methods combine single-pointed meditation with rigorous nonattachment to phenomenal mental states, carried out within a context informed by rational philosophical inquiry.

In passing, I have noted a residual tension in Sāṃkhya philosophy concerning the sense in which it can be *Puruṣa*—the subject of pure nonintentional consciousness—who awakens to the fact that he has "seen" the display of *Prakṛti* (SK 66) and hence cannot be identical to her (SK 64). There remains much more that could be said about this tension, for which I do not have space here. In brief, we might understand *Sāṃkhya Kārikā* 64 as voicing, as it were, the "last breath" or "last gasp" of intentional consciousness—the consciousness *of* or *about* something. Insofar as the realization of non-identity with *Prakṛti* is an intentional (contentful) mental state at all, it is an expression of *buddhi*, but (*pace* Larson) it does not follow that the referent of "I" and "mine" in the phrase "'I am not,' 'not mine,' 'not I'" must be *buddhi* and that what is being denied is that *buddhi* is genuinely conscious. Rather, I take it that what is being figuratively portrayed here is a conscious human being's realization that their true identity is *Puruṣa* and not *Prakṛti*. Since this realization is itself an intentional state, there is a sense in which it is an instantiation of *buddhi* and not the final abiding of *Puruṣa* in unalloyed "aloneness" (*kaivalya*). But it is precisely this last breath of intentional consciousness that, as the image of the dancer returning to inactivity suggests (SK 65), precipitates that aloneness, "which is both absolute and conclusive" (SK 68).[47]

Notes

1. Cf. Gerald James Larson, "Preface," in Gerald James Larson and Ram Shankar Bhattacharya, eds, *Sāṃkhya: A Dualist Tradition in Indian Philosophy* (Princeton, NJ: Princeton University Press, 1987), xi–xiv, at xi.

2. For the text of the *Sāṃkhya Kārikā*, see Mikel Burley, *Classical Sāṃkhya and Yoga: An Indian Metaphysics of Experience* (London: Routledge, 2007), 163–79. For the *Sāṃkhya Sūtra*, see *The Sánkhya Aphorisms of Kapila, with Illustrative Extracts from the Commentaries*, trans. James R. Ballantyne, 3rd ed. (London: Trübner & Co., 1885). Translations from these and other Sanskrit texts are my own unless otherwise stated. In citations I shall use the abbreviations "SK" and "SS" respectively.

3. See, e.g., the respective commentaries by Gauḍapāda and Vācaspatimiśra: *Sāṁkhyakārikā of Īśvarakṛṣṇa, with the Commentary of Gauḍapāda*, trans. T. G. Mainkar, 2nd ed. (Poona: Oriental Book Agency, 1972), 37; *Tattva-Kaumudî (Sânkhya) of Vâchaspati Miśra*, trans. Gangânâtha Jhâ (Bombay: Tookaram Tatya, 1896), 2–3.

4. *evaṃ tattvābhyāsān nāsmi na me nāham ity apariśeṣam / aviparyayād viśuddhaṃ kevalam utpadyate jñānam //* (SK 64).

5. I am not here assuming a strict demarcation between Sāṃkhya's soteriological practice, on the one hand, and its philosophy, on the other, for these are intimately intertwined. Rather, I am distinguishing between Sāṃkhya's soteriological practice—that is, what Sāṃkhya practitioners *do*—and how the philosophy's conceptual framework is presented in textual sources.

6. Richard Garbe, *Die Sâṃkhya-Philosophie. Eine Darstellung des indischen Rationalismus nach den Quellen* (Leipzig: Haessel, 1894).

7. John Davies, *Hindū Philosophy. The Sānkhya Kārikā of Īśwara Kṛishṇa: An Exposition of the System of Kapila* (London: Trübner & Co., 1881), v.

8. Gerald James Larson, "Introduction to the Philosophy of Sāṃkhya," in *Sāṃkhya: A Dualist Tradition in Indian Philosophy*, 1–103, at 3.

9. Georg Feuerstein, *The Philosophy of Classical Yoga* (Manchester: Manchester University Press, 1980), ix.

10. Gerald James Larson, "Introduction to the Philosophy of Yoga," in *Yoga: India's Philosophy of Meditation*, ed. Gerald James Larson and Ram Shankar Bhattacharya (Delhi: Motilal Banarsidass, 2008), 19–159, at 23.

11. Feuerstein, *The Philosophy of Classical Yoga*, 113, 115.

12. Ibid., 117–118.

13. Ian Whicher, *The Integrity of the Yoga Darśana: A Reconsideration of Classical Yoga* (Albany, NY: SUNY Press, 1998), 49–53.

14. *dṛṣṭam anumānam āptavacanaṃ ca sarvapramāṇasiddhatvāt* (SK 4).

15. *The Sāṁkhya-Kārikā: Iśvara Kṛṣṇa's Memorable Verses on Sāṁkhya Philosophy with the Commentary of Gauḍapādācārya*, trans. Har Dutt Sharma (Poona: Oriental Book Agency, 1933), 75–76.

16. *The Sánkhya Káriká, or Memorial Verses on the Sánkhya Philosophy, by Íswara Krishna*, trans. Henry Thomas Colebrooke; *also the Bháshya or Commentary of Gaurapáda* [*sic*], trans. Horace Hayman Wilson (London: Valpy, 1837), 178.

17. *Tattva-Kaumudî (Sânkhya) of Vâchaspati Miśra*, trans. Gangânâtha Jhâ (Bombay: Tookaram Tatya, 1896), 107.

18. *sattvapuruṣānyatākhyātimātrasya sarvabhāvādhiṣṭhātṛtvaṃ sarvajñātṛtvaṃ ca* (YS 3.49). For the Sanskrit text, see http://gretil.sub.uni-goettingen.de/gretil/1_sanskr/6_sastra/3_phil/yoga/patyog_u.htm (accessed April 9, 2018), based on the edition by Kāśinātha Śāstrī Āgāśe (Pune: Ānandāśramamudraṇālaya, 1904). I use "YS" in citations as an abbreviation for *Yoga Sūtra*.

19. *tadvairāgyād api doṣabījakṣaye kaivalyam* (YS 3.50).

20. See, e.g., the characterizations of *Puruṣa* as "witnessing, aloneness, equanimity, awareness, and inactivity" at SK 19, "neutral" or "non-engaged" (*udāsīna*) at SK 20, and "consciousness" (*cetana*) at SK 55.

21. S. S. Suryanarayana Sastri, ed. and trans., *The Sāṅkhyakārikā of Īśvara Kṛṣṇa*, 3rd ed. (Madras: University of Madras, 1948), 98–99.

22. *tattvābhyāsān neti netīti tyāgād vivekasiddhiḥ* (SS 3.75, in *The Sánkhya Aphorisms of Kapila*, 277). Cf. *Bṛhadāraṇyaka Upaniṣad* 2.3.6, 3.9.26, 4.2.4, in Patrick Olivelle, trans. and ed., *The Early Upaniṣads: Annotated Text and Translation* (Oxford: Oxford University Press, 1998), 67, 101, 111.

23. Feuerstein, *The Philosophy of Classical Yoga*, 115.

24. Gerald James Larson, *Classical Sāṃkhya: An Interpretation of Its History and Meaning*, 2nd ed. (Delhi: Motilal Banarsidass, 1979), 274.

25. For the translation "remaining fixed like a spectator," see for example S. G. M. Weerasinghe, *The Sāṅkhya Philosophy: A Critical Evaluation of Its Origins and Development* (Delhi: Sri Satguru, 1993), 236.

26. *tena nivṛttaprasavām . . . / prakṛtiṃ paśyati puruṣaḥ prekṣakavad avasthitaḥ svacchaḥ // dṛṣṭā mayety upekṣaka eko dṛṣṭāhamity uparamaty anyā / sati saṃyoge 'pi tayoḥ prayojanaṃ nāsti sargasya //* (SK 65–66).

27. There are discrepancies between different traditional commentaries over whether the final word in this phrase should be *svasthaḥ*, *susthaḥ*, or *svacchaḥ*. I have here followed the *Yuktidīpikā* and Vācaspati's *Tattvakaumudī*

in opting for the third of these. The significance for the meaning of the phrase as a whole is negligible.

28. Attempts to date the *Maitrāyaṇīya Upaniṣad* have not noticeably advanced since the time of Arthur A. Macdonell, who categorizes it as post-Buddhist in his *A History of Sanskrit Literature* (London: Heinemann, 1900), 226, 230. Following Macdonell, Crangle places it around the first century CE; see Edward Fitzpatrick Crangle, *The Origin and Development of Early Indian Contemplative Practices* (Wiesbaden: Harrassowitz, 1994), 65.

29. *Maitrāyaṇīya Upaniṣad* 2.7, trans. S. Radhakrishnan, *The Principal Upaniṣads* (London: George Allen & Unwin, 1978), 804.

30. *Maitrāyaṇīya Upaniṣad* 2.7, trans. J. A. B. van Buitenen, *The Maitrāyaṇīya Upaniṣad: A Critical Essay, with Text, Translation and Commentary* ('s-Gravenhage: Mouton & Co., 1962), 128; my square brackets.

31. See, e.g., Radhakrishnan, *The Principal Upaniṣads*, 804: "he covers himself with a veil made of qualities."

32. B. David Burke, "Transcendence in Classical Sāṃkhya," *Philosophy East and West* 38, no. 1 (1988), 19–29, at 20.

33. . . . *sākṣitvam . . . kaivalyam mādhyasthyaṃ draṣṭṛtvam akartṛbhāvaś ca* (SK 19).

34. SK 56 and 63 both refer to "each" or "every" (*prati*) *Puruṣa*, thereby implying that there are more than one, but neither of these verses helps to nuance or embellish the principal analogies by means of which the relationship between *Puruṣa* and *Prakṛti* is articulated.

35. See the translation of *Yogabhāṣya* 2.22 in Swāmī Veda Bhāratī, *Yoga Sūtras of Patañjali with the Exposition of Vyāsa: Translation and Commentary*, Vol. 2: *Sādhana-Pāda* (Delhi: Motilal Banarsidass, 2001), 371.

36. See, e.g., *Tattvakaumudī* 20; *Yogabhāṣya* 1.4.

37. See, e.g., Feuerstein, *The Philosophy of Classical Yoga*, 118; Whicher, *The Integrity of the Yoga Darśana*, 53.

38. Whicher, ibid.

39. Rodney J. Parrott, "The Experience Called 'Reason' in Classical Sāṃkhya," *Journal of Indian Philosophy* 13, no. 3 (1985), 235–264, at 240–241.

40. Albrecht Wezler and Shujun Motegi, eds, *Yuktidīpikā: The Most Significant Commentary on the Sāṃkhyakārikā*, Vol. 1 (Stuttgart: Steiner, 1998); Edeltraud Harzer, *The Yuktidīpikā: A Reconstruction of Sāṅkhya Methods of Knowing* (Aachen: Shaker, 2006), 103.

41. *jñānaṃ dvividhaṃ śabdādy upalabdhilakṣaṇaṃ guṇapuruṣāntaropalabdhilakṣaṇaṃ ca* (*Yuktidīpikā* on SK 23). My translation is a slightly amended version of Parrott's; see Parrott, "The Experience Called 'Reason' in Classical Sāṃkhya," 260n41.

42. Compare the translation of *apūrva* as "innate" by Shiv Kumar and D. N. Bhargava, *Yuktidīpikā*, Vol. 2 (Delhi: Eastern Book Linkers, 1992), 190.

43. The "reflection" (*ūha*) in question is held to differ from the three standard means of knowledge, namely perception, inference, and authoritative testimony. For discussion, see James Kimball, "The Relationship between the *bhāvas* and the *pratyayasarga* in Classical Sāṃkhya," *Journal of Indian Philosophy* 44, no. 3 (2016), 537–555, at 548–549, 552.

44. *abhyāsajaṃ punar vairāgyaparvāvajayapṛṣṭhalabdhaṃ śāntam amalaṃ dhruvaṃ sakalabhavābhavapratipakṣabhūtam* (*Yuktidīpikā* on SK 23).

45. See esp. *Yoga Sūtra* 1.12: "Through practice and nonattachment, that cessation [is achieved]" (*abhyāsavairāgyābhyāṃ tan nirodhaḥ*).

46. Cf. *Yoga Sūtra* 1.15–16: "Nonattachment is the controlled consciousness of one who is without craving for objects, whether perceived or [merely] heard about. Higher than that is the knowing of *Puruṣa*—the absence of craving for the *guṇas*" (*dṛṣṭānuśravikaviṣayavitṛṣṇasya vaśīkārasaṃjñā vairāgyam // tat paraṃ puruṣakhyāter guṇavaitṛṣṇyam*).

47. *aikāntikam ātyantikam ubhayaṃ kaivalyam āpnoti* (SK 68). For discussion of an earlier version of this chapter, I am grateful to participants in the conference, *The Sāṃkhya System: Accounting for the Real*, at Loyola Marymount University, March 2018. Geoff Ashton generously provided written comments on a subsequent draft.

Chapter 4

The Determinative Nature of the Guṇas and Bhāvas in the Sāṃkhya Karikā

CHRISTOPHER KEY CHAPPLE

This chapter will focus on the discussion of *guṇas* and *bhāvas* in the *Sāṃkya Kārikā,* topics that pervade much of the text. Some traditional commentators on the text as well as modern interpreters have chosen a path that tends to de-emphasize the significance of the three-fold *guṇa* assessment of reality. Furthermore, though much has been written about the seemingly "dualistic" relationship between *Puruṣa* and *Prakṛti,* less attention has been given to their relationship as manifested through the *bhāvas* of the *buddhi,* the dispositions and predispositions situated within the "intellect" better explained as the platform of human impulse. The state of the *guṇas* and *bhāvas* determine the nature of lived experience.

Revisiting Sāṃkhya Kārikās 25–36

Sāṃkhya Kārikā verses 25–32 describe human behaviors or fluctuations (*vṛittis*) in the world. Īśvarakṛṣṇa argues that the world is construed according to the constitution of one's own particular set of *guṇas*. A suggestion will be made below that the repeated use of the number three in these verses can be seen as a reference to the *guṇas,* not to the threefold organ as defined later in the text (33).

The number three appears prominently in the *Sāṃkhya Kārikā*. More than just serving as a descriptive number, it carries a code-like message that signals three simultaneous core philosophical aspects. In the beginning of the text, the author signals that the key to freedom is a threefold process that involves arriving at the discernment of the manifest, the unmanifest, and the knower (*vyakta, avyakta, jña*, SK 2). The text delineates three means of knowledge: that which is apparent, inferred, or declared authoritatively (*dṛṣṭaṃ, anumānaṃ, āptavacanaṃ* SK 4). Most importantly and insistently, three *guṇas* create the manifest realm. They are first mentioned in *Sāṃkhya Kārikā* 11 and are further described in eighteen additional verses (12–14; 16, 18–20, 23, 25, 27, 29–30; 33, 36, 46, 48, 54, 60). Their centrality cannot be over-emphasized. This paper will focus on one instance where the commentator Gauḍapāda overlooks a key reference to the *guṇas* which has influenced successive commentators, detracting attention away from their determinative power. This chapter will also suggest that in addition to the *guṇas*, insufficient focus has been placed upon the *bhāvas*, the topic of no less that thirteen verses (23, 43–51, 63–65, 67).

As argued in chapter 15 of my book *Yoga and the Luminous*, a commentator can miss the flow of a text's intent, as seen in four instances in the *Yoga Sūtra*. The length of a comment can interrupt the argument being pursued in prior and subsequent passages. A commentary is generally read, not recited. "The memory is not engaged to the extent as when reciting a text, and insights derived from hearing 'echoes' within the recited text cannot be gleaned . . . In nearly all cases the commentary is several times longer than the *sūtra* itself, and by the time one reads through it, the continuity or flow from one *sūtra* to the next is lost. The commentarial tradition focuses primarily on *sūtras* in isolation from one another" (Chapple 2008, 221). In a close reading of the *Sāṃkhya Kārikā* over the course of more than a year, one such instance surfaced, wherein Gauḍapāda seemingly misinterpreted the number three in such a way that de-emphasizes the constitutive role of the *guṇas*. This paper will discuss not only this occurrence but also how it may distract from the emotional and constitutive roles of the *bhāvas* which, despite their significant presence, tend to be overlooked by many interpreters.

As noted above, the discussion of the *guṇas* begins with verse eleven and proceeds through verse twenty:

11. An object is discerned due to the three *guṇas*.
It is held in common and is not conscious.
It proceeds according to its constitution (*dharma*).
The manifest is therefore linked to the *pradhāna*.
The *pumān* stands apart from it.

12. In regard to the *guṇas*,
their nature is delight, dis-rest, and despair.
Their purpose is luminosity, activity, and restraint.
Their fluctuations combine so one overpowers the others.
One predominates while the others support.

13. *Sattva* is light and luminous.
Rajas stimulates and moves.
Tamas is heavy and concealing.
A fluctuation is like a lamp.
Its purpose is to make a thing apparent.

14. The humble jumble of nondiscernment
arises from the three *guṇas*.
The absence of that results in the contrary (the *pumān*).
The material cause be found in the nature of the *guṇas*.
The unmanifest is thus established in the effect.

15 and 16. The *avyakta* is the cause
(1) Because of the number of distinctions.
(2) Because all things hold a common origin.
(3) Because activity follows its own power.
(4) Because there is a distinction
between cause and effect.
(5) Because all distinctions disappear
back into a universal form.
(6) All things arise from the three *guṇas*
like the emergence of water as steam, liquid, and ice.
(7) All specificity relies upon the particularity of the *guṇas*.

17. *Puruṣa* exists
(1) Because combinations exist for the sake of another.
(2) Because there must be something distinct from the *guṇas*.

(3) Because there must be a superintendent.
(4) Because there must be an enjoyer.
(5) Because both activity and freedom
exist for its sake.

18. It is established that there are many *puruṣas*.
(1) Because of the diversity
of births, deaths and faculties.
(2) Because activities take place at different times.
(3) Because the distinctions of the proportions of the
three *guṇas* vary.

19. Hence it is established that the *Puruṣa*
is the opposite of the three *guṇas*.
It is the witness.
It is solitary (*kaivalyaṃ*), neutral (*madhyastha*).
It is the seer. It does nothing.

20. Furthermore, due to *saṃyoga*,
the unconscious appears as if marked by consciousness.
Because of the fluctuations of the *guṇas*,
the indifferent one appears as if active.

These verses assert the primacy of the *guṇas*. They characterize all aspects of the movement from the unmanifest to the manifest. They bring into specificity the existence of the material world, *Prakṛti*. They stand apart from *Puruṣa*. When their operations cease, then *Puruṣa* emerges. They give rise to and define the "humble jumble (*viparyaya-abhāva*) of nondiscernment (*aviveka*)."

The next verse describes the process of *saṃyoga*, which Geoff Ashton skillfully translates as "compresence." *Saṃyoga* allows the dance between action and the witness to unfold, providing experience and freedom (SK 21). The following verses itemize the specific ways in which the *guṇas* congeal into other *tattvas*, cascading from *buddhi*/*mahat* into ego, mind, the five sense organs, the five action organs, the five rudiments, and then, from the rudiments, into the elements. Verse 23 introduces the *bhāvas*, to be explained in fuller detail much later in the text (43–52).

23. Mental effort in its elevated state (*sattvika*)
leads to *dharma*, knowledge (*jñāna*),
freedom from attachment (*virāga*), and power (*aiśvarya*).
From *tamas*, the reverse arises.

Both this verse and 25 and 27 emphasize the *guṇas*.

25. From the energization of the ego,
arises the illuminating (*sattvika*) eleven
(the mind and the ten organs)
and the heavier (*tamasika*) elements, rudimentary and gross.
Both are suffused with *tejas* (*rajasika*).

27. The mind is of the nature of both
(the sense organs and action organs).
The organs follow its intention.
From the distinctions of its constitutive *guṇas*,
the various aspects of the external world arise
correspondingly.

The latter part of verse 27 requires special attention: *guṇapariṇāma-viśeṣān nānātvaṃ bāhyabedāśca*. Every manifest thing within the world owes its existence to its constitutive *guṇas*.

The three verses following verse 27 affirm the centrality of the *guṇas*, stating that every fluctuation (*vṛtti*) generates from this process. Without constitutive *guṇas* there can be no experience. Without experience there can be no freedom.

Despite the obvious emphasis that Īśvarakṛṣṇa places on the power of the *guṇas* in the shaping of reality, and despite the usage in seven prior verses of the number three as *tri* or *traya* in clear reference to three *guṇas* amid six other verses that describe the *guṇas*, Gauḍapāda makes an assertion even before the start of verse 29 that a new topic is being introduced. This assertion, which I rebut, muddies the meaning of this verse. At stake here is the word *trayasya* in verse 29. Grammatically, it indicates "of the three." Because the thirteen antecedent verses that use or refer to the number three involve the three *guṇas*, it makes sense that the reference to three in verse 29 indicates the constitutive *guṇas*. Hence, we have translated this verse as follows:

29. A fluctuation has the three characteristics (*guṇas*).
No [fluctuation] is held in common.
The five winds, expressed through the breath,
form a fluctuation that is common in every operation.

In addition to reinforcing the primacy of the *guṇas,* this verse also contrasts the changing and distinct nature of fluctuations (*vṛtti*) generated by the *guṇas* with the omnipresence of the five breaths (*prāṇas*), adeptly examined by Ana Funes in this volume. However, the verse does not in any way indicate the meaning given by Gauḍapāda. Guaḍapāda opens his commentary with *adhunā buddhi ahaṃkāra manasām ucyate* which translates as "Now the conversation turns to *buddhi,* ego, and mind." However, this threefold designation, which introduces an entirely new topic, does not appear in the text until verse 33.

Other translators have grappled with understanding verses 29 and 30 because of Gauḍapāda's assertion. Larson states that the "three" refers to the *buddhi,* the *ahaṃkāra,* and senses (1979, 265) while Burley rebuts him, stating that "three" refers to *buddhi, ahaṃkāra,* and *manas* (Burley 204). Although these three inner organs emerge later in the conversation as important, both in verse 29 and the two following verses, the emphasis seems to still reside in documenting and asserting the role of the *guṇas.*

30. A fluctuation, it is said,
arises in steps and simultaneously due to four
[functions of *buddhi, ahaṃkāra, manas,* and an
indriya].
Furthermore, it can be seen that every action
has an unseen precedent [governed]
by the three (*guṇas*).

The use of the number four makes sense here, and duly anticipates the role of the interplay between the threefold inner organ (*antaḥ karaṇa*) specified in verse thirty-three and the external world made known through one of the senses (*buddīndriya* or *karmendriya*). Additionally, the use of the term *trayasya,* as in verse twenty-nine, makes sense when seen as referring to the *guṇas.*

At stake here is laying out the premises for the relationship between the experience of activity through a fluctuation in service of the silent, inactive witness.

31. Each fluctuation arises
due to its mutuality of cause and resulting condition.
Each occurrence is created
for nothing other than for the purpose of *Puruṣa.*

Īśvarakrṣṇa continues this reasoning in the following verse, again indicating the suffusion of the threefold process in every occurrence, every event:

32. Occurrences happen through a thirteen-fold process
resulting in holding, sustaining, and revealing.
The result of this is tenfold,
allowing all that is to be held, sustained, and revealed
[through the ten sensory and action organs].

In a delightful play on words involving assonance and alliteration, the author invokes the word *āharaṇa* for holding (*tamas*), *dhāraṇa* for sustaining (*rajas*), and *prakāśa* for illuminating (*sattva*). This suggests that all activities manifest through the *guṇas.*

Two more nearby verses emphasize the importance of the *guṇas* in determining the tenor and tone of experience. Verse thirty-three fully and unambiguously introduces the threefold organ. It also includes a statement that alludes to the importance of the *guṇas.* Perhaps the inner organ itself might reflect the *guṇas, buddhi* occupying a space of *sattva, ahaṃkāra* the movement of *rajas,* and *manas,* which lands through the senses and organs into the realm of the material, *tamas.*

33. The inner occurrence is threefold
  [*buddhi, ahaṃkāra, manas*].
The external is tenfold
  [involving sense and action organs].
The context for experiencing an object
is predicated by the three (*guṇas*).

The external always exists in the present.
The internal occurrence (*karaṇam*) resides
in all three times (past, present, future).

The objective world becomes construed through the threefold nature of the *guṇas* and the *antaḥkaraṇa*.

Verse 36 emphasizes that all experience is shaped by the *guṇas*:

36. These [experiences], like a lamp, are distinct,
one from another, determined by the *guṇas*.
They are brought to light in the *buddhi*,
utterly for the purpose of *Puruṣa*.

The *guṇas* provide specificity to experience (*guṇaviśeṣa*). This verse underscores the purpose of experience: to be witnessed by *Puruṣa*.

Liṅga as Personality

One term that eludes easy translation is *liṅga*. Whereas Larson styles the *liṅga* as a sort of "proto person . . . comprising . . . psychological characteristics" (as summarized in Burley 129), Burley suggests that *liṅga* be seen as the "fluctuating experiential content of any individual conscious subject" (Burley 130). Burley seems to be contrasting the ever-changing aspects of the individual subject with the ultimate soteriology of Sāṃkhya which proclaims *nāham, nāsmi, na me*, "no ego, no acting, no possessions." This Buddhistic formula emphasizes the ultimate futility of all identity, all undertakings, and all identifications. This also mirrors the Upaniṣadic adage, *neti, neti*. However, this might put the emphasis too much on the negation side of the Sāṃkhya formula. It takes diligent, vigilant effort in order to arrive at this epiphany. The primary practice of Sāṃkhya, known as *tattva-abhyāsa*, requires a thorough understanding of the three *guṇas*, the twenty-five *tattvas*, the eight *bhāvas*, and the fifty *bhāvas*. Freedom or the *upavarga* side of the formula arises as a desideratum at the very start and as a culmination at the end of the text, verses 59–68. In the algebra of Sāṃkhya, far more attention is given to *Prakṛti* rather than to *Puruṣa*.

The term *liṅga* remains difficult to render into English. To call it a mark or a characteristic or sign, while technically correct and reflects its usage in logic, fails to capture the emotionality wrapped up in its function. Similarly, "experiential content" borders on the clinical and analytical without conveying much texture or flavor. However, the text itself uses the term as found in logic, a technological application for laying out the premises for the Sāṃkhya argument. Īśvarakṛṣṇa proclaims that "inference is threefold: from a clear mark (*tal liṅga*), from a prior mark (*liṅga-pūrvakaṃ*), and from reliable authority" (SK 5). Whereas the term mark or signifier works best in this context, later usages of the term lend themselves to the more psychological rendering of the word "personality." In verse ten, *liṅga* is one of nine qualities used to describe manifest reality (*vyakta prakṛti*). We have elongated our translation to read "marked with personality," whereas Burley uses the term "cipher," Larson "supported," and Mainkar "dependent." Another way to interpret SK 5 is to see the "mark" as indicating the role of personality in perception. In the first instance of a clear mark, the personality is operating in the present moment. In the second instance of the prior mark, it could refer to those aspects of the personality influenced by past impressions and experiences.

A sequence of verses later in the text describes the important linkage between *guṇas* and *liṅga* and *bhāva*, verses 40–42, 52, and 55. In these instances, Burley chooses to leave the term untranslated. However, the word personality works consistently in these instances, as given below. Though we appreciate the critique of personality offered by Burley with his emphasis on no-self as the goal, in this context the personality becomes determinative. It is only through the personality that one gathers and garners experiences of suffering that provide the impetus to move toward freedom. As the Jains and Buddhists and Īśvarakṛṣṇa point out, difficulty and darkness (*duḥkha*) serve as the catalyst in the pursuit of freedom. Here are the verses on personality (*liṅga*):

40. The marked personality,
which is cloaked with the *bhāvas,*
has already arisen but is not yet empowered.
It endures within the Mahat to the edge of the subtle.

Because it has not experienced enjoyment, it
transmigrates.

41. Just as art requires color,
just as without pillars there can be no shadow,
similarly, the personality cannot exist
without the specifics [of the *bhāvas*].

42. The personality performs like an actor
due to its connection (*yoga*)
with the allurement of Prakṛti.
This is the cause of human exertion:
yearning for both the secular (*nimitta*)
and the transcendent (*naimittika*, freedom).

52. Without the *bhāvas*, there is no personality.
Through the personality, the *bhāvas* can be quelled.
Therefore, the resultant created world (*sarga*)
emerges in a two-fold manner [subtle and gross].

55. . . . Due to the *svabhāvas* of personality
not being turned back,
there is suffering.

The personality (*liṅga*), staged from the platform of human impulse (*buddhi*) determines the qualities of one's experiences and interactions within the world.

Personality as *Bhāva*

The first thirty-eight verses of the SK deal with hardware, both philosophical and physical. To cohere, the Sāṃkhya system posits its principles of consciousness monads (*puruṣas*) interacting with materiality, both potential (*avyakta, mūla, pradhāna*) and manifested (*vyakta*) as realities. In Jain tradition, and in *Yoga Sūtra* IV:3, these manifestations of karma are known in the plural as *prakṛtis* or, in the word suggested by Ashton in this volume, procreativities. These realities include the gross elements, the subtle or rudimentary elements, the sense organs, the action organs, and, to a certain extent, the operations of the mind and ego. Starting with *Kārikā* 39, we see a shift in emphasis away from the hardware to a granular analysis of human software. This conversation continues to the very end, consuming nearly half the text. This transition is signaled by the term *sūkṣma,* generally translated as subtle or incipient. These subtle influences, as noted above, shape the human personality. This section of the chapter will systematically examine the two sets of descriptions of the factors that determine personality. The first, an eightfold analysis, is divided into two, one set of four deemed to be "lightening" or *sattvika,* the other set of four deemed to be downward trending (*tamasika*). The second description of *bhāvas* is more complicated. Its fifty-fold analysis outlines five varieties of ignorance, nine states of contentment, eight forms of success, and twenty-eight incapacities. The permutations of these *bhāvas,* from either list, determine the experience of the human person in the realm of experience.

Eight Bhāvas

Though only four *kārikās* describe the eight *bhāvas,* the language used by Īśvarakṛṣṇa is emphatic and emotional:

> 23. Mental effort in its elevated state (*sattvika*)
> leads to *dharma,* knowledge, freedom from attachment,
> and power.
> From *tamas,* the reverse arises.
>
> 43. The *bhāvas,* including *dharma* and the others,
> are primary.
> They are seen in the way life occurrences unfold,
> and in the unfolding growth of an embryo.
>
> 44. With *dharma* there is movement upward.
> Without *dharma,* things move downward.
> With knowledge freedom arises.
> From its opposite, bondage.
>
> 45. From nonattachment, things resolve themselves
> back into *Prakṛti.*
> From passionate attachment, *saṃsāra* arises.

From power, obstacles dissolve.
From its opposite, they persist.

The four positive attributes, in reverse order, are power (*aiśvarya*), nonattachment (*virāga/vairāga*), knowledge (*jñāna*), and *dharma*. Associated with uplift into the realm of *sattva*, they chart the path toward freedom, with knowledge as the portal that leads to the final goal. The opposites are lack of power or weakness (*anaiśvarya*), attachment (*rāga*), ignorance (*ajñāna*), and absence of virtue (*adharma*). These qualities drag a person downward into states of darkness (*tamas*). Although deceptively simple, this eightfold analysis provides a foundation for personality assessment. It also implicitly issues a moral challenge: how could one not desire, given the premises, to move from vice to virtue, from ignorance to knowledge, from attachment to nonattachment, and from weakness to power? As noted in this volume's chapter 2 by Ana Laura Funes Maderey, this assessment has been interpreted by Oberhammer as comprising an ethical mandate, a call to action that is inherently a form of spiritual practice. Though the text does not provide a list of precepts to be followed, the implied response to each negativity is clear: be good, seek knowledge, renounce attachments, and become effective.

Chart One	
The Eight *Bhāvas*	
Aiśvarya / Powerful	*Anaiśvarya* / Incompetent
Virāga or *Vairāgya* / Nonattached	*Rāga* / Attached
Jñāna / Knowledgeable	*Ajñāna* / Ignorant
Dharma / Virtuous	*Adharma* / Bereft of Virtue, Vicious

Fifty *Bhāvas*

Relatively little attention has been given to the second set of *bhāvas*, and for good reason. The description is dense and requires careful unpacking. Upfront, one must grapple with four categories: errors, contentments, successes, and incapacities. To understand the last category, one must revisit all the philosophical and physical *tattvas* painstakingly described in the first half of the text. Only after delving into the errors and incapacities can one begin to understand the categories that lead to contentment and success.

First come the lists: five states of ignorance, twenty-eight incapacities (shortcomings within the philosophical and physical domains), nine contentments, and eight perfections. Before we "get into the weeds" and risk losing ourselves in the details, it is important to hearken back to Ashton's chapter. These fifty *bhāvas* provide granular descriptions of the Ortegan category of circumstance, what Ashton refers to as "lived experience." Each of these variants and combinations of variants unfolds within manifest reality, what Ashton refers to as procreativity (*vyakta-prakṛti*). For the details on how Īśvarakṛṣṇa and Gauḍapāda delineate the *bhāvas*, please consult the charts within this chapter and the charts prepared by Ana Funes Maderey on pages 55–57. After a short narrative recap of the four major forms (error, incapacities, contentments, successes), hypothetical illustrative examples will be offered.

According to Gauḍapāda, the five states of ignorance (*viparyaya*) correspond to the five *kleśas* delineated by Patañjali in the *Yoga Sūtra* (II:3–9): ignorance (*avidyā*), egoism (*asmitā*), attachment (*rāga*), repulsion (*dveṣa*), and a desire to return and continue to live (*abhiniveśa*). Verse 48 seems to delineate further difficulties that arise from the five basic errors, compounding into eight forms of *tamas*, eight forms of delusion, ten forms of great delusion, as well as eighteen forms of extreme delusion and eighteen forms of "utter darkness." Under the category of error alone, Īśvarakṛṣṇa lists sixty-two possibilities. Gauḍapāda explains that the first pitfall can occur when the aspirant attributes consciousness to any one of the aspects of procreativity as expressed through the ten operations of the sense and action organs. The second pitfall arises when one becomes addicted to any of the eight powers. Gauḍapāda waxes eloquent in describing the morass of disappointments that arise through attachment, saying "the profound grief felt by one who dies amidst the abundance of sensual pleasures in the very season of enjoyment or who falls from the command of power [into] Utter Darkness,"[1] whether experienced by a human or a divine being.

Chart Two	
The Fifty *Bhāvas*:	Five Forms of Error (*viparyaya*)
1. *Tamas* (darkness)	Lack of wisdom (*avidyā*) in *Yoga Sūtra* II:4–5.
2. *Moha* (delusion)	Egotism (*asmitā*) in *Yoga Sūtra* II:6.
3. *Mahāmoha* (extreme delusion)	Attachment (*rāga*) in *Yoga Sūtra* II:7.
4. *Tāmisra* (thick darkness)	Aversion (*dveṣa*) in *Yoga Sūtra* II:8.
5. *Andhatāmisra* (total darkness)	A desire to hold onto and return to life (*abhinivśa*) *YS* II:9.

Continuing an assessment of *tamasika bhāvas*, Īśvarakṛṣṇa next delineates twenty-eight incapacities (*aśakti*): failure of the sense organs, the action organs, and the mind (eleven) as well as failure in the nine contentments and eight success that will be delineated in the next two paragraphs. If the mind fails, one becomes insane. If the action organs fail, one becomes impotent, constipated or plagued with diarrhea, incapable of using one's legs and feet, paralyzed in the arms and hands, and dumb. If the sense organs fail, one loses the sense of smell, of taste, of touch, and becomes blind and deaf.

Chart Three
The Fifty *Bhāvas*: Twenty-Eight Incapacities (*aśakti*)
1. Failure in the nine contentments
2. Failure in the eight successes
Failure of mind, sense organs, and organs of action, resulting in:
3. Madness
4. Deafness
5. Blindness
6. Paralysis
7. Loss of taste
8. Loss of smell
9. Inability to speak
10. Mutilation of hands
11. Lameness
12. Constipation or other eliminatory problems
13. Impotence

The first group of more positive occurrences comprise what are called the nine contentments (*tuṣṭi*). Though they do not lead to liberative knowledge, they do bring about a state of complacency. The first four are philosophical in nature. First one takes comfort in the mistaken notion that the nature of Prakṛti herself will resolve all problems. The second comfort arises when one adopts a materialist point of view and rejects the efficacy of meditative practice. The third misguided thought happens when one capitulates to the notion that "time heals all wounds." And the fourth false, though happy, notion asserts that freedom depends on good luck.[2] The second group of five contentments is physical in nature, found in happy fragrances, flavors, forms, feelings, and sounds.

Chart Four
The Fifty *Bhāvas*: The Nine Contentments (*tuṣṭi*)
Internal Contentments: Four Mistaken Notions:
1. Prakṛti will arrange for her own liberation.
2. Meditation is of no avail.
3. When time ripens, liberation will naturally occur.
4. Only by luck (*bhāgya*) does knowledge arise.
External Contentments in the Realm of the Senses:
5. Pleasant fragrances.
6. Delicious tastes.
7. Warmth and radiance.
8. Caress.
9. Gentle sounds and music.

Īśvarakṛṣṇa identifies eight additional forms of positivity. They begin with a reversal of the three modes of pain that are described at the very beginning of the *Sāṃkhya Kārikā*. One can, at least temporarily, find respite from inner psychological or spiritual pain (*ādhyātmika duḥkha*). One can take shelter from inclement weather or other forms of pain inflicted externally (*ādhibhautika duḥkha*). One can also seek protection from the wrath of the gods and goddesses (*ādhidaivika duḥkha*) through propitiation enacted in sacrifices. To these three, five other sources of happiness are added: the joy that comes from study, the elation that one feels when teaching, the satisfaction of making a good argument, the delight that one feels in the company of friends, and the pride that comes when one attains a state of purity. However, again echoing the very start of the text, no singular instance of positivity provides freedom. Like Vedic rituals, they can lead only to temporary abatement of suffering. In the final analysis, they prove to be fleeting.

Chart Five
The Fifty *Bhāvas*: Eight Forms of Success (*siddhi*)
1. Avoidance of Internal Pain
2. Avoidance of Externally-induced Pain
3. Propitiation of Deities
4. Study and Learning
5. Effective Teaching
6. Reasoning and Argumentation
7. Friendly Companionship
8. Purity

Here are a few hypothetical examples. A non-reflective person operates from the mistaken notion that happiness can be found in material wealth. Meditation does not interest such a person, who seeks pleasures in fine food and extravagant forms of entertainment. Having found great success in gathering a posse of friends, this person for several years seems to want nothing and in fact is envied by peers. However, disasters happen: bankruptcy, loss of the fancy cars and ability to pay for expensive meals, the death of beloved friends, and eventually debilitating illness. Slowly, all the illusions are dispelled. The truth taught at the beginning of the *Sāṃkhya Kārikā* is revealed: the torment of threefold suffering. The personality that had relied upon pleasure and reveled in friendly company sours. A bitterness sets in.

In another instance, the darkness of ego governed the life of another individual. Craving recognition, this person became a teacher and took great joy in the adulation of students. However, with old age, this person developed arthritis and could no longer write. Hearing began to fail, and the teacher could no longer respond to questions. And as the memory and voice fail, it becomes impossible to communicate in a helpful manner. Frustration and anger came to replace pride.

Although these two examples are perhaps simplistic, they nonetheless speak to the wisdom contained in Sāṃkhya. Sāṃkhya, rather than being tone deaf on ethics, indicates that there is general agreement that the better path in life would be to pursue virtue. In the case of the eight *bhāva* system, one would seek to understand the fleeting nature of pleasure, to rise above attachment, to gain power through the pursuit of higher meaning rather than being subservient to materialist or egotistical drives. In the case of the fifty-*bhāva* system, one would discern the pitfalls of mistaken notions. Sāṃkhya, by implication, exhorts one to understand and then distance oneself from the *guṇas* in their specific *bhāva* forms of expression.

During the lifetime of the Buddha, five hundred individuals attained nirvana. In every instance, they uttered the same pronouncement as given in *Sāṃkhya Kārikā* 64: *nāsmi, na me, nāham,* "nothing to do, nothing to have, nothing to be." Each of these individuals then automatically took up a life within the Brahmavihāra, manifesting friendliness, compassion, sympathetic joy, and equanimity. Their afflictions ceased. Though this value-added moment is not included in the *Sāṃkhya Kārikā,* one can only imagine that as the force of karma ceases, that one would take up the path informed by the four *sattvika bhāvas*: certainty, nonattachment, knowledge, and virtue. These qualities bear a family resemblance to the Brahmavihāra. One attains the good life through the cultivation of positivity, eventually leading to freedom.

Two Modern Interpreters of Sāṃkhya

Earlier in this section of the book, Ashton has explored the implications of Sāṃkhya for making sense of the human condition, focusing on the broad concepts of self and circumstance. Burley has focused on the underlying ethical imperatives implied in the text. Funes has examined the centrality of the breath in light of the *Yuktidīpikā* and its interpreters. This chapter has taken a decidedly psychological approach to understanding Sāṃkhya. To conclude this chapter, two modern interpreters will be cited in regard to the importance of affect in Sāṃkhya: Anima Sen Gupta (1969) and Frank R. Podgorski (1984).

Anima Sen Gupta, like Frauwallner as summarized in the chapter by Ana Funes, emphasizes the centrality of ethics in Sāṃkhya. She writes:

> According to the Sāṃkhya, *apavarga* or liberation arising from discriminative knowledge of Puruṣa and Prakṛti (seemingly unified through ignorance) is the real good or *śubha*. . . . this discrimination will enable the experiencer[s] to understand [their] own contribution to experience and also [their] own essential nature [and thus] dissociate from . . . elements which are by nature painful.[3]

She continues by invoking the centrality of the emotional life and the need to undertake constant vigilance: "Analysis of experience, thus, becomes a moral obligation in the empirical life of every soul." Noting the importance of the first of the eight *bhāvas* and then delineating the fifty *bhāvas*, she asserts that "Worldly life . . . is thus a life of constant struggle against error and evil so as to be able to reach the ream of truth and good . . . The bound souls are therefore striving ceaselessly to reach the highest goal of Self-realization, which is the culminating point of the evolutionary flow of Prakṛti."[4] Her assessment of Sāṃkhya states

> . . . it is the duty of a bound soul to help the seed of liberation grow and bear fruits after rejecting the seed of bondage . . . What a [person] thinks, feels, and wills is therefore of very great importance . . . by [one's] own thought, feelings, and emotions, an individual determines [one's] own nature, existence, and environment in this life as well as in the next . . . purification of intellect or the psychical apparatus is therefore regarded in Sāṃkhya as the most essential step towards attainment of peace and perfection.[5]

Moving the dispositions (*bhāvas*) away from *tamas* and *rajas* into *sattva* holds the key to understanding experience and moving into freedom.

Frank Podgorski lauds the real-world appeal of Sāṃkhya, writing that "this *darśana* (system of thought) takes as its starting point the common experience of the human person firmly situated within our surrounding, real world . . . Sāṃkhyan thinking may be described as nature-centered, human-focused, matter-oriented, and including toward a probing exploration of the human psyche. . . . Who and what is a human being? What is the meaning of human experience?"[6] After summarizing the functions that determine states of being (*bhāvas*) which we have been surveyed earlier in this chapter, Podgorski emphasizes the liberating power of knowledge (*jñāna*) as

> a bridge which enables the Yogi to transcend, cross over and claim another identity. The Yogi no longer identifies as *Prakṛti* in any of its diverse forms or costumes; rather precisely because of the transforming realization effected by *jñāna*, the Yogi now recognizes and proclaims authentic identification as *Puruṣa*. *Jñāna* terminates that metaphysical suffering (*duḥkha*) traceable to *ahaṃkāric* exaltations of matter . . . the cyclical unfolding and refolding of *Prakṛti* for sake of *Puruṣa* has revealed a lesson of supreme value . . . our identity cannot be properly carved out within any form of matter . . . all that remains is for this ever more illuminating consciousness to recognize and appreciate its unique value.[7]

Rather than rejecting the difficulty and suffering that has been overcome by re-identification with consciousness, Podgorski suggests that what he calls the "unfoldings and refoldings of *Prakṛti*" may be seen as "a prerequisite, a necessary purgative which must be experienced before *jñāna* can be appreciated . . . lessons that must be mastered before the uniqueness of *Puruṣa* can be recognized."[8] In the final pages of his book, Podgorski quotes Thomas Merton on contemplation, defined as "the awareness that this I is really not I."[9]

Conclusion

In this chapter we have examined the central role of the *guṇas* and *bhāvas* in determining the place of the human within the cosmos, and the place of the cosmos in the human. After critiquing Gauḍapāda's interpretation of *Kārikā* 29, a case is made that the tenor of the first part of the text overwhelming asserts the primacy of the *guṇas* in regard to the configuration of the manifest world. Everything, from the gross and rudimentary elements, to the sensory and active organs, to the mental constitutions from the predispositions to specific thoughts and actions, finds expression through the modalities of *tamas*, *rajas*, and *sattva*. This supports a view of Sāṃkhya that leans on the side of Prakṛti and her complexities rather than on the side of the-one-who-cannot-be-named, the experience of pure consciousness or Puruṣa. A verse count affirms this stance: twenty-six *kārikās* deal directly or indirectly with Puruṣa[10] while forty-seven address Prakṛti and her manifestations.

The *bhāvas* are the specific states of being that color one's experiences of self and the world. They provide granularity within the more generalized fields of the three *guṇas*. By learning the origins of things, whether physical or emotional, one comes to understand how actions and reactions work. Through this understanding, a discernment can arise that makes good on Īśvarakṛṣṇa's optimistic prognosis regarding the human condition: one can build and maintain freedom from ignorance.

Dedication

This chapter is dedicated to the memory of Eugene Paul Kelly, Jr. (1949–2022). Gene, known for many years as Yogi Anand Viraj, was Assistant Director of Yoga Anand Ashram in Amityville, New York, where we both studied with Gurāṇi Añjali Inti. We attended Stony Brook and Fordham Universities, studying with Antonio T. DeNicolas and John B. Chethimattam. Gene taught at Roanoke College for many years. Gene taught a class for several months on the *Sāṃkhya Kārikā* in 1978 at Yoga Anand Ashram that introduced Ashram members to this important text.

Notes

1. T. G. Mainkar, *Sāṃkhyakārikā of Īśvarakṛṣṇa with the Commentary of Gauḍapāda*, Second Revised Edition (Poona: Oriental Book Agency, 1972), 164. (First edition, 1964.)

2. These correspond loosely to the second verse of the *Śvetāśvatara Upaniṣad* that attributes the first cause to time (*kāla*), inherent nature (*svabhāva*), necessity (*niyati*), or chance (*yadṛcchā*). See Robert Ernest Hume, *The Thirteen Principal Upanisads* (Oxford: Oxford University Press, 1931), 394.

3. Anima Sen Gupta, *Classical Samkhya: A Critical Study* (Lucknow: Monorajnjan Sen Gour Ashram, 1969), 149–150.

4. Ibid., 150–151.

5. Ibid., 162–163.

6. Frank R. Podgorski, *Ego: Revealer-Concealer, A Key to Yoga* (Lanham, MD: University Press of America, 1984), xvi.

7. Ibid., 223–224.

8. Ibid., 225–226.

9. Ibid., 230. For more on Merton, contemplation, and Hinduism, see David M. Odorisio, *Merton & Hinduism: The Yoga of the Heart* (Louisville, KY: Fons Vitae, 2021).

10. 3, 7, 14, 17, 18, 19, 20, 21, 30, 31, 36, 37, 55, 56, 57, 58, 59, 60, 61, 62, 63, 64, 65, 66, 68, 69.

References

Burley, Mikel. 2007. *Classical Sāṃkhya and Yoga: An Indian Metaphysics of Experience*. London: Routledge.

Chapple, Christopher Key. 2008. *Yoga and the Luminous: Patañjali's Spiritual Path to Freedom*. Albany: SUNY Press.

Larson, Gerald James. 1979. *Classical Sāṃkhya: An Interpretation of Its History and Meaning*. Delhi: Motilal Banarsidass.

Chapter 5

प्रत्यय Pratyaya

State of Mind in Yoga and Sāṃkhya

SRIVATSA RAMASWAMI

The term *pratyaya* is found in Patañjali's *Yoga Sūtra* in *sūtras* I-10, I-18, I-19, II-20, III-2, III-12, III-17, III-19 and III-35, IV-27.[1] *Pratyaya* or *pratyayam* is *prati* + *ayam* or *ayam prati pratyayam*. While *prati* itself has different shades of meaning it is here "to" or "toward" and *ayam* is "this" as well as a noun derived from the verb root "I," to go. Since this word is used in the context of the mind, or *citta*, many scholars refer to *pratyaya* as a state of *citta* or mental state at a given moment. Some scholars relate *pratyaya* to *citta-vṛitti* itself. In YS II-20 referred to above, while describing *puruṣa* or *draṣṭā* as the consciousness/Self, Patañjali explains it as *pratyaya anupaśya* or one who completely sees the *pratyaya*. According to Patañjali the innumerable *citta-vṛttis* are grouped into five: correct cognition, error, imagining, sleep, and memory (YS I:6).

A detailed interpretation of *pratyaya* can be found in the *Sāṃkhya Kārikā*. Its classification of *pratyayas* helps us to understand all twenty-five Sāṃkhya *tattvas*, especially the all-important *Puruṣa*, the consciousness or the knower (*jña*). Such knowledge provides the means for overcoming the three types of grief (*duḥkha*) referred to by both yogis and followers of Sāṃkhya. The *pratyayas* as enunciated by Īśvarakṛṣṇa in his *Sāṃkhya Kārikā* are fifty in number, in contrast to the five groups of *citta-vṛittis* in Patañjali. The fifty are grouped into the four categories delineated in the chapter by Chapple in this volume: error, incapacities, contentments, and successes. Of the four categories, only one is favorable to the spiritual aspirant: success.

The first group is *viparyaya pratyayas*. *Viparyaya* as is known from Patañjala Yoga is believing falsehood as true, à la believing fake news as factual or the classic mistake that the body–mind complex is the Self—a universal misconception berated by the followers of Sāṃkhya, Yoga, and Vedānta—and not the consciousness or *Puruṣa*. *Viparyayas* are *kleśas*: *avidyā* and its four off-shoots: *asmitā* (I-feeling with the body–mind complex), *rāga* (intense attachment), *dveṣa* (enmity), and *abhiniveśa* (fear, especially of death). The five *viparyayas* are explained differently by other *darśanas* and scholars as *tamas* (eight shades of darkness), *moha* (eight delusions), *mahāmoha* (ten intense delusions), *tāmisra* (eighteen-fold gloom) and *andhatāmisra* (eighteen-fold panic).

The next group of *pratyayas* is known as *tuṣṭi*. These comprise states of complacency, compromise, or a mental state of "rising with the tide and rolling with the punches." Even having heard of the nature of the Self by studying Sāṃkhya, Yoga, or Vedānta, one may not be proactive. That state of mind, or *pratyaya,* is of nine types, four internal and five with external objects. Having a second-hand knowledge of the self (*parokṣa*), one may make no further efforts to know directly (*aparokṣa*) through appropriate efforts like *antaraṅga sādhana* as in Raja Yoga. The attitude that "I have heard about the nature of *Prakṛti* and *Puruṣa,* and *Prakṛti* will bring about *kaivalya* in due course" is called *Prakṛti tuṣṭi*. This can be extrapolated to mundane activities as well. The second *tuṣṭi* is called *upadāna* or trying to pay attention only to the external means for *kaivalya*. Having understood that the external universe is full of pain, as mentioned by Sāṃkhya, Yoga and Vedānta, one may decide to become a renunciate or a *vairāgī* taking on the life of a *sannyāsī*. Here, there is no further attempt to get to know the *ātman* by *antaraṅga yoga sādhana* but following the rules and lifestyle of a recluse, like wearing orange or other color robes, leaving home and becoming a nomad, and showing other external signs as having a staff, shaving the head (*muṇḍa*), or the other opposite, having long matted hair (*jaṭa*) or having a tuft (*śikhaṇḍaka*). The belief that merely becoming a recluse and following the rules will somehow get one to *kaivalya* is the second internal complacency. Next is the complacency that *kaivalya* will happen in due course. "Time will solve all the problems." With this *tuṣṭi pratyaya* one may remain content. The fourth *adhyātma tuṣṭi* (internal contentment) depends on luck, or *bhāgya*. It suggests the belief that, "If I am lucky, I will attain *kaivalya* and one day hit the spiritual jackpot."

The contentment with the outside universe is of five types. Once the bookish knowledge of the *ātman* and *Prakṛti* takes place in an individual, one may become complacent with the activities that need to be done. Different scholars explain these differently. One approach is to look at the *duḥkha* that the external world produces to the individual and decide to put up with it with a smile. The following is an example. When finding that earning the means of livelihood like money and possession is strenuous, one may stop working to earn money and decide to live in poverty (*anarjana duḥkham*). Even if one earns and saves, protecting it causes *duḥkha* (*rakṣana duḥkham*). Once one starts to use savings, they become depleted, and that also is a source of sorrow (*jīrṇa duḥkham*). Wastage or loss due to theft or taxes is another *duḥkha*. And finally, acquisition usually causes harm to other beings. Some scholars refer to the five senses and developing dispassion toward the objects of the five senses as not being able to produce permanent satisfaction and require more and more efforts for the same satisfaction. These nine *pratyayas*, called *tuṣṭi pratyaya*, do not per se lead to the ultimate goal of the *kaivalya* state where the three types of *duḥkha* (*adhyātmika*, *ādhidaivika*, and *ādhibhautika*) are permanently and definitively removed. These *tuṣṭi pratyayas* are impediments to achieving the goal—whether spiritual or mundane.

The next twenty-eight *pratyayas* are termed *aśakti*, described as depravity or weakness. As noted earlier, they are delineated as eleven deficiencies of the sense and motor organs, failure to achieve the nine contentments listed above, and the eight successes described in the next paragraph.

The last group of *pratyayas* are favorable for removing the three groups of pain or sorrow. There are called *siddhi pratyaya*, the mental states conducive to leading one to *kaivalya*, freedom from three types of *duḥkha* forever. Yogis are usually familiar with the *siddhis* explained by Patañjali in the third chapter of the *Yoga Sūtra*.

The best of all *siddhis* is the direct perception (*yaugika pratyakṣa*) of the unwavering consciousness, the *Puruṣa* or Self. *Siddhis* refer to the mental states that lead to that *kaivalya* and also the very state of the mind in *kaivalya.*

The eight *siddhis* are divided into the categories of principal (*mukhya*) and contributory (*gauṇya*). The principal ones correspond to freedom from the three sufferings (*duḥkhas*) due to one's body/mind, those due to other creatures, and those caused by acts of God. The means of attaining everlasting freedom require five more forms of success: reasoning, listening, studying, generosity, and receptivity.

The first is *ūha,* or reasoning and contemplation. This would also include the whole set of internal practices that are familiar to yogis. Once an aspirant receives all the information, it must be thoroughly analyzed and internalized. A classical example is that of Bhṛgu, the son of Varuṇa in the Taittirīya Upanishad. Bhṛgu, who came to know about Brahman, the ultimate reality, sought his father's help to completely understand it, know it, and directly experience it. The father gives a leading definition of Brahman as that from which everything is created, sustained, and finally into which everything merges. The father, Varuṇa, acted truly as an *Ācārya,* or one who is showing the path rather than carrying his son/disciple on his shoulders. Bhṛgu realized the true nature of Brahman by rejecting the five layers of the physical self: body, *prana,* mind (*indriyas*), intellect, and emotion as not the real self. Thus, it could be seen that the individual yogic mental effort called *ūha* in Sāṃkhya is absolutely necessary to reach the ultimate sorrow-free state of *kaivalya.* It may be said that the mental states of individual efforts, independent reasoning—sometimes not even found in texts—would come under *ūha.*

The other four helpful mental states in this category begin with *śabda,* or hearing the exposition of texts like the *Sāṃkhya Kārikā.* The second, *adhyayana,* requires study of the Vedas, especially the philosophical portions like the Upanishads and texts that teach Sāṃkhya. Generosity (*dāna*) requires paying appropriate guru *dakṣina* and studying with a competent teacher. Receptivity (*suhṛt prapti*) is the right knowledge obtained from friends, including within one's family traditions of wisdom. These eight favorable *pratyayas* are the mental states to be cultivated by one who is looking for a way to overcome the three types of perennial pain. The purpose of Sāṃkhya, Yoga, and Vedānta is to permanently and definitively eradicate suffering within one's lifetime.

As mentioned earlier, Patañjali uses the term *pratyaya* ten times in the *Yoga Sūtra*. He defines the *Puruṣa* as the seer (*draṣṭṛ*) or the one who merely sees (*dṛśimātra*). This state is pure, untainted and untarnished by any of the *guṇas*:

द्रष्टा दृशिमात्रः शुद्धोपि प्रत्ययानुपश्यः

draṣṭā dṛśimātraḥ śuddhopi pratyayānupaśyaḥ (YS II:20)

The *Puruṣa* observes every object, every intentional mental state (*pratyaya*). Even the physical person is to be considered as emerging from an intentional mental state. However, this ever-changing ego state is part of the body–mind complex. The true subject is not the body–mind complex but the unchanging consciousness called the *Puruṣa*. Each activity (*vṛtti*) in the objective realm is no more than a *pratyaya,* one of the fifty states of the active mind trapped in ignorance. No object of the outside world is known directly without the interpretive lens of *pratyaya*. One's state of mind (*bhāva*) determines everything. All activities, all thoughts, all intentions serve the purpose of providing experience to the witness, the *Puruṣa*. By cultivating adept contemplation, listening, learning, generosity, and receptivity, one can skillfully prepare for the ultimate knowledge found in the *jñāna bhāva* that leads to freedom.

Note

1. *Yoga Sūtra* I:10: The sleep fluctuation depends on an intention (*pratyaya*) of non-becoming.

I:18: The other has *saṃskāra* only and is preceded by practice and the intention of cessation.

I:19: The ones absorbed in *Prakṛti* and free from the body still have an intention of becoming.

II:20: The seer only Sees; though pure, it appears intentional.

III:2: There, the extension of one intention is meditation.

III:12: Hence again, when there is equality between arising and quieted intentions, there is the *pariṇāma* of one-pointedness of the mind.

III:17: From the overlapping here and there of word, purposes, and intentions, there is confusion . . .

III:19: From perception of another's intention, there is knowledge of another mind.

III:35: When there is no distinctuion of intention between the pure *Puruṣa* and the perfect *sattva,* there is experience for the purpose of theother; from *saṃyama* on purpose being for the self, there is knowledge of *Puruṣa.*

IV:27: In the intervening spaces of that, there are also other intentions, due to *saṃskāras.*

Translations from Chapple, *Yoga and the Luminous* (Albany: SUNY Press, 2008).

II

Living Expressions of Sāṃkhya

Chapter 6

Kāpil Maṭh

A Contemporary Living Tradition of Sāṃkhyayoga

MARZENNA JAKUBCZAK

Introduction

Although some of the writings of Swāmi Hariharānanda Āraṇya (1869–1947), such as *Yoga Philosophy of Patañjali*,[1] are well known and have been discussed among scholars specializing in Indian philosophy, he is not commonly recognized as a great modern Yoga teacher and as the founder of a living tradition, unlike some other Bengali figures of his time such as Swāmi Vivekānanda (1863–1902) or Śri Aurobindo (1972–1950). Apparently, the fact that he established Kāpil Maṭh, an *āśrama* dedicated to the legendary sage Kāpila, whose members wish to cultivate the strict ancient model of renunciation (*saṃnyāsa*), did not give him due fame. According to Hariharānanda Āraṇya it was Kāpila, dated to the seventh century BCE, who was the first to attain liberating knowledge (*mokṣa*) and establish the worldview of both Sāṃkhya and Yoga. Therefore, both philosophical schools are perceived by Hariharānanda as being embedded in one integrated tradition, and their followers are labeled as Sāṃkhyayogins (Jacobsen 2018, 2–41).[2]

In this chapter I am going to present Hariharānanda Āraṇya as a unique spiritual seeker who managed to re-establish Sāṃkhyayoga[3] as a living tradition, thus initiating a new phase of its development, which may be called "neo-classical." I aim to consider what it actually means to re-establish a philosophical school that was regarded as extinct for centuries. In the first section of the chapter, I will briefly summarize the characteristics of Hariharānanda. This will be followed by the answer to a major question: What makes Kāpil Maṭh really "Sāṃkhyan"? In the subsequent sections, I will present some comparative ideas and Buddhist inspirations of Hariharānanda Āraṇya, and discuss the hybrid identity of the reinterpreted Sāṃkhyayoga theory and practice cultivated by the founder of Kāpil Maṭh and his followers.

When Did Neoclassical Sāṃkhyayoga Start?

Presenting the history of Sāṃkhyayoga tradition, Gerald J. Larson points to three main historical stages of its development that seem to echo three dimensions of meaning in the word "*sāṃkhya*," namely: (1) an enumerated set or grouping (*sāṃkhya* as an adjective); (2) someone who calculates, enumerates, or discriminates properly and correctly (*sāṃkhya* as a masculine noun); (3) and a specific system of dualist philosophizing that proceeds by a method of enumerating the contents of experience (*sāṃkhya* as a neuter noun) (Larson 1987, 3–41). Hence, the three historical phases of Sāṃkhya development cover accordingly: (1) the period when Sāṃkhya denotes intellectual inquiry and grouping attempts at systematic thinking, which are documented in the oldest learned traditions of ancient India (from the Vedic period ca. 1500 BCE through the third century BCE); (2) the second period when Sāṃkhya becomes linked to a methodology of reasoning that results in spiritual knowledge leading to liberation from the cycle of rebirth (ca. eighth century BCE until the first centuries of the Common Era); and (3) the third phase when Sāṃkhya technical philosophical terminology and normative formulation is complete and begins to circulate in the form of *Yogasūtra* ascribed to Patañjali (ca. 4th century), or rather *Patañjalayogaśāstra*,[4] and *Sāṃkhyakārikā* compiled by Īśvarakṛṣṇa (ca.

5th century), which are the main texts of two currents of Sāṃkhya that emerged from the common source.

We can label the above stages of tradition development as follows: proto-Sāṃkhya period, pre-classical Sāṃkhya, and the classical period when Sāṃkhya and Yoga gain the status of separate schools. Further, we can distinguish the fourth stage labeled as post-classical Sāṃkhyayoga when its texts reading undergoes the influence of other traditions, especially monistic and theistic currents of Vedānta, as well as the *tapas* tradition of Indian ascetics and the Haṭhayoga tradition. The Vedāntic interpretations have been developed since the tenth century and brought about such important texts as *Tattvasamāsasūtra* (fourteenth century), *Sāṃkhyasūtra* (fifteenth century), and some commentaries of Aniruddha and Vijñānabhikṣu. Although the Haṭhayoga tradition, present in India from the eleventh century, differs significantly from the classical Sāṃkhya and Yoga, teachers of modern postural Yoga have often linked their practices to the *Yogasūtra*, ignoring the fact that this text emerged within a wider Sāṃkhyayoga lineage. Paradoxically, Sāṃkhya philosophy—being the conceptual ground for *Patañjalayogaśāstra*—has not attracted much attention until now, although *Yogasūtra* attracts millions of readers worldwide. The revival of Yoga in modern Hinduism and its global popularity, which has been increasing gradually since the 1960s, has been predominated by Vedāntic and Haṭhayogic interpretations, which usually underestimate the historical context and ignore the philosophically relevant background of *Patañjalayogaśāstra*.

Here, I propose to highlight the fifth stage of the Sāṃkhyayoga tradition initiated by Hariharānanda Āraṇya, a Bengali philosopher and ascetic, whose interpretations remain fully in line with the spirit of classical Sāṃkhya. What makes him unique and outstanding among many other modern teachers of Yoga is not only his writing, which consists of a number of in-depth commentaries written mostly in Sanskrit and Bengali, but also the fact that his genuine lifelong practical engagement led to the establishment of a small monastery aiming to revive Sāṃkhyayoga as a living philosophical tradition. This new period, which started with the founding of Kāpil Maṭh in 1924, may be labeled as neoclassical Sāṃkhyayoga.

Table 6.1. Stages of the Sāṃkhyayoga Tradition Development

STAGE OF THE SĀṂKHYAYOGA TRADITION DEVELOPMENT		MAIN FIGURES / BRIEF CHARACTERISTICS	DATING
1	Proto-Sāṃkhya period	Kāpila, Āsuri	1500 BCE–3rd c. BCE
2	Pre-classical Sāṃkhya	Pañcasikha, Paurika, Vārṣagaṇya, Vindhyavāsin, Mādhava	8th c. BCE–2nd c. CE
3	Classical period of Sāṃkhyayoga	Sāṃkhya and Yoga become separate schools; Patañjali, Īśvarakṛṣṇa	4th c. CE–9th c. CE
4	Post-classical Sāṃkhyayoga	Influenced by Vedānta and Haṭhayoga; Vācaspati Miśra, Bhojarāja, Aniruddha, Vijñānabhikṣu	10th c. until present
5	Neo-classical Sāṃkhyayoga	Initiated by Hariharānanda Āraṇya	Since 1924 until present

Thanks to the extraordinary charisma of Hariharānanda Āraṇya, manifested in his involvement in personal meditative and ascetic practice, monastic activity, and philosophical reflection, this tradition, considered extinct for centuries, has been brought back to life. Although the renewal movement of the classical Sāṃkhyayoga associated with the center of Kāpil Maṭh, based in Madhupur, has not gained much popularity in the past century, its very existence until this day and the rich legacy of the *quasi*-classical Hariharānanda's commentaries, successively translated into English and published thanks to the efforts of the Kāpil Maṭh community,[5] is a unique socio-philosophical phenomenon, and as such should be acknowledged as an example of a living tradition. A similar opinion is expressed by Knut A. Jacobsen, who argues for including Kāpil Maṭh in modern Hinduism, as one of the forms of Yoga and new orthodox Sāṃkhyayoga. He believes that "this inclusion may bring about greater awareness of Sāṃkhyayoga as the philosophy of the *Patañjalayogaśāstra*" (Jacobsen 2018, 207).

Who Was the Founder of Kāpil Maṭh?

Little is known about the life story of the founder of Kāpil Maṭh. We can only mention a handful of basic facts since he firmly forbade his disciples from writing any form of biography whatsoever. Hariharānanda Āraṇya was born to a well-to-do, upper-caste Bengali family (*bhadralok*) and started his intellectual and spiritual quest at an early age. He joined the famous Presidency College in Kolkata, but after progressively losing interest in formal education, decided to leave before graduation. Soon after, he was to adopt an ascetic lifestyle and dedicated himself entirely to the pursuit of liberating knowledge. Patañjali's *Yogasūtra* was to be a huge inspiration on his spiritual path. In approximately 1890 he was initiated into *saṃnyāsin* by Swāmi Trilokī Āraṇya, who was at that time returning from a pilgrimage to Gaṅgāsāgar, south of Kolkata, and was maintaining a vow of silence (*mauna*). Trilokī might possibly have been a Kāpila worshiper since Kāpila is the main divinity worshiped at the Gaṅgāsāgar festival on the island of Sagar. Instead of verbal instruction, the *muni* handed to Hariharānanda a locked wooden box with the key deposited inside it. The young monk grasped the message and needed his teacher no more. Hariharāndra Āraṇya probably never met his guru again. Shortly afterward, he spent some time in complete renouncement, in the solitary caves of the Barābar hills near Gaya, in Bihar, built during the reign of King Aśoka (3rd century BCE). He described some of his experiences of that time in an allegorical form in *A Unique Travelogue* (Āraṇya 2001). After 1898, he returned to live in monastic society where he continued his meditative practice and his studies of the ancient Hindu and Buddhist philosophical texts independently. First, he spent some years at a small hermitage in Tribeni, on the bank of the Ganges, and then he went to Kurseong, near Darjeeling. Finally, in 1924, he decided to reside for good in Kāpil Maṭh, in Madhupur.

While leading a hermit's life, Swāmiji continued his spiritual practice and at the same time occupied himself with writing. He wrote numerous philosophical commentaries and essays, including *Sāṃkhyatattvāloka*, an interpretation of the Sāṃkhya texts, and *Bhāsvatī* (alias *Yogakārikā*), a masterly annotation to Patañjali's *Yogasūtra* and *Yogabhāṣya* (Āraṇya 2000), and *Karmatattva*, an insightful explanation of the doctrine of *karman* (Āraṇya 2008). Most of his contributions prove great erudition and philosophical insight of a practising *yogin* with a nonsectarian outlook and were written in Sanskrit and Bengali. He was able to read Pāli, Sinhalese, and Burmese, which was helpful while preparing the first rendering of *Dhammapada*, the collection of the Buddha's sayings, from Pāli to Sanskrit, and the first Bengali translation of Śāntideva's *Bodhicaryāvatāra*: a Buddhist manual for the practice of Yoga for *bodhisattvas*.[6] Thus, to revive Sāṃkhyayoga as a living tradition, Hariharāndra Āraṇya contributed his own original commentaries on the core texts of the tradition. Since his interest was not merely intellectual but rather spiritual, he wanted to test his understanding as self-experience (*sādhāna*) by personally following the strict discipline of the renunciant (*saṃnyāsin*). Therefore, he undertook long periods of silence in isolation following in the footsteps of the Jain and early Buddhist monks, and those who were described in Hindu texts such as the *Saṃnyāsa Upaniṣads* and the *Dharmaśastra* literature.

His main interest was to rediscover and purify the tradition of Yoga and to revitalize the original Sāṃkhyayoga philosophical framework of the *Yogasūtra*. As Knut A. Jacobsen rightly suggests, the modern rebirth of Sāṃkhyayoga represented by Kāpil Maṭh was based on the assumption spread in the late nineteenth-century Bengal—the center of the intellectual encounter between India and the West—that it was Kāpila and not Patañjali who was the originator of the philosophy of Yoga as being a part of the Sāṃkhya philosophical tradition (Jacobsen 2018, 204)—whereas Patañjali, who has become central to modern Yoga, and in the nineteenth century was celebrated mostly by Orientalists and proponents of Western Esoterism, plays no special role in Kāpil Maṭh. Moreover, no element of postural Yoga is promoted there. Instead, among the eight limbs that constitute Patañjali's yogic practice (*aṣṭāṅgayoga*, YS II.28–30), the emphasis is on the five restraints (*yama*), five observances (*niyama*), and concentration (*samādhi*), while bodily posture (*āsana*) is understood as just sitting comfortably on the floor in the lotus position (*padmāsana*), and *prāṇāyāma* is focusing on the breath as a way of calming the mind.

After 1900, Hariharānanda's writings and conceptions became increasingly popular, and the *aśrama* he founded attracted many interested people from all parts of India and even abroad. Among them were powerful people, teachers, intellectuals, and politicians. However, Hariharānanda was quite aware that Sāṃkhyayoga appeals to a relatively small number of people. He emphasized the difficulty of Yoga and suggested that to attain the goals of Yoga one needs to become a *saṃnyāsin* living outside of society. In 1926, he decided to isolate himself even from his students, closing off the entrance to his artificial cave (*guha*).[7] From 1939 onward, due to his poor health, caused by diabetes, Hariharānanda was regularly visited by his closest student, Dharmamegha Āraṇya. In 1947, at the age of seventy-eight, he decided to stop maintaining his life and died after five days of total fasting.[8] Before his death, Hariharānanda Āraṇya addressed two interdicts to his disciples: first, after his passing away, he wanted his body to be laid to rest in the cremation ground, placed close to the surface so that dogs and jackals could have easy access to a sumptuous feed; and secondly, he forbade the building of a memorial temple or the organizing of a commemorative service after his death or annually. Responding to a request from the devotees and his successor, Hariharānanda ultimately agreed to modify his will as follows: his body was to be laid within the Maṭh, though no memorial edifice could be erected there; no biography was to be written or monument built to commemorate his person (Āraṇya 2003, 141). Dharmamegha Āraṇya, who after his master's death became the leader of the *aśrama*, was highly appreciated by the Kāpil Maṭh devotees for his charismatic personality, and he put effort into the translation and publication of some of his Bengali writings. When he died in 1985, Bhāskar Āraṇya, the current guru born in 1942, took over the duties of leader and maintains the same lifestyle of austere seclusion that both his predecessors did.

What Makes Kāpil Maṭh Really 'Sāṃkhyan'?

Now let us consider some questions that arise when we try to characterize and appraise such a phenomenon as Kāpil Maṭh. One can doubt if it is possible at all to re-establish a philosophical tradition that has broken down and has had no succession for centuries. Can we respect such a lineage of self-identity declared by a modern thinker despite the obvious discontinuity of the tradition he wants to identify with? And is it sufficient for a contemporary philosopher, who is an outstanding *yogin* and a knowledgeable, brilliant commentator of the canonical *sūtras*, to proclaim the texts of a particular ancient tradition, like Sāṃkhyayoga, to be the best articulation of his own insights and therefore an authoritative source for the followers of the "new," revived philosophical school identified with the "old," or "genuine" *darśana*?

Before giving a negative answer to the questions above, one should reflect on the fact that there are also some time gaps within the earlier history of Sāṃkhya: between its proto- and classical periods, that is, between the seventh century BCE and the fifth century CE. Thus, looking suspiciously on the modern revival of this philosophical school, one ought also to query the continuity of the tradition between Kāpila and Pañcaśikha, and between the latter and Vārṣagaṇya, and subsequently Īśvarakṛṣṇa. Perhaps it was the case that the subsequent Sāṃkhyayoga philosophers, whose names have been recorded, had to recover and re-establish this school numerous times by updating the old issues with their own exegetical insights, and thus were contributing to the tradition text. The "tradition text," as Eliot Deutsch explains (Deutsch 1989, 165–173), refers to no particular text but rather to the ongoing process of philosophy-making within a certain school. Each tradition text has its authoritative sources grounded in the oral transmission, its summaries, and its ongoing written elaborations. The exegetical material gradually expands, refines, and modifies arguments, sometimes adding new ideas, usually with increasing precision. The philosopher-commentator seeks to remain faithful to his sources and to bring greater systematic coherence, but in his own creative terms. Surely, Sāṃkhyayoga has been developed over centuries as an influential textual tradition. Yet, apart from some discrete flourishing periods—traced thanks to a few luckily preserved texts—there were also several longer scopes of time when some few *saṃnyāsin*s scattered around India were practicing some form of Sāṃkhyayoga that was transmitted orally. The example of Kāpil Maṭh shows that tradition may be understood as a succession of "reincarnations" aiming to rediscover the message of Kāpila and to develop it on the Sāṃkhyayoga path through a unique combination of theory and practice or "practiced theory."

So, our initial inquiry needs to be rephrased as follows: on which grounds can we regard the revival of Sāṃkhyayoga, carried out by the Kāpil Maṭh founder, to be the opening of another period of development in this long-lasting and, most likely, at times discontinuous tradition? There are two arguments I would like to provide when giving the answer: one is to argue for the Sāṃkhyayoga orthodoxy of Kāpil Maṭh, and another is to demonstrate the uniqueness and originality of Hariharānanda Āraṇya's contribution. Together, they allow us to label Kāpil Maṭh as a "neoclassical" phase of Sāṃkhyayoga, not just as an epigonic or imitative phenomenon. The second argument will be discussed in detail in the following sections devoted to a comparative perspective and pan-Indian universalism of Hariharānanda Āraṇya, and to the hybrid identity of this new manifestation of Sāṃkhyayoga.

First, let us look closer at the inheritance of Kāpil Maṭh. A contemporary reinterpretation of the classical texts is worthy of consideration as long as it is philosophically coherent, nonsectarian, inspiring, and, above all, *really* Sāṃkhyan. It means that we expect it to be in agreement with "the spirit of the school," as Daya Krishna puts it (Krishna 1996, 146), and to contribute to the "tradition text" by incorporating the philosophical content of a school in a creative and consistent way (Deutsch 1989, 169–170). Naturally, we cannot make the definition of "the Sāṃkhya spirit" too narrow or too rigid, as the tradition has been interpreting and re-interpreting itself over the ages. In a sense, the search for the "true spirit" or "pure form" of a school seems to be closer to the Indologist's romantic dream rather than a historical observation (Ganeri 2002, 40).

Nonetheless, if one wants to attribute the Sāṃkhyan core to a worldview or to detect the philosophical perspective typical of this school, we should examine some crucial assumptions and claims. The points that define the unique identity of Sāṃkhya are captured in its classical period, codified by Īśvarakṛṣṇa in his *Sāṃkhyakārikā*.[9] Let us start with the four most important rudimental claims. First and foremost, to think in the "Sāṃkhyan way," one needs to assert the ultimate dualism between the objective and subjective realm (*prakṛti–puruṣa*): discrimination between the self (*puruṣa*)—being the principle of consciousness—versus the unconscious and spontaneously creative nature (*prakṛti*), is considered crucial and effective for liberation (*mokṣa*) from worldly suffering. The second key assumption is the recognition of the twenty-five principles, or categories of reality (*tattvas*), and the distinction between the evolvent and the evolute of nature (*prakṛti–vikāra*). Third, the recognition of three constituents of nature (*guṇas*), or the substantive "threads" of objective reality, which account for pleasure, thinking, and clarity (*sattva*); craving, activity, and attachment (*rajas*); and depression, restraint, and delusion (*tamas*). Fourth, emphasis on egotism (*asmitā*) and misattribution of the self (*ahaṃkāra*) as the basic manifestation of fivefold ignorance (*avidyā*), the root of all suffering.

The list of crucial assumptions and claims may be extended, of course, but here it is interesting to refer to the Sāṃkhyayoga teachings as they are summarized by Hariharānanda Āraṇya himself. Apart from acceptance of the authority of Kāpila, the founder of the neo-Sāṃkhya tradition, he emphasizes the significance of such concepts as *mokṣa, puruṣa, prakṛti, citta, samādhi, duḥkha, karman, vāsanā,* and *īśvara*. In his introduction to *Yoga Philosophy,* he summed up the core of Sāṃkhya doctrine in twelve points: (1) liberation (*mokṣa*) consists in the complete cessation of all suffering (*duḥkha*); (2) on attainment of liberation one abides in one's immutable and attributeless self (*puruṣa*); (3) in the state of liberation, the mind (*citta*) returns to its original cause (i.e., *prakṛti pradhāna*); (4) cessation of the mind can be brought about by renunciation and supreme knowledge acquired through concentration (*samādhi*); (5) concentration is attainable by observance of the prescribed codes of conduct and practice of meditation; (6) liberation brings about cessation of the cycle of rebirths (*saṃsāra*); (7) this cycle is without a beginning and is the result of latent impressions (*saṃskāra, vāsanā*) left by our physical and mental activities (*karman*); (8) nature (*prakṛti*) and the countless selves (*puruṣas*) are respectively the constituent and efficient causes of the creation; (9) *prakṛti* and *puruṣa* are non-created realities with neither beginning nor end; (10) *īśvara* is the eternally free self (*puruṣa*); (11) he has nothing to do with the creation of the universe or life; (12) the lord of the universe is demiurge, called

Prajāpati or Hiraṇyagarbha, and the whole universe is being held and sustained by him (Āraṇya 2000, xxv).

As we can see, Hariharānanda clarifies that Yoga is primarily a philosophical teaching that must be complemented with renunciation, which is a prerequisite for every serious practitioner of Yoga discipline. His idea of the living Sāṃkhyayoga tradition contrasts sharply with modern postural Yoga institutions, which primarily promote bodily practice to influence and improve mental and physical health.

Comparative Perspective of Hariharānanda

The writings left by the founder of Kāpil Maṭh are original, thorough, and consistent. Although he uses philosophical Sanskrit vocabulary quite freely, citing from a variety of Indian sources, Āraṇya's interpretations are coherent, based on profound scholarship and formulated clearly from the classical Sāṃkhyayoga perspective, which is, as he says, "logical and systematic right through" (Āraṇya 2005, v).

In his *Karmatattva*, a comprehensive elucidation of the Sāṃkhyayoga theory of action, the Bengali ascetic tries to apply an intercultural comparative perspective, referring frequently to Western philosophical thought, both ancient and modern, and also making numerous remarks on the findings and popular theories of the late nineteenth-century science right up to the 1930s (Āraṇya 2008, 1–58). He mainly cites or comments on physical chemistry, biology, materialist theories in modern physics, evolutionism, and Darwinism. Hariharānanda refers to such authors as Ernst Haeckel (*Riddle of the Universe*, 1900), James Hopwood Jeans (*The Universe around Us*, 1929), Oliver Lodge (*Life and Matter*, 1905), William H. Conn (*The Story of the Living Machine*, 1899), John B. Burke (*The Origin of Life, Its Physical Basis and Definition*, 1906), and Arthur S. Eddington (*The Nature of the Physical World*, 1928). The most influential among them was probably Haeckel, a German adherent of Darwin, who was an outstanding biologist, physician, philosopher, and artist who discovered and named thousands of new species, and who coined many terms in biology, including "anthropogeny," "ecology," "stem cell," and "Protista." Āraṇya must have also been inspired by James H. Jeans, an English physicist and mathematician, known for his popular books about astronomy. He was the first to propose the continuous-creation theory: claiming that matter is continuously created throughout the universe. Darwinism, which seemed to Hariharānanda Āraṇya to be in tune with the Sāṃkhyayoga vision of spontaneous evolution of nature (*prakṛti parināma*), originally gained scientific acceptance after Charles Darwin published *On the Origin of Species* (1859), but later in the mid–twentieth century became a synonym of a simplified theory, and has been used within the scientific community only to distinguish the modern evolutionary synthesis, sometimes called Neo-Darwinism, from the outdated theory of Darwin himself. Thus, nowadays, Darwinist terminology in the comparative remarks of Hariharānanda does not imply the same up-to-date and intellectually attractive connotation as it did in his lifetime.

Yet in the comparative studies of the Kāpil Maṭh founder, the main focus is on intra-Indian discourse. His argument, inspired by a sort of pan-Indian universalism,[10] is not devoid of syncretism and remains open to criticism, either from the perspective of the idealistic Vedānta or the theistic currents of Indian philosophy. First of all, he strongly believes that the philosophical positions of Sāṃkhyayoga and early Buddhism have much more in common than was conventionally acknowledged, arguing that "they are the branches of the same tree, nourished by the same roots." Like the orthodox Hindu traditions respecting the authority of Vedas (*āstika darśanas*), heterodox Buddhism belongs to the tradition of the sages (*ṛṣi*s) called *ārṣa dharma*, or "*ārṣaism*," inaccurately termed "Brahmanism" (Āraṇya 2003, 22). As Hariharānanda puts it, the lineage of the sages (*ārṣa dharma*) was broadly divided into two currents: one, called *pravṛtti dharma* (the creed of worldliness), preached and practiced the performance of religious rites leading to worldly happiness, while the other, called *nivṛtti dharma* (the creed of renunciation), propounded the path of liberation from all worldly conditioning. The latter, of which Paramaṛṣi Kāpila was known to be the greatest exponent, owed its origin to those *ṛṣi*s who had discovered the way to self-realization and developed from their own spiritual experience a complete system of theory and practice for guiding others along that path toward liberation from the cycle of rebirth (Āraṇya 2000, xxi–xxv).

Attainment of the ultimate aim of the creed of worldliness (*pravṛtti dharma*) involves the worship of God or saints, the practice of virtues along with the performance of good deeds (*puṇya*), and proper rituals (*yajña*). The creed of renunciation, on the other hand, points out that the ultimate aim of liberation from *saṃsāra* can be achieved only through a perfect knowledge of one's true self. In his introduction to a rendering of the *Dhammapada*, an early Buddhist text, Hariharānanda claims that the majority of mankind can only follow the creed of worldliness by practicing good deeds, which he calls "the lower rungs of the great ladder," which leads to "blowing out" (*nirvāṇa*) (Āraṇya 2003, 22). He emphasizes that in this matter there is no difference between the Buddhists and the *ārṣas*, as both may promote either *pravṛtti* or *nivṛtti dharma* aspirations. Āraṇya admits that the Buddha spoke of rituals as possessing little merit, although he never put them altogether beyond the pale of meritorious actions. And, as we can easily see in the further development of Mahāyāna Buddhism, especially in Tibet, cult and ritualism expanded and eventually, paradoxically, became an essential aspect of Buddhist life. The *Mahābhārata,* Hindu epics of ancient India, on the other hand, appreciate the value of knowledge and even prize it beyond ritual by saying that a single truth is of greater merit than the sacrifice of a thousand horses (*aśvamedha*)[11] (Āraṇya 2003, 22).

Thus, the author of *Bhāsvatī* argues for a special kind of pan-Indian universalism that challenges such entrenched categories as orthodox *versus* heterodox (*āstika/nāstika*), accepting the doctrine of the self *versus* no-self (*ātman/anatman*) or believing in god *versus* rejecting god (*seśvaravāda/nirīśvaravāda*). The only essential distinction one should never overlook when describing a particular school or philosopher is the one between *pravṛtti* and *nivṛtti*. What Āraṇya tries to emphasize above all is the uniqueness of human endeavor focused on self-knowledge-through-renunciation and presents it as a very narrow current within the multiple and disparate Indian philosophical traditions. He generalizes that "unlike *pravṛtti dharma* which has been prevalent in all parts of the world, *nivṛtti dharma* originated in, and belonged exclusively to, India" (Āraṇya 2000, xxii). However, it must be stressed here that this historical claim serves no cultural or sectarian usurpation because, as Āraṇya sarcastically or just realistically observes, every genuine spiritual tradition centered on renunciation cannot continue unbroken for a long time. Each philosophical school or yogic monastery of this kind, he predicts, can function properly and stick closely to its founder's recommendations for a generation or two, after which irregularities creep in and various sects and fractions arise (Āraṇya 2003, 21). Moreover, Āraṇya was aware that the living tradition he revived appeals to a relatively small number of people: namely, those who are capable of getting free from the objects of experience (*apavarga*) and seek for knowledge leading to liberation (*kaivalya*). The path to *kaivalya* is comprised of restraint, concentration, and knowledge, and the institution of *saṃnyāsa* (Jacobson 2018, 204). The majority of people are focused on their own enjoyment (*bhoga*) while experiencing the world, which entangles them in further activities (*karman*) and persists *saṃsāra*.

Interestingly, despite the fact that he considers the stability and durability of transmission of the creed of renunciation to be extremely fragile, Hariharānanda had no doubt about its eternal, universal accessibility to highly motivated and persistent seekers, no matter the time or the place, or from which religious tradition or philosophical school they come. According to his successor's account, Swāmiji maintained that yogic lore conducive to self-knowledge, unlike any physical science and other branches of knowledge, has not evolved over time or, in other words, undergoes no substantial historical development.[12]

A Hybrid Identity of the Living Sāṃkhyayoga Tradition

A close connection between the Sāṃkhya and Buddhist ideals is openly declared by Kāpil Maṭh members.[13] Hariharānanda maintains that undeniable affinities exist between Buddhism and Sāṃkhyayoga, and that the Buddha's teachings were profoundly influenced by the ancient doctrine of Sāṃkhya, as transmitted to the Buddha through Ārāḍa Kālāma and Rudraka. The current guru, Bhāskar Āraṇya, in his public talks calls the Buddha Śākyamuni the greatest of all Kāpila's disciples and the most accomplished philosopher within the whole Sāṃkhya tradition. In interviews, devotees describe their two late Swāmijīs' personalities as "Buddhist-like." A visitor to the *āśrama* may be surprised that a contemporary non-Buddhist monastic community, which regards itself to be a re-established lineage of Sāṃkhyayoga, expresses such deep respect for the authority of the Buddha, none less so than for Pañcaśikha, Patañjali, or Īśvarakṛṣṇa.

On the other hand, it is no secret that the Buddha favored the doctrine of no-self (*anātman*). His criticism of the concept of the permanent unchanging self (*puruṣa*) accepted by Sāṃkhya and Yoga, however, does not diminish the close relationship between these comparable traditions. As Hariharānanda assumes, his own in-depth reading of the Sāṃkhyayoga and Buddhist core texts can go beyond the seeming contradictions between both conceptions. What is more, he offers a new perspective that shows that the living Sāṃkhya tradition can benefit from the Buddhist challenge and gain a new, more precise, formulation of its classical position. To see how this is achieved, let us trace a few Buddhist counter-arguments and the way in which they may be addressed from the neoclassical Sāṃkhyayoga perspective.

As we learn from Aśvaghoṣa's famous Sanskrit poem *Buddhacarita* (1st or 2nd century CE), Siddhārtha Gautama (to become the Buddha) was initially inspired but then disappointed with the philosophical teachings of a popular Sāṃkhya *yogin* named Ārāḍa Kālāma, who was believed to have gained insight into absolute bliss.[14] In *Buddhacarita* 12.69–88, the Buddha claims that the self—declared to be pure and eternal—is a seed and the causal root for continued existence and rebirth. So the very concept of the self is recognized as an obstacle on the path to ultimate freedom from all suffering. Therefore, he rejects this concept by discrediting its Sāṃkhyan definition which is as follows: the true self, being eternal and contentless, by no means can be objectified, even by or for itself. First, Siddhārtha undermines the permanence of the self, noting that as long as there is a knower, there is something for him to know, and since there is something for him to know, he can never be released (*Buddhacarita* 12.80). The early Sāṃkhya philosopher could easily refute such criticism by saying that to capture the meaning of "self," one must distinguish between the upper or true self—being pure consciousness, transcendent to nature (*prakṛti*), but also absolutely passive, not involved in the process of doing or knowing—and, on the other hand, the lower embodied self, or empirical "I," that is the psycho-physical organism fully engaged in all bodily and mental activities. In the next passage of the *Buddhicarita*, Śakyāmuni seems to react to this possible Sāṃkhya defense by asking sarcastically, if the "field knower" (*kṣetrajña*) can also refer to the one who is actually *not* a knower, as a non-engaged upper or transcendent self, then why should we call this not-knowing self "the self" or a subject, after all? This strong concept of the self (*ātman/puruṣa*) sounds to him illogical and simply invented, so he mocks it by saying that we can do without the self, since absence of knowing exists in a log or a wall (*Buddhacarita* 12.81). Bodhisattva refuses to accept a distinction between the lower and the upper self for one further reason. He asserts that getting rid of the imperfections of the self by abandoning action, ignorance, and desire cannot be successfully realized as long as one keeps identifying oneself with the self—no matter lower or upper—and upholds its permanent existence (*Buddhacarita* 12.73). While Ārāḍa, the early Sāṃkhya teacher, assumes eradication of the wrong I-sense (*ahaṃkāra*), together with the egotism it causes, to be the essential prerequisite for achieving the highest meditative absorption and liberation, Siddhārtha doubts if the ego may really be abandoned unless belief in the eternal self has been completely given up (*Buddhacarita* 12.76).[15]

Thus, what makes the pure self (*puruṣa*) inevitable for the Sāṃkhyayoga conception of human nature, since—as a Buddhist opponent suggests—every psycho-physical function may be accounted for by the transient empirical self, called *antaḥkaraṇa* in Īśvarakṛṣṇa's *Sāṃkhyakārikā* or *citta* in *Patañjalayogaśāstra*? What is this concept good for, and why is it worth upholding, despite all the criticism directed at the Sāṃkhyayoga idea of subjectivity? Why should a metaphysical claim about the existence of a permanent, immutable, and inactive subjective being be favored over the view that everything, including the self, undergoes continued change, which is just a continuum of dependently originated events and phenomena?

While specifying the rationale for the absolute self, the principle of consciousness, one cannot forget the ultimate purpose of any cognition or meditative insight, but also the conceptual view following the act of directly acquired knowledge. Any view (*darśana*) worth maintaining is to be beneficial and useful for attaining liberation. Therefore, the Sāṃkhya claim that whatever happens in *saṃsāric* reality is for the sake of the self, including the discriminative knowledge (*vivekakhyāti*) of the known *versus* the knower,[16] must be *of some use* for the ultimate enterprise, namely, achieving liberation (*mokṣa*).

Now, if we dare to reinterpret the Sāṃkhya conceptual framework through a Buddhist lens, the first benefit of adhering to the concept of the self (*puruṣa*) could be expressed in terms of skilful means (*upāya kauśalya*). A strong conviction of the existence of "the true self" may act as an efficient motivation, or useful means, which generates or intensifies the practitioner's spiritual aspiration. Although initially it may seem quite like all other egoic motivations and manifest itself in the form of feelings like "I envy the self for being so pure and free from suffering," or "I am proud of *my*self" and "I desire to become as pure and free as the self is," etc., this spiritual aspiration to become the self-in-itself (*svarūpa*; YS 4.34)—if supported by a proper meditative practice—is gradually transformed into the realization of self-knowledge and acts "for the sake of *puruṣa*" (*puruṣakāra*). Thus focusing on the self, being an independent and uninvolved witness, eventually results in a non-afflicted (*akliṣṭa*) endeavor toward discriminative knowledge opposed to egotic (*ahaṃkāra*) or afflicted (*kliṣṭa*) activity of identifying oneself with variable *prakṛtic* reality.

But of what benefit can the assumptions of passivity and non-cognoscibility of the absolute self be to a seeker of freedom from suffering? Again, this serves as a pedagogical device, since the self can do nothing apart from witnessing what is done *for* it; every activity and all responsibility for doing or forsaking belongs to this present "I-am-ness" (*asmitā*). If this present "I-consciousness"—being the involved, knowable, and ever-changing agent—is not approaching liberation, it will never happen. Therefore, the transcendent nature of the self proves to be the inevitable and most beneficial presupposition and anchorage of meditative practice. What we call "the absolute self" connotes an absolutely unknowable entity, unconditioned, independent of mind, like the Kantian thing-in-itself (Gr. *noumenon*) opposed to all phenomenal realm accessible to observation, or like Fichte's "absolute consciousness." That is why a Sāṃkhya-*yogin,* when cultivating concentration and advancing in discriminative insight (*samādhi*), never tends to identify with the ultimate self (as the Advaita Vedāntins would do), because the aim is not to identify directly with *puruṣa* but rather to keep dis-identifying with the present phenomenal self by means of constant realization: "I am not, not mine, not I" (*nāsmi na me nāham*).[17] And last but not least, all these superhuman efforts to bring the advantageous, non-afflicted results must be undertaken for the sake of "the other," not for myself (*ahaṃkāra*) but for the self that has nothing to do with my present "I" (*aham*), or "mineness" (*mamakāra*), nor "self-conceit" (*abhimāna*). In other words, the entire task is completed by me, but no virtues or profits are ever enjoyed by myself, since having achieved self-knowledge—which in Sāṃkhyan terms is but negative, namely, knowledge of what-I-am-not, or what I am absolutely distinct from—there is no point in continuing *my* phenomenal existence or expecting any rewards for *my*self, these being nothing one can identify with. Does this not echo somehow a Bodhisattva's mission? (see note 6). Thus, the metaphysical theory of Sāṃkhya, if reinterpreted in such a manner, might be, surprisingly, much less alien to the Buddhist worldview than it is commonly thought.

Although the above discussion on "the self" was not directly expressed but only inspired by Hariharānanda Āraṇya's writings, and encouraged by oral explanations and conversations with the current *sannyāsins* and devotees of Kāpil Maṭh, the conclusion seems to the present author sufficiently grounded in the neoclassical Sāṃkhyayoga worldview. Yet it must be noted that this quasi-Buddhist reinterpretation is articulated merely "on behalf" of the living Sāṃkhya tradition, which may certainly carry a risk of over-interpretation.

Conclusion

When reconsidering the fundamentals of Sāṃkhyayoga philosophy, especially the conception of the self, in the light of the comparative remarks of Hariharānanda Āraṇya and his followers, we can see that they do not only try to defend their doctrine against criticism of other Hindu and Buddhist philosophers but also to reinterpret it creatively, taking into account some of the critical arguments and the advances of contemporary natural science. What is also significant is that they do not mind using *vipassana* Buddhist meditative practice.[18] Apparently, neoclassical Sāṃkhyayoga can benefit from Buddhist critiques. Its strategy of dealing with the alternative conception of the self, proposed by the Buddha, seems to be in line with the general Indian agenda of cultural adaptation and assimilation: a rival Buddhist view is not rejected or dismissed right away, but rather mitigated by reinterpreting it according to one's own perspective and also used to better formulate, rephrase, and re-evaluate the Sāṃkhyan conception of the self.

Thus, the revived Sāṃkhyayoga's spirit can persist, despite an obvious historical discontinuity, but also gain a new hybrid identity thanks to embracing some supplementary assumptions. First, Buddhism as such is considered to be a re-establishment of Kāpila's tradition. This is why the Buddha's conception of no-self (*anātman*) is not perceived as being totally opposed to Sāṃkhya's position, but rather as a radical presentation of the universal self-knowledge that may be expressed differently and more adequately in terms of neoclassical Sāṃkhyayoga. Second, the fact that in the canonical Buddhist texts there are references to a supposed Sāṃkhya teacher, a hermit Ārāḍa Kālāma,[19] who was abandoned by Siddhārtha after mastering his teachings, does not prove the Buddha's total rejection of the Sāṃkhya path but rather testifies to his high motivation for attaining self-knowledge through direct insight, which he valued higher than any verbal testimony. Third, a textual reference to Ārāḍa's and Udraka's meditative achievements when describing the gradual process of meditation shows that the Buddha followed his teachers' footsteps, although he contributed some essential innovations to the method used by his predecessors. Fourth, although the Buddha rejects certain features of the early Sāṃkhya metaphysics and further develops its method of meditation, elevating the new concept of *vipassana*[20] (i.e., insight and thorough penetration of an object), he integrates it with a pre-Buddhist yogic system of *dhyāna* (Pāli *jhāna*), based on the *śamatha* method of meditation,[21] which leads to a well-balanced, tranquil mental state. This invention of the Buddha does not infringe on the Sāṃkhyayoga theory of self-development and was successfully adjusted and fit into its own methodology, at least in *Patañjalayogadarśana*.[22] Studying the contemporary example of the Sāṃkhyayoga living tradition, practiced and discussed in Madhupur, we can see how the spirit of innovation and fidelity to tradition interact to produce another hybrid identity that can be defined as the *quasi*-Buddhist orthopraxy synthesized with the Sāṃkhyan orthodoxy.[23]

Notes

1. Originally, *Yoga Philosophy of Patañjali,* aka *Patañjala Yoga-darśana*—considered to be his *magnum opus*—was published in Bengali by the University of Calcutta, and then in Hindi by the University of Lucknow. During the last years of his life, Swāmi Hariharānanda Āraṇya asked some Indian and non-Indian scholars to take up the work of rendering it into English. The English edition was published in 1963 by the University of Calcutta (cf. *Preface* to the first edition in: Āraṇya 2000, xiii–xiv). Since then it has been reprinted several times, revised, and enlarged.

2. Knut A. Jacobsen has recently published a comprehensive and insightful monograph *Yoga in Modern Hinduism: Hariharānanda Āraṇya and Sāṃkhyayoga* (Jacobsen 2018), devoted to the contemporary manifestation of Sāṃkhyayoga as a living tradition. He explores the Yoga teaching of Hariharānanda and connects Kāpil Maṭh to the nineteenth-century transformations of Bengali religious culture of the educated upper class.

3. Notation without a hyphen "Sāṃkhyayoga," instead of "Sāṃkhya-Yoga" or "Sāṃkhya and Yoga," is used here to emphasize both the integrative perspective promoted by Hariharānanda Āraṇya and the multi-stage process of development of this philosophical tradition.

4. As Philipp A. Maas argues (Maas 2013), the so-called *Yogabhāṣya* or *Vyāsbhāṣya,* considered to be the oldest commentary to Patañjali's *Yogasūtra,* is not an independent work but an auto-commentary since in old manuscripts *sūtras* and *bhāṣya* are always found together. Therefore, Maas argues that both texts should be thought of as a unified work and called *Patañjalayogaśāstra sāṃkhyapravacana* (being the full title of the work written in the colophon in the manuscripts of the text), which can be translated as "the exposition of Yoga of Patañjali, the doctrine of Sāṃkhya."

5. Some basic information on Sāṃkhyayoga philosophy, the issued publications, and ongoing activities taking place in the Kāpil Maṭh Campus are available on the website http://kapilmath.com.

6. In Mahāyāna Buddhism, the Sanskrit term "*bodhisattva*" refers to anyone who has generated *bodhicitta,* that is, "a spontaneous wish and

compassionate mind to attain Buddhahood for the benefit of all sentient beings" (Kelsang 1995, 1).

7. To learn more about the meaning and historical context of the cave tradition see Jacobsen (2005, 333–349).

8. Such a method of meeting death is a centuries-old Indian tradition, practiced mostly in the Jain community (Kakar 2014). It is a respected ritual, also called "fasting facing north" (*sallekhanā,* also known as *santhara, samādhi-maraṇa* or *saṃnyāsa-maraṇa*). *Sallekhanā* is seen to be nonviolent, the most peaceful and satisfying form of "greeting death when it approaches" (Amritchandra 2012, 175). Nowadays, it is observed in India by monks and nuns, as well as lay people. Interestingly, it is practiced statistically more often by women than men (Braun 2008, 913–924). Jain texts make a clear distinction between *sallekhanā* and suicide; the one who practices the former is free from passion, desire, anger, and delusion, contrary to a person committing suicide (Amritchandra 2012, 116–117).

9. *Sāṃkhyakārikā* is the oldest preserved text of the Sāṃkhya school, although the school surely had existed by then for over a thousand years. Presumably, the original title of Īśvarakṛṣṇa's work was *Sāṃkhyasaptati* (Wezler 2001, 360n45) but became commonly referred to as *Sāṃkhyakārikā* due to Colebrooke's 1827 essay "On the Philosophy of the Hindus" (Maas 2017, 30n4).

10. The comments on Āraṇya's idea of pan-Indian universalism are partly repeated after Jakubczak (2012, 31–33).

11. *Aśvamedha* was a particularly lavish and abundant kind of sacrifice, performed only by ancient Indian kings to prove their imperial sovereignty.

12. Dharmāmegha Āraṇya states: "Every yogic practitioner who has attained liberation has comprehensive knowledge of the principles of reality and is fully enlightened. From this perspective there is no such thing as *originality* among the enlightened yogic practitioners and preceptors. They have only organized the yogic principles in new ways to suit their own times so that their contemporaries may comprehend them properly. There may be originality in the presentation but not in the ultimate knowledge of Yoga" (Dharmāmegha 2003, 148).

13. Until recently, connections between Sāṃkhya philosophy and Buddhism have been under-researched but, fortunately, more and more scholars are undertaking this topic. For instance, Ferenz Ruzsa in summing up his original interpretation of the Sāṃkhya dualist position argues that the Buddha inherited his substance-reductionist ideas from the proto-Sāṃkhya circles of Āruṇi and Yājñavalkya (Ruzsa 2019, 153–181).

14. A reference to this episode can be found in *Ariyapariyesana Sutta, Majjhimanikāya* 26 (cf. Bodhi 2005, 72). Also see Olivelle (2008, 322–323).

15. In later Buddhist tradition there are more arguments against Sāṃkhya metaphysics given in the Abhidharma texts (cf. Bronkhorst 1997, 393–400), but to mention only the key ones hitting at the very heart of classical Sāṃkhya, we should highlight those that refute: (1) the conception of self-existent nature (*svabhāva, prakṛti*) evolving spontaneously by itself (*pariṇāmavāda*); (2) the doctrine of the inner dynamics of nature caused by its three constituents (*guṇas*), or the strands of *prakṛti,* which explains the plurality and diversity of phenomena but also implies a deeper unmanifest source of the world, namely primal nature (*pradhāna, mūlaprakṛti*); (3) the theory of causation according to which the effect preexists in its cause in an unmanifest condition prior to its manifest production (*satkāryavāda*).

16. *Sāṃkhyakārikā* 2 defines liberating insight (*vivekakhyāti*) as recognizing a distinction between the manifest (*vyakta*) and the unmanifest (*avyakta*), and the knower (*jña*), that is, the self (*puruṣa*).

17. Noteworthy, the phrase "*nāsmi na me nāham*" occurs in the core texts of both traditions, in *Sāṃkhyakārikā* 64 as well as in *Majjhimanikāya* 109.15–16.

18. When I visited *aśrama* for the first time in 2010, there were two monks, including Ṛtaprakāśa Āraṇya, the younger one who was the chief editor of their journal *Sāṃkhyayāna*. When asked about the practical method helpful for the Sāṃkhyayoga monks in realizing their philosophical and spiritual purpose, Swāmi Ṛtaprakāśa Āraṇya pointed to the *vipassanā* technique (i.e., meditative insight into impermanence) as it is taught nowadays at the Vipassanā Meditation Centres initiated by Satya Narayan Goenka, who mastered it under the guidance of his Burmese teacher U Ba Khin.

19. Apart from the above-mentioned episode of the Buddha's life recorded by Aśvaghoṣa in *Buddhacarita,* which refers to Ārāḍa Kālāma, also in the Pāli canon the Buddha makes a passing remark upon Āḷāra Kālāma (cf. the *sutta* on *The Noble Search—Ariyapariyesana Sutta, Majjhima Nikāya* 26). (Cf. Bodhi 2005: *passim*).

20. As Ayon Maharaj proves in his insightful paper, Hariharānanda Āraṇya opted for a quasi-Buddhist interpretation of *smṛti* being the mental precondition for the establishment of *dhyāna* in Patañjali's *aṣṭāṇgayoga; Yogasūtra* I.20 (Maharaj 2013, 57–78).

21. The Sanskrit term *śamatha* (Pāli, *samatha*) refers to a state of concentration (*samādhi*) that consists in achieving the utmost one-pointedness of thought (Pāli, *cittassa ekaggata*) upon a given subject of salutary nature, and then raising one's conception of the subject to an abstraction (cf. Mahāthera 1962, 4–5).

22. Gerald J. Larson characterized Yoga as a hybrid form of Sāṃkhya or neo-Sāṃkhya, which reflects the interaction between Ṣaṣṭitantra and

Abhidharma of Sarvāstivāda and Sautrāntika (Larson 1989, 135; Larson 1999, 723–732).

23. This chapter is based on research that could not have been possible without the long-lasting support of a number of persons more or less formally associated with the contemporary tradition of Sāṃkhyayoga located in Madhupur. I owe my thanks to Swāmi Bhāskara Āraṇya, the current head of Kāpil Maṭh, and Professor Arindam Chakrabarti, who helped me to contact the Kāpil Maṭh devotees in Kolkata. I am particularly grateful to Adinath Chatterjee and his son Abhiprasun Chattopadhyay for their continued and whole-hearted assistance.

References

Amritchandra, Shri Suri. 2012. *Purushartha Siddhyupaya: Realization of the Pure Self*, translated by Vijay K. Jain. Dehradun: Vikalp Printers.

Āraṇya, Swāmī Hariharānanda. 2000. *Yoga Philosophy of Patañjali with Bhāsvatī*, translated by P. N. Mukerji. Kolkata: Calcutta University Press.

Āraṇya, Swāmī Hariharānanda. 2001. *A Unique Travelogue. An Allegorical Exploration of Spirituality and Yoga*, translated by S. Guha. Madhupur: Kāpil Math.

Āraṇya, Swāmī Hariharānanda. 2003. *Progressive and Practical Sāṃkhya-Yoga*, ed. A. Chatterjee, Madhupur: Kāpil Math.

Āraṇya, Swāmī Hariharānanda. 2005. *Sāṃkhya across the Millenniums*, ed. Adinath Chatterjee. Madhupur: Kāpil Math.

Āraṇya, Swāmī Hariharānanda. 2008. *The Doctrine of Karma (Karmatattva): A Philosophical and Scientific Analysis of the Theory of Karma*, translated by I. Guptā. Madhupur: Kāpil Math.

Bodhi, Bhikku ed. 2005. *In the Buddha's Words: An Anthology of Discourses from the Pāli Canon*. Somerville, MA: Wisdom Publications.

Braun, Whitny. 2008. "*Sallekhana*: The Ethicality and Legality of Religious Suicide by Starvation in the Jain Religious Community." *Medicine and Law* 27(4): 913–924.

Bronkhorst, Johannes. 1997. "Sāṃkhya in the Abhidharmakośa Bhāṣya." *Journal of Indian Philosophy* 25: 393–400.

Deutsch, Eliot. 1989. "Knowledge and the Tradition Text in Indian Philosophy," in G. J. Larson and E. Deutsch (eds.). *Interpreting across Boundaries: New Essays in Comparative Philosophy*. Delhi: Motilal Banarsidass, 165–173.

Ganeri, Jonardon ed. 2002. *The Collected Essays of Bimal Krishna Matilal: Ethics and Epics*, Delhi: Oxford University Press.

Jacobsen, Knut A. 2005. "In Kapila's Cave: A Sāṁkhya-Yoga Renaissance in Bengal," in *Theory and Practice of Yoga. Essays in Honour of Gerald James Larson*, ed. Knut A. Jacobsen. Leiden: Brill, 333–349.

Jacobsen, Knut A. 2018. *Yoga in Modern Hinduism: Hariharānanda Āraṇya and Sāṁkhyayoga*. London & New York: Routledge.

Jakubczak, Marzenna. 2012. "Why Didn't Siddhartha Gautama Become a Sāṃkhya Philosopher, After All?" in Kuznetsova, eds. Irina and Ganeri Jonardon and Chakravarthi Ram-Prasad, *Hindu and Buddhist Ideas in Dialogue: Self and No-Self*. Farnham, UK: Ashgate, 29–45.

Johnston, E. H., translator. 1972. *Aśvaghosa's Buddhacarita*. A complete Sanskrit text supplemented by the Tibetan version and Chinese translation. Delhi: Motilal Banarsidass (reprint of the 1936 Lahore edition).

Kakar, Sudhir. 2014. "A Jain Tradition of Liberating the Soul by Fasting Oneself," in *Death and Dying*. London: Penguin.

Kelsang, Gyatso. 1995. *The Bodhisattva Vow: A Practical Guide to Helping Others*. Ulverston: Tharpa Publications.

Kent, S. A. 1982. "Early Sāṃkhya in the *Buddhacarita*," *Philosophy East and West* 32: 259–278.

Kimball, James. 2013. "The Soteriological Role of the *ṛṣi* Kapila, According to the *Yuktidīpikā*." *Journal of Indian Philosophy* 41(6): 603–614.

Krishna, D. 1996. "Is Īśvarakṛṣṇa's *Sāṁkhya-Kārikā* Really Sāṁkhyan?," in *Indian Philosophy: A Counter Perspective*. New Delhi: Oxford University Press, 144–155.

Larson, G. J. 1989. "An Old Problem Revisited: The Relation between Sāṁkhya, Yoga and Buddhism." *Studien zur Indologie und Iranistik*, vol. 15, 129–146.

Larson, G . J. 1999. "Classical Yoga as Neo-Sāṃkhya" in *Asiatische Studien / études Asiatiques*, vol. 52. *Proceedings of the Conference on Sāṃkhya*, Lausanne 5–8.11.1998, 723–732.

Larson, G. J. 2000. "The 'Tradition Text' in Indian Philosophy for Doing History of Philosophy in India," in *The Aestethic Turn: Reading Eliot Deutsch on Comparative Philosophy*, ed. R. T. Ames. Peru, IL: Carus Publishing Company, 59–69.

Maas, Philip A. 2013. "A Concise Historiography of Classical Yoga Philosophy," in Eli Franco (ed.), *Periodization and Historiopgraphy of Indian Philosophy*, De Nobili Series, 53–90, Vienna: Institute für Südasien-, Tibet- und Buddhismuskunde der Universität Wien.

Maas, Philip A. 2017. "From Theory to Poetry: The Reuse of Patañjali's *Yogaśāstra* in Māgha's *Śiśupālavadha*," in Elisa Freschi and Philipp A. Maas (eds.), *Adaptive Reuse: Aspects of Creativity in South Asian*

Cultural History, 29–62, Abhandlungen für di Kunde des Morgenlandes 101. Wiesbaden: Harrassowitz.

Maharaj, Ayon. 2013. "Yogic Mindfulness: Hariharānanda Āraṇya's Quasi-Buddhistic Interpretation of *Smṛti* in Patañjali's *Yogasūtra* I.20." *Journal of Indian Philosophy* 41: 57–78.

Mahāthera, P. V. 1962. *Buddhist Meditation in Theory and Practice. A General Exposition According to the Pāli Canon of the Therevāda School*. Colombo: M. D. Gunasena.

Majjhimanikāya, translator, in Ñāṇamoli, Bhikkhu and Bhikkhu Bodhi. 1995. *The Middle Length Discourses of the Buddha. A New Translation of the Majjhima Nikāya*. Boston: Wisdom Publications.

Olivelle, Patrick, translator. 2008. *Life of the Buddha by Aśvaghoṣa*. New York: New York University Press.

Osto, Douglas. 2018. "No-Self in Sāṁkhya: A Comparative Look at Classical Sāṁkhya and Theravāda Buddhism," *Philosophy East and West*, 68(1): 201–222.

Ruzsa, Ferenc. 2019. "Sāṁkhya: Dualism without Substances," in Joerg Tuske (ed.) *Indian Epistemology and Metaphysics*, 153–181. New York: Bloomsbury Academic.

Sāṃkhyakārikā, translator, in Gerald J. Larson. 1979. *Classical Sāṁkhya. An Interpretation of its History and Meaning*, 255–277. Delhi: Motilal Banarsidass.

Shevchenko, Dimitry. 2017. "Natural Liberation in the Sāṃkhyakārikā and Its Commentaries," *Journal of Indian Philosophy* 45: 863–892.

Wezler, Albrecht. 2001. "Zu der Frage des Strebens nach äußerster Kürze in den Śrautasūtras." *Zeitschrift der Deutschen Morgenländischen Gesellschaft* 151: 351–366.

Chapter 7

Observing Sāṃkhya Categories in a Mid-Twentieth-Century Village

McKim Marriott

I had vowed early in 1951 to reside in Parhil (Paḍīl), as complete an average-sized, old-fashioned village as my Jeep could find me in a roadless corner of Aligarh District in Uttar Pradesh state, about one hundred miles southeast of New Delhi, India's capital since her independence as "Bharata" in 1947. One of my objectives was to see how that diverse, still largely peasant, country from which American social scientists had been barred by Britain for many years could achieve the unity desired by most modern nations, given her illiteracy, class disparities, Hindu–Muslim hostilities, and the allegedly rigid ranking of tens of thousands of castes in tens of thousands of villages that were still homes to 85 percent of her people, the lowest of whom were treated as untouchable. European armchair scholars had imagined Hindu religion to be a principal cause of India's ailments, while British officials generally scorned Hindu ideas and had commissioned separate descriptions of hundreds of castes as if they were independent tribes. None of those authorities, nor I, seemed aware of the internal workings of India's rural communities or knew anything about *Sāṃkhya* ("the Inventory"), India's oldest and, for Hindu peasants, the most relevant philosophy.

I was an admirer of the growing style of a wholly cultural anthropology at the time that privileged no outsider's queries or complaints but sought to understand any people through the categories and logics of their own worldviews, as urged by Ruth Benedict in her 1934 *Patterns of Culture*. I had planned to live and observe in Parhil for at least a year, learning the local language, meeting everyone, and participating as far as I could in its social life and means of subsistence. Adding several subsequent stays in the same village for a total of nearly four years, I found myself witnessing the abolition of landlord tenures plus half a century of massive improvements in the country's agriculture and Parhil's schools (Mayer 1958; Marriott 1971). But most improved for me were my understandings of the recent and innumerable earlier Hindu villagers who must have seen themselves as parts of a three-stranded (*triguṇa*) material universe like that assumed in the enduring fourth-century Sanskrit *Sāṃkhya Karikā*, a text generally puzzled over by recent Indologists, but freshly interpreted by Gerald James Larson in 1969, and extensively annotated by him with Ram Shankar Bhattacharya in 1986.

Spoken as well as written languages are essential to cultural studies, but in 1951 no university in the United States taught any language generally spoken in India other than English, and the few U.S. soldiers like me posted in India during our war with Japan had been forbidden to fraternize with Indians. Learning classical Sanskrit in the United States would require additional years of study, but linguistic anthropologists advised me that a quicker way of learning a local variant of Hindi would be to find bilingual helpers and imitate their ways of speaking, which I attempted to do. When I began graduate study in 1947, the University of Chicago offered classical Sanskrit but no other language of South Asia. Since cultural anthropologists considered the *in situ* learning of the local language a desirable part of fieldwork in any unknown society, I prepared instead by gathering ideas from linguistics, psychology, sociology, and mathematics that I supposed might be of use anywhere.

I had chosen to work in one of Hindi-speaking Aligarh district's most primitive villages whose strengths were only those of farmers with their animals, plows, and hand tools because I wanted to see how people could manage without the new energies, materials and devices that the twentieth century would soon be offering them. I had turned down several rural landlords' offers of places to park my Jeep because I wanted to live with and observe people of all economic classes. I liked the fact that Paḍīl's twenty-four caste groups in what the 1950 Census said were only 861 people (both figures probably undercounts) gave it twice the average number of different castes in villages so small (Marriott 1960, 23) because I wanted to observe intercaste relations. To discourage outsiders from interfering with my plans I gave Paḍīl a fictional name—"Kishan Garhi"—that could not be found on any published map, although Aligarh's places bore many other such Vaisnava names.

Relying largely on British sources, armchair scholars of Europe had imagined India to be handicapped, some like Max Weber (1958) by the diversity of her castes, others like Louis Dumont (1970) by her Church-like repression of personal diversities, but neither had proven their imaginings to be true. Colonial officials had published separate descriptions of a thousand castes, each as having distinct occupations, gods, and territories, but rarely as connected with each other as they are in kingdoms, towns, and cities, and never in her half million of small villages. Admission to India from outside had been granted to English school teachers, physicians, agronomists, sight-seeing tourists, and missionaries, but never to social scientists for the needed whole-community researches.

I housed my wife and small children in a modern suburb of Aligarh city near the national Muslim University to which I had an introduction, planning myself to reside solo five days a week in Paḍīl village, fifteen miles away, for at least a year, meeting all residents, learning their dialects, and participating as far as I could in their present, old-fashioned means of subsistence and social life, hoping thereby to learn more of their ways of thinking about their world, each other, and themselves.

I had first gone to Lucknow, the U.P. state capitol, to meet its newly elected political leader. He welcomed my aims and interests, hoping that I would also tell the world about his state's imminent abolition of its landlord tenure system, granting full ownership of their holdings to all cultivators willing just once to pay ten times their present low annual rents directly to the state. This would enable it to end ineffective planning from above and provide people's strongly felt needs for expensive things such as electricity and more all-weather roads. Also imminent were new, state-supervised elections of a representative council in each village to replace its landlords' powers.

From the immediacy of these plans I saw that a study of Paḍīl's old customs could not wait for clearer understandings of *Sāṃkhya's* founding text but would have to begin at once empirically, seeking older ways not just from memories but perhaps from observing them still in active practice. I began with fifteen months of participant observation in 1951–1952, of which some findings are reported in my papers listed below as published in 1995 and 1996.

Holi, the Essential Riot

The first week of my Parhil residency in March 1951 took me to what villagers said (through a local translator) would be the greatest festival of their year, a central event I should not miss. With the midnight rising of their full moon of Phalgun, I awoke to join some two hundred men and boys of the village and a few older women, both Hindu and Muslim, at a huge, ritually prepared bonfire celebrating the incineration of *Holika,* an egoistic, anti-Vaisnava demoness. Each of us circumambulated the fire, greeting and embracing from head to foot whomever we chanced to meet, old or young, who were circumambulating it in the opposite direction. Home fires were later rekindled with coals brought from the common bonfire. The water first heated by this fire was thought to have special curative value. Condolences, too, were given to unrepresented families who had lost members during the past year, with pleas that they rejoin the living community at its *Holi* bonfire next year.

The rest of the festival lacked a text but felt like a riot: stones struck my door at dawn and bricks came over my wall from the lane, thrown by youngsters challenging adult residents to give up hiding in their houses and come out where the past year's clay pots were being smashed. Sand and ashes were also flying. Adult celebrants shortly handed me some of *Holi*'s potent drink—the sweetened juice of a wild cannabis plant that grew along the rural cart tracks—and offered me their shoulders' support when my knees began to feel wobbly. One young man, declared a bully, was being forced by youngsters who were his usual victims to ride a donkey around the village seated backwards. A mock dirge was being sung outside a wealthy moneylender's door. A priestly scold found her ancestral hearth fouled with dog-doo. One wife had been found in another man's bed, and many other infidelities were suspected. "But no one should get angry," I was repeatedly warned, as buckets of cows' urine were being thrown while friends and enemies smeared each other's faces with soot, oil, mud, or almost anything else.

In the afternoon, wives began beating with sticks any husbands (like me) whom they could catch, administering punishments that we could escape only by running away or by dodging behind our sticks planted firmly on the ground. "It shows how much they love you!" other husbands assured me. After sundown, two of Parhil's *Jogi*-caste professional ballad singers for Lord Shiva began writhing through an elaborate choreography applauded by crowds of people throwing flower- or dye-colored water upon each other. A chorus of devotees sang Ganga Devi hymns as I floated with them, and another crowd through two or maybe three nearby villages.

What did it all mean? Whoever I asked, the answer was "*Holi* is Lord Krishna's festival of love!" "Love" is a bit different from his romp in the *Bhagavat Purāṇa* that is pictured in Alfred Collins's chapter 8 in this volume. One may only experience such passions again fully in Phalgun after eleven months of ordinary living, but how were those months to be understood? How were they ordered?

The Naturally Ordered Villagers

After a cleanup, I began mapping Parhil's twisted lanes and meeting with some of its 166 families, each understood as the people eating from one hearth behind their dwelling's windowless mud walls. Each family belonged to one of nineteen different hereditary, endogamous Hindu castes (*zat*) or five Muslim hereditary but not endogamous tribes (*kaum*). Dwellings of these twenty-four categories were closely intermingled below the hilltop mansions of Parhil's seventeenth-century Jat conquerors whose descendant landlords had largely become absentees by 1951. The dissolving and rebuilding of mud-brick dwellings for perhaps three millennia had evidently helped to raise the village's bastion-like hill thirty feet above its large pond, as its residents cultivated square miles of the surrounding alluvial plain.

Half of the village men were cultivators of that plain, three-quarters of them belonging to a single ancient Brahman (i.e., priesthood-qualified) caste called *Sanādhya*. The *Sanādhya* Brahmans had long ago imposed their vegetarian rule on hundreds of villages for miles around. This kept everyone "cool" according to Hindu humoral (*doṣa*) theory. These Sandhaya Brahmans, unlike most Brahmans, warmed themselves bodily by working in the fields they rented. They often worked alongside laborers they hired from "lower" ranking castes. They could give these laborers food but could not accept cooked food from them.

The non-Brahman quarter of the village's other large cultivators belonged to five different high- or middle-ranking Hindu or Muslim groups and two lower castes, the rank of each being calculated by its particular food-giving and -taking relations with the others. Among these cultivators, two Jat and two Muslim families worked their fields together and shared raw foods, though they cooked at four hearths rather than one.

The non-cultivating half of the village population only occupied enough land for their dwellings and practicing their trades. Parhil was thus clearly stratified by caste and landholding, more steeply than most other villages in India's north but not so steeply as many others in her far south (e.g., D. P. Mines 2005; M. Trawick 2017). During the 1947 partition of India, five locally landless Muslim men were said to have walked eight hundred miles to Karachi in Islamic Pakistan in hopes of receiving land. When this did not happen, they walked back to Parhil where they could resume working for their mostly Hindu neighbors.

More than its surrounding villages, however, Parhil was a place to find many specialists including Hindu priests, blacksmiths and carpenters, barbers, watercarriers, ballad singers, potters, brick-makers, cotton-carders, weavers, tailors, brass players, bangle-sellers, dancers, beggars, oilpressers, laundrymen, former "Chamar" leatherworkers (*jatavs*), sweepers (*bhangis*), and forest hunters. Ranking from very high to very low in food transactions (detailed in Marriott 1968), some of these non-cultivating others provided agricultural labor part-time as well as their crafts and services to cultivators. There were no shops or bicycles in Parhil, but vendors occasionally came through on foot selling matches, country cigarettes, fruits, or other small things not made or grown locally.

Among Parhil's total population of 861 residents, twelve literate men daily sent their boys to learn writing in a nearby hamlet and just two had their sons enrolled in more distant high schools. One priest had gone to Trinidad, one *Jat* had joined the British Indian army, and two of a scribe caste had arranged their transfer to Agra on state jobs. One young Muslim briefly taught Hindi writing to a dozen local youngsters, but Parhil had never had its own school, which means that the 1951 villagers were generally nonliterate.

Each of Parhil's families took its name and direction from its eldest man. Others in the family were usually ranked and commanded by seniors of their gender, as M. G. Davis also describes from rural W. Bengal. Adult men supplied their labor, any special abilities, and hopefully male heirs to continue the family, enlarge, or divide it. Men generally slept in a group near their dwelling's door, while women, young children and inactive senior men retired to the inside and rear. Although their daily labor kept men outdoors most of the time, their nighttime and lifelong attachments remained with their Parhil homes "where their placentas were buried." Muslims had distinct Urdu-language kin terms, but the Hindi kin terms of address used throughout the village made all residents feel somewhat like members of a single patrilineal clan, one into which they quickly absorbed me.

Brides for Hindu males were acquired in their protected, virginal teens from genealogically unrelated families of the same castes in other villages averaging five to thirty-five miles away through their parents' searching, bargaining, viewing, and inspecting, followed by duties that were often felt by the girls as physically and psychologically stressful. As protection, the bride might bring with her a token of some small deity from her original family. A new wife in her husband's family served primarily by doing the (for Hindus, untouchably polluting) work of coupling, bearing, and then caring for her young children until the years when she again became clean enough to assist in the family's food preparation. Her presence might be blamed for any quarrel or other inauspicious turn in the family that she had just joined. But ultimately, she could expect to succeed her husband's mother as feeder of the family—a management position—until she retired and was succeeded by her son's wife. The senior woman's duties included scheduling the dates when intercourse between any younger couple was believed likely to produce offspring. Women of higher class were not seen alone outside their homes. Among lower classes and castes, matches, women, and families were less controlled and less formal, and among Muslims matches were often arranged between well-acquainted patrilineal cousins.

Everybody and Thing Is Naturally Ranked by Age and Gender

According to the anthropological methods developed by British scholars as their empire expanded, understanding any unfamiliar society is best begun by learning its people's particular ways of reckoning kinship, which in Paḍīl involved houses. Birthings were done outside houses to avoid polluting them, but a house was named after its eldest living male whose afterbirth had been buried beneath the house. Females fathered there held the same right and duty as males to stay and be supported there until married out. There was only one such person still in Paḍīl—a woman whose young husband had died before she and he could be united, so she had never left her birthplace.

Males of each house were introduced to me first by their personal names in older-before-younger age order without numbering, and before the introduction of any in-married females of the same house with their female children who were also introduced to me by name in their declining age order. Such age-rank orderings were felt to be essential: if followed in action as said in Bengali villages like Davis's (1971), they made all other requirements of life go smoothly, but if not followed, endlessly troublesome.

Females, too, had house rights and duties where they were fathered and given birth, but lost those and gained new ones in their husband's house by marriage, sometimes accompanied by a dowry to compensate them for the risks or losses they might bring with them (Raheja 1988, *The Poison in the Gift*). Their two houses had to be of the same caste and of distinct patrilineal descent and located in villages that I found averaged ten to thirty-five miles apart—distances great enough to mark brides' permanent separations from their original homes and unity with their new ones.

The fathers and/or brothers arranging a girl's marriage generally presented their decision as a step upward for the girl, although words for the prime duty of her new position is often the same that Hindi speakers use for prostitutes, and although giving a daughter in marriage is commonly also believed to rid the giving family of any problem it may have been feeling.

Girls marrying into or out of Paḍīl often showed how they still treasured ties with their origins by returning there for their first birth-giving, by sending a wrist charm to, or by herself performing an annual foot-washing for a potentially further generous, dowry-giving father or brother whose house she had left behind her (Wadley 1975, 170b, 175). Once in 1952, three husbands who had recently taken Paḍīl girls as brides to their their different villages returned briefly with their wives to run a male's foot race in *Paḍīl* for everyone's amusement on that special day. The rule of village exogamy thus produced not isolated villages but a rural society of distantly intersecting ties among dozens of different caste groups.

Ranking caste groups by their seniority in Paḍīl resembled the ranking of persons by their ages in a household, but did not exercise their powers so easily. "*Sanādhya* ('Genuine') *Brahmans*" (simply "*Sanādhyas*" hereafter)—were its largest and probably the earliest among Paḍīl's presently seven different cultivating castes. People of the Aligarh area assumed that all had been ruled by nonresident *Rajputs* (Hindu princes), often as agents for *Mogul* or other foreign, often Muslim military groups settled in Delhi or Agra.

Sanādhyas of Paḍīl included four or five *Saṃskrit*-teaching families who had received gifts or payments from others sufficient to relieve them from the necessity of earning a living by cultivation; they could give priestly services to any other Hindus requesting and paying for those services.

Sanādhya priests did not serve the single small, locally resident *Maithil Brahman* artisan caste group of eight carpenter or blacksmith houses whose own traveling priests visited Paḍīl occasionally to service just them. This group claimed descent from artisans whom they say originated in a village of Bihar state named *Maithil*. It and the local *Sanādhya Brahman* caste disagreed on their relative ranks and consequently their members did not interdine, but were otherwise friendly.

Sanādhyas or other castes might differ politically among themselves by liberal or conservative factional views that joined them with or opposed them to some members of other local castes who held different opinions on practical matters such as village schools, lanes, lights, and government.

During the disorderly eighteenth century, Paḍīl was ruled briefly not by *Moguls* or their agents but by Indian *Marāthas*, and then by French forces moving up the Ganges, simultaneously in part by Indian *Jāt Thākur* ("Cultivator Lord") armies advancing eastward across the Yamuna river. Some of those *Jāts* became Paḍīl village's landlords, collecting revenue for the conquering British, whose formal rule after 1850 was interrupted only in 1857 by a short rebellion of native Indian soldiers in a nearby district who burned the French-built Aligarh District office containing Paḍīl's earlier land records.

In the following ninety years, the British colonial government extended canal irrigation and recruited some local *Jāts* as fighters in World Wars I and II. It also dealt with growing Indian nationalism until the British forces gave up and departed in 1947.

By building on top of a small hill augmented by the dissolved remains of previous centuries of mud-brick dwellings by others, successive ruling groups or their agents had constructed and fortified their own mansions in Paḍīl until by 1951 they had reached thirty feet above the otherwise mostly flat Ganga-Yamuna river delta.

The mansion of the one still hill-resident *Jāt Thākur*, a small landlord named Kishan Singh, contained the only table and chair in Paḍīl, both of solid, painted wood and standard equipment for small rent-collectors—along with a shotgun, ammunition, and a guard's uniform for his servant.

The only furniture, if any, in commoners' houses was one or more cots—each roughly six-feet by eighteen-inch wooden frames on two-feet corner legs, its strings woven smoothly at the "higher" head end and tightened less comfortably by ropes at the "lower," foot end. They served their owners as instruments of hospitality or its lack, and supplied sitters with estimates of their own ranks, since one heard frequent urges to "sit higher," "lower," or off the cot and on the ground, no houses having other than clay floors. "Equality" was thought non-existent in nature, impossible for any two humans, not even between twins. My Jeep's two seats and steel benches, fenders, and tow-bar were similarly used to observe rank by the up to eight villagers who might occupy such perches on my weekly trips past Aligarh city.

I began to draw a conceptual "table" (see table 7.1) with at least ten horizontal rows to allow for the ever-present possibility of finding further small degrees of ranking as perhaps at feasts. Like aging, other rankings could be understood as fundamental to the rest of village thinking about the uneven, changing properties of nature.

Building a *Sāṃkhya* Table for Humans

Harvesting of the main winter grain crops was begun shortly after *Holi* by each field's proprietor using mostly male laborers whom he hired for the day, wielding their own small hand sickles. They started work in the darkness of early mornings to minimize their exposure to the dependably fiery (110° F +) heat of the spring sun. Later threshing their grain under the feet of all available cattle, they winnowed it when the wind was right—moderate and steady. During the summer monsoon rains, everyone defended the flat-roofed parts of their largely unroofed homes, as well as their stacks of fodder and cowdung fuel, from violent south winds and possible floods. In the gentler fall and winter weather that followed, cultivators plowed manure and trash into the moist earth, then planted and undertook the long labor of weeding the growing crops. Crops were irrigated with melted snows from the Himalayas brought closer underground by Ganga Devi, or Allah, and raised by those few large tenants who had wisely dug wells thirty feet deep. They then bought or borrowed sufficient bullocks to lift in thirty-gallon leather scoops some of the water that every crop needed. Such techniques never produced enough surface water, so a third of the fields remained dry and subject to later rainfall vagaries.

Water (rain), fire (heat), and air (wind) were three elements (*mahābhūtas*) with variations of which every villager contended and which everyone spoke of throughout the year. Such environmental variations produced moods and characteristics like those attributed to people and animals—helpful or not, hot or not, steady or not. A generous employer or lactating cow was bountiful; a "hot" man or bull could be aggressive sexually; a steady man or water buffalo was essential, an angry one dangerous, and so on.

Such preoccupations and comparisons indicated that villagers were given to thinking materially and systematically, encouraging me to ask further about the roles of natural categories in their thinking. Adding space (*ākāś*), a term whose meaning includes sky or heaven, and adding earth (*pṛthvī*) to the varying water, fire, and wind, I heard villagers agree that there are five gross elements (*pañcamahābhūtas*) of which everything and everyone in the universe consists in various proportions.

After hearing Gerald Larson lecture at the national meeting of the Association of Asian Studies about his textual findings and later seeing his chart of the *Sāṃkhya Karikā*'s whole natural universe (1979, 236), I saw that this reflected the village wisdom shared in Parhil. I created my own chart (table 7.1) of the five gross elements, rearranging the middle three in *triguṇa* order (see rows 2, 3, and 4 of column [E]).

Horizontal entries in Larson's chart and my table are connected by homology, imputed cause and effect, or necessary preexistence, such as the assumed necessities of space (not air) for sound and speech, and fire's energy for motion and vision. Homologous relations are common in Vedic literature where they are identified by the brotherly term *bandhus*, writes Brian K. Smith (1994).

From the 1970s onward, I listened to Parhil conversations to learn what other human matters such a table might accommodate. Some immediate finds were the three kinds of inner, that is, psychological, functions (*antaḥkaraṇas*) that villagers reported feeling inside themselves. The Hindi names of these functions reproduce the *Kārikā*'s Sanskrit trio of intellect (*buddhi*), heart-mind (*manas*), and ego (*ahaṃkāra*), terms from between verses XXII and XXXII that I ultimately assigned to the table's column [B] and to that column's vertically middle rows 2, 3, and 4.

Column [B]'s row 2 top inner function intellect (*buddhi*) is for a person's accumulating knowledge—knowledge worth "emitting" to others in its higher sub-row labeled 2a and worth "tasting" by

Table 7.1. Functioning of Sāṃkhya Tattvas and Other Hindu Categories

[A] Three strands ***triguṇas*** **of Prakṛti**	**[B] Inner Functions antaḥkaraṇas**	**[C] Motor & Sensory capacities**	**[D] Subtle Sensations** ***tanmātras***	**[E] Gross Elements** ***mahābhūtas***	**[F] Humors** ***tridoṣas***	**[G] Goals** ***trivargas***	**[H] Actions**
		Speaking		Space			Mandate
		Hearing	Sound				Worship
Goodness *sattva*	Intellect	Emitting		Water	Wind and *Vāta*	Coherence	Give
		Tasting	Taste				Accept
Passion *rajas*	Heart–Mind	Walking		Fire	Bile *Pitta*	Attachment	merge
		Seeing	Sight				Unmerge
Darkness *tamas*	Egoity	Grasping		Air	Phlegm and *Kapha*	Advantage	Unmatch
	Sociality	Touching	Feeling				Match
		Coupling		Earth			Place
		Smelling	Odor				
Puruṣa		Nonmateriality		Consciousness		Release / *Mokṣa*	

someone else in its lower sub-row labeled 2b (like mother's milk?). Both sub-rows are homologous with column [A]'s row 2, the strand of "goodness." Goodness' virtues are respectively homologous with the high values of "water," "phlegm," and "coherence" in columns [E], [F] and [G], knowledge of which is gained by "giving" and "taking," according to the extra-*Sāṃkhya* column [H].

Column [B]'s functions of the two translations "heart" and "mind" I join by a hyphen because I found that both are homologous with column [A]'s row 3, the strand of "passion." The *Kārikā*'s single term *manas* (Hindi *man*) can feel both intense wanting and intense thinking. But *manas*' homologies with column [C]'s and column [H]'s sub-rows suggest distinguishing between these two kinds of passion. One kind of passion is in sub-row 3a's movements like "walking," which requires column [E]'s "fire" and column [F]'s "bile" and can lead to column [G]'s "attachment" and column [H]'s act of "merging." The other, cooler kind of "passion" assigns to columns [C]'s and [D]'s sub-row 3b only the capacity for analytic "seeing" (of differences?) that may lead to the opposite action of "unmerging."

Further down in column [B], at "darkness'" row 4, Larson notices two partly contrary meanings of the single Hindu moral term "egoity" (*ahamkara*), meanings similarly distinguished by Michel Hulin. The table first offers a possibly heroic but sometimes socially irresponsible meaning that is homologous with sub-row 4a's "grasping," "air," "wind," "advantage" and "unmatching." (The demoness *Holika* was destroyed for being such a socially irresponsible egotist.) Second, with the term "sociality," the table describes a socially responsible meaning of *ahamkara* that is homologous with the "touching," "feeling," and "matching" terms that appear respectively in columns [C],'s [D],'s and [H]'s sub-row 4b.

The *Holi* festival, a carnival of passions, made much use of both the contrasting sub-rows 4a and 4b almost as if they were primal, undivided (*avyakta*) terms, from which 4b's term "sociality" seems to point back toward column [A]'s row 2 strand of moral "goodness." Row 5's final sub-rows a and b under column [C] offer a fragrant regeneration ("coupling" with "smelling"), and in sub-row 5a of column [H] a kind of oblivion ("placing" in the earth).

In the table's column [C] the sensory and motor capacities are distinguished but combined vertically because the *Kārikā*'s list of five "gross senses" (*jnanendriyas*) in verse XXVI are correlated with its five "gross actions" (*karmendriyas*) in verse XXVIII. When interdigitated the two capacities form upper sub-row a and lower sub-row b pairs contextually distinguishing outer and inner, cause and effect, or active and passive. All these terms have their vernacular equivalents.

With the table's column [D] featuring what the *Kārikā* calls "subtle sensations" (*tanmātras*)—"sound" (*śabda*), "taste" (*rasana*), "sight" (*dṛṣṭi*), "feeling" (*vedanā*), and "odor" (*gandha*)—I could match stories of several ghosts (*bhūts*) known to people in Parhil and learn a little about ghosts' faint sensory manifestations—mostly apparitions, speakerless voices, or otherwise unexplained drafts of air. How ghosts may be created by late-life attachments was later described by Sarah Lamb in a village of West Bengal. But Larson (1979, 267) tells us that the *Kārikā*'s verse XXXVIII may refer to other subtleties that remain unclear to him.

Then for the *Kārikā*'s and villagers' five underlying, omnipresent, and therefore highly variable "gross elements" (*mahā bhūtas*) themselves one could envision the sturdy column [E].

Correspondences of columns [B]'s and [C]'s, if not also [D]'s human functions with the central three of the five elements sky, water, sun, wind and earth in [E] were explicitly and repeatedly heard in the work of agriculture. All those central three were also readily correlated both with the popular ayurvedic (*tridoṣa*) humoral terms "phlegm," "bile," and "wind" of column [F], and with the often observable interactions in column [H].

Should one's highest goal in life be achieving "coherence" (*dharma*) with others or should it be gaining "advantage" (*artha*) over others? These were two of the three goals (*trivargas*) discussed in the Brahmanic *Manusmṛti* text represented in column [G] that must have been argued among members of the intercaste committee who collected funds for Parhil's first elementary school building in 1969. Answering this question divisively was avoided by their going to another text on which the committee could agree—the *Bhagavad Gītā* (discussed below). To inspire the students, two words were molded in the plaster on the school's roof—the *Gītā*'s "*sattva*" (goodness) along with Manu's "*dharma*." The issue here was like that between the "egoity" and "sociality" interpretations of *ahaṃkāra* in column [B]'s rows 4a and 4b.

Differing from the Western scientific preference for precision, the content of each cell in this Hindu Table varies naturally and therefore verbally between its a and b sub-rows, which generally mean "cause" and "effect," or "more" at their tops and "less" at their bottoms. But only nine of the table's sub-row variants are specified, leaving sixteen other contextually appropriate variants to be supplied by the reader. For example 2a, "goodness," in column [A] could be opposed to biological rottenness as well as to moral evil in 2b. Water in column [E] may be contrasted with its lack as "drought" or as "thirst," in 2B, according to its context as fields or persons. In column [C] of the table, the initial action words of sub-rows a—"speaking," "emitting," and "walking" (or otherwise "moving") etc.—are paired with their respective passive, sensory sub-rows b—"hearing," "tasting," and "seeing," etc., as in *Karika* XXXIV. Appropriate variants may generally be found thus—by pairing them with homologous words elsewhere in the same row.

Arguments between variants of Hindu moral thought similar to the physical and social variants of this table are presented from the Tamil Nadu villagers studied by Sheryl Daniel. Variation itself appears to be natural everywhere in Sāṃkhya's Hindu universe—not only in Sheryl's moral-conceptual "toolbox."

Appended by the present anthropological author, the eighth column [H] titled "interactions observed" ventures beyond the *Sāṃkhya Kārikā* text but pursues other varying human activities homologous with previous columns [C]'s motor and [E]'s elemental contents. In its sub-row 1a column [H] adds one new term—"mandating"—for (gods?) speaking from heaven, issuing mandates which require hearers in sub-row 1b to respond by "worshiping." And in sub-row 5a's "earth," column [H] adds another new term—"placing," which there means planting, burying or hiding something, such as the seed of new life.

Detailed in column [H]'s sub-rows 2a and 2b are the frequent "givings" and "takings" of invisible "marks"—analytic terms for caste ranking borrowed from animal ecology by Marriott (1990, 19–20). These terms of marking are analogous to the "emitting" and "tasting" of column [A]'s sub-row 2a's "goodness" and of column [B]'s "intellect" by unmentioned others.

Also included in column [H]'s givings and takings are disposals of the many negative inauspiciousnesses (reported from a village in Saharanpur U.P. by Gloria Raheja 1988, ch. 2) and the plethora of constructive personal "polishings" (*saṃskāras*) including not only those leading up to marriage but also the Sanskrit postmortem gifts, connections, and services concisely analyzed by Diane Mines in 1990.

Column [H]'s givings and takings (like column [C]'s emittings and tastings) are interactions in both worshiping and inter-caste ranking that are further described below under "Food and Caste Ranking." Similar interactions occurred frequently also in the playing-card games in which some villagers were experts.

Looking back to the above descriptions of Parhil's Hindu families, their marriages, and their female transitions—originally protecting their daughters, then "unmerging" them from their origins and "merging" them by wedding them with categorically "matched" (by caste) but genealogically "unmatched" families and astrologically appropriate (thus "unmatching") persons, one sees that five other complex but common interactions of column [H] rows 3 and 4 have already also been described.

This table might be improved by further research and extended beyond column [H], but why does it begin as it does with a trio of ideas in its first column [A]?

Three Dimensionality (*triguṇas*)

When Hindu preachers occasionally visited Parhil in the twentieth century, one of their favorite texts was the *Bhagavad Gītā,* a battle episode of the *Mahābhāarata* in which Lord Kṛṣṇa directs Prince Arjun to fight, but to choose his actions first by their moral and legal goodness (*sattva*), second by the sufficiency of his passion (*rajas*) for doing the act as a warrior, and third by his personal darkness (*tamas*), meaning his anger against his victim's previous relations with him or with someone he loved. Arjun is advised to perform in the battle only those violent actions which meet *all three* criteria.

Although popular through earlier centuries this formula of the "three strands" (*triguṇas*) was not attributed to the *Gītā* by Īśvarakṛṣṇa, the fourth-century author of the *Sāṃkhya Kārikā*. Apparently he derives the formula rather from the much older

Chāndogya and other *Upaniṣads*, a more inclusive and authoritative body of Hindu wisdom. Following Īśvarakṛṣṇa's lead by entering the three words "goodness, passion, and darkness" at the beginnings of the vertically central rows 2, 3, and 4 in column [A] of the table means that corresponding row entries in all the other columns [B]–[H] should be understood as homologous with, that is, equal or similar to, causal of, necessary to, or effects of those initial three entries.

This three-strand formula may be pictured in Indian textile terms as a thread or rope made of at least three intertwining "strands" (*guṇas*). As their ancestors may have been doing for at least a millennium, women in 1951 Parhil were still spinning thread from strands of home-grown, locally carded cotton, the thread next to be locally woven into sleeping mats or fabrics for local tailoring into clothing. Men, too, had long been twisting strands of wild hemp fibers on their thighs, making guide-ropes for their animals (and swings for their sisters' amusement) and were still doing so in 1951, although factories had by then taken over manufacture of much heavier well-ropes made of stronger materials.

As the *Kārikā*'s verses XII–XIV (and likewise Larson's 1969, 162–164) state, the interactions of Sāṃkhya's three *guṇas* are qualities thought to structure the whole Hindu universe—a notion that resembles but exceeds Western "solid" geometry's users' findings that three-dimensional structures are very common. Another caution about comparing Sāṃkhya ideas with geometric thought is that soft, fibrous "strands" may form lines, but are not inherently lines, nor are they straight; in fact, they are often curved or orthogonal, thus ready for intertwining. Also, they need not have fixed or measurable lengths as geometric dimensions often do. Like the Fluid Signs of which the title of E. V. Daniel's 1984 Tamil village monograph warns us, plural *guṇas* (Tamil *kunams*) may combine or clash without physical contact and without their combined quantities being parametric, as vividly exemplified in his pages on houses, sexuality, and *passim*.

Nevertheless, because geometry's three-dimensional relationships are better understood by modern readers, I use them as metaphors for the many jobs that the more flexible *triguṇas* do in Hindu social thought. They help, for example, to define each combination of the three rows 2, 3, and 4 in the present table or elsewhere as a cube of human relations. They depict with such cubes many Hindu ideas and practices that structure whole households, communities, lifetimes, conflicts, and pantheons, some of which are represented visually in my "A Hindu Way of Thinking," a work presently in process.

The *Sanādhya Brāhman* and Other Castes

*Sanādhya*s were one of Aligarh District's largest caste populations in 1951, forty families of them working as tenants on about half of Paḍīl village's total one square mile of arable land. Unusual among the hundreds of other Brahman castes elsewhere who intensely valued cattle, but less often personally worked them, *Sanādhya Brāhman* cultivators themselves proudly plowed with castrated male bulls purchased from *Panjāb*. They might have, but did not assert their being themselves descended from the area's first-ever Vedic bovine cultivators. Having been fixed around Aligarh for centuries, they had less need to have an origin story or to keep track of their exact genealogies than did some of the more mobile, equine-inclined *Jāt Thākurs,* who nevertheless also plowed with bullocks. Only four or five of the forty-three local *Sanādhya* families practiced the priesthood and did not plow.

One rarely saw cows of the same species as bullocks since more and far richer milk came from water buffalo cows, the main source of highly valued ghee. I met one *Sanādhya* priest who kept unplowed land as a retirement home for old bovines of all species.

Mainly *Sanādhyas'* homes and barns lined the favored southern edge of the dwelling area, which included Paḍīl's single large paved and walled eastern well from which drinking water was mostly carried by family women and partly by men of the specialized water-carrying caste.

Grudgingly, the *Sanādhyas* had accepted the recently arriving *Jāt Thākur* families as landlords under the conquering British, each controlling its shares of the fields and dwelling area of Paḍīl, although all but one of those families had moved their own residences to towns or cities where their numbers were greater by 1951.

The southern of two polluting *Bhangī* Sweeper caste houses of Paḍīl was dug an extra three feet deep at the south street's west end to make its presence tolerable to a new, directly adjacent *Sanādhyas* house, possibly because their older surface position had been vertically convenient for quickly serving some earlier ruler's mansion that stood directly above.

Respected elder males among the *Sanādhyas* and a few others gathered in 1951 as an informal *panchayat* ("council of five") to hear me state my aim of residing for a year in Paḍīl to learn about India's rural life in order to describe it for my college students in America. They approved my announced intention of meeting every local family and drawing their genealogy, but cautioned me (seen as a former soldier and lusty meat-eater, or a secret missionary who might in a famine steal starving children to feed, convert, and adopt) never to enter any house where females and children were but no man was present to approve.

As I sketched a map of the houses (see figure 7.1 below), I was usually offered information on the occupants by passers-by or neighbors, if not by the residents themselves, showing that almost every adult male recognized by name almost every other adult of the village. Wives of cultivators gestured as if hiding their faces from all equal or superior adult males and avoided appearing in public alone. Unmarried young women did not hide their faces from me if they categorized me, as most did, as one of their unmarriageable village brothers.

Males conventionally slept in a group near the door of most houses, females in a group toward the back, but the presence of more than two sexually adult couples in most houses seemed to keep the possibility of incest alive, as suggested by occasional curses during quarrels and by the everyday vulgar Hindi term for any unnamed man—*bahenchoḍ* ("sister fucker"). I heard one household of five mobile *Jāṭav* adult couples disapproved by others as wife-swapping, and heard one absent older brother's wife's scream to protest a nighttime approach by her husband's younger brother—a kind of occurrence that seems likely, although usually dismissed as a joke. A senior female seemed to manage times and places for the intercourse of juniors in higher-ranking houses.

My partial overriding of any undesirable roles was to offer in my later village abode a weekly clinic to which mothers might bring their children for treatment of simple injuries from my own first-aid kit. This gave me intrafamily-like roles to play and enlarged my acquaintance with local domestic manners, while my effective applications of DDT to hated bedbug infestations of cot frames ultimately got me invited by males into more houses.

Interactions of Worship (*puja*)

Apart from the collective Vaishnava victory celebration at Krishna's *Holi,* some Hindus of Parhil in 1951 domestically celebrated twelve other heavenly mandated anniversaries—two others by Krishna, three by Ganga's sisters Durgā and Lakṣmī, and one by Śiva, plus six by regional or local deities (Marriott 1955, 192–215). Families celebrated such divine acts by fasting, offering and eating special foods, modeling figures or painting designs on walls or floors. Each year one or two men also walked forty miles each way to fetch Ganga water for their local Shiva shrines, and in rare years a few male pilgrims traveled four hundred miles to worship Durgā at her fiery pit at Nagarkot in the Kangra district of Panjab.

While acknowledging some of the above widely celebrated and largely space- (heaven-) constituted major gods (*devas*), one or more members of probably all Parhil Hindu families daily worshiped "small gods" (*devatas*) which were the family's, a wife's, or another member's choice. They did so by "giving *back*" divinely given water and/or food to the god, and then "marking" themselves by "taking *back*" the god's mark in his or her "leavings" (*jutha*), just as a wife might eat leavings from her husband's plate to show her devotion to him. These worshiping interactions to elevate the god or husband are reversals of the usually lowering, "marking" formula for working or feeding among humans that is described below.

Parhil's small gods themselves—190 of them were named in a partial local survey—were rarely shared between unrelated families, since the names of most were brought to Parhil by different brides from as many different places, or by men from their personal travels. They were usually represented by small, inconspicuous tokens in a niche of some interior wall of the house, close to the hearth. They were often represented and worshipped also at dedicated spots in the fields of those families who had a bit of land.

Muslims were not seen to pray publicly in the village but did so daily in their homes. Muslim men walked three miles on

Fridays to pray at a small regional mosque established by a past Shiite landlord.

Only four of Parhil's forty *Sanādhya* Brahman men had been tutored by their seniors to work as professional priests. They provided astral dates of births and deaths, performed weddings and more elaborate Sanskrit versions of any other, optional ritual, the most popular being a reading about the piety of a Vaisnava figure, *Satya Narayan*. The *Sanādhya* priests served all other high castes excepting the blacksmiths, who considered themselves equal in rank to *Sanādhyas* and had traveling priests of their own caste. Men of the low *Jatav* and *Bhangi* castes improvised such actions for their groups, sometimes co-opting an untrained *Sanādhya* to help them approximate the higher castes' ritual forms.

Any person could directly approach a major Hindu deity for help in or rescue from a negative variant of the table's columns [G] and [H], for general shelter as a continuing devotee (row 3), for getting a specific earthly reward (row 2), or for heavenly abode in the afterlife (row 1). These degrees of prayer are described by Susan Wadley (1975, ch. 6) from her observations in Karimpur, a Brahman-dominated village seventy miles to the southeast, degrees that are like those made in Parhil.

Beyond all materiality might be a Hindu's desired (but in Sāṃkhya terms impossible) exit from life into the table's column [G] row 0, which would "release" one from rebirth anywhere in the material universe. I never met such an explicit aspirant but did meet two *Sanādhyas* of Parhil who meditated in the early morning facing north across the fields toward what they firmly described in Hindi as "nothing," perhaps referring to the *Kārikā*'s nonmaterial category *Puruṣa* (table row 0).

The *Gītā*'s Three-Dimensionality

During my 1951–1952 observations in Paḍīl I had heard a sermon by a visiting male Sāṃkhya preacher on warriors' motivations in the intertribal war described in the *Bhagavad Gītā*, the sixth book in the *Mahābhārāta*. About forty listeners seemed especially to appreciate hearing there about the divine Lord Kṛṣṇa's revelations to *Arjun*—the names and variable quantities of each of the three most significant qualities in each warrior and relationship (*triguṇas*)—the Sanskrit words *sattva, rajas,* and *tamas,* translated to "goodness," "passion," and "darkness."

To abbreviate these three famous words in the revolving vertical middle of my Revised *Sāṃkhya* table rows 2, 3, and 4, I use the bold italic capital letters ***S***, ***R***, and ***T***. Villagers repeated those words emphatically as they continued discussing them. I did not myself further consider the novelty and reality of this declaration of psychosocial three-dimensionality until 1979 when I had in hand the second edition of Larson's book *Classical Sāṃkhya.*

The Gangā Devi Cult

Most surprising for me about Paḍīl was finding that while every Hindu house that I knew had placed a small token of its unique family god in a niche near its hearth and also in its garden or in one of its fields, and that three families had built larger outdoor shrines primarily for their own devotions to *Viṣṇu* or *Siva,* the village as a whole had no human-sized *Gangā Devi* temple. This was so, although all the Hindus I met strongly agreed that Paḍīl and other villages for hundreds of miles upstream and down owed worship to the goddess *Gangā Devi* who summoned local men in their dreams.

Villagers sometimes used the Devi's name instead of the more usual "Rām Rām!" as part of their mutual greetings, and separately offered personal prayers to her at a raised, smooth "pilgrim stone" in the field they said was owned by her below the southwest end of the village mound. (An offering there is pictured in Marriott 1955 opposite page 217 in which a *Sanādhya* man prays for the goddess to move his caste to accept as its member the woman of uncertain caste to whom he has recently been married.)

A household of just four wifeless *Jāt* men known as the "Singers"(of *Gangā Devi's* hymns at *Holi*) managed that field for her, especially at the local fair celebrating completion by Paḍīl's women and children of their annual collective wagon pilgrimage to the flowing river's edge about thirty miles to the northeast.

During the days and nights of the pilgrims' absence elder home-bodies slept outdoors in the goddess's field, trusting her to protect them all, as well as to continue replenishing their land with the water she brought them underground from the melted snows of the visible Himalayan peaks over 150 miles away.

Paired brass vessels of Gangāji's flowing water were also brought on Siva's birth and wedding days yearly on foot in yokes by men of two cultivator castes in order to bathe the *lingams* enshrined near their respective homes in the village.

When in some years men felt summoned in their dreams by *Gangā Devi,* groups of men from Paḍīl and nearby villages were said to have traveled over five hundred miles to Nagarkot in the Panjab Himalayas to worship where she was said to live in a cave, responding to worship by emitting fire and smoke. Although I had pledged by sipping curds with the other pilgrims from a brass tray to accompany them on this pilgrimage, its astral date proved incompatible with my 1979 University of Chicago calendar.

Food and Caste Ranking

Village-wide outdoor feasts began soon after the spring harvest, most of them celebrating weddings, in which my Jeep's job became the leading of a parade of the Parhil groom with his kin and loud Muslim band into his bride's village, then bringing the wedded couple home together quietly.

At the twelve wedding-connected feasts feeding two hundred or more males during my first fourteen months in Parhil I recorded twelve almost identical, twenty-four caste-ranked orders of the eaters' silent self-seatings. Cooks were women of the host's caste (who were all also fed), servers were male teams rank-matched to each of eight ranked groups of feasters, absent wives and children were often carried food, and Sweepers collected the used banana leaf plates and broken clay cups used in the feast which might bear remainders of food for their swine or themselves.

Calls to such feastings of the whole community were issued *viva voce* and excuses had to be offered for a man's failing to show up if he did not want publicly to insult the host (Marriott 1966).

The few and uniform foods customarily offered at these large feasts were also matched—whole-grain, stone ground, ghee-assisted, wok-baked wheat or barley flatbread (*roti*) served with yogurt and water. Superior feasts might also or alternatively include a potato curry. Such meals might be criticized when the grain was inferior to these, or when the cooking fat was of cheaper, vegetable origin rather than the prized bovine ghee. Yogurt was liked but not thought unusual, given the village's many cows, the rich plenitude of their milk, the warm climate, and the lack of refrigeration; milk's usual alternative product was ghee, sold to urban markets.

A caste group whose members were forgotten or thought they might be seated too low—at what the table's column [H] 4a calls an "unmatching" rank—in a feast might fail to attend, but the host's effort, especially at wedding feasts, which were very public events, was always to assure every caste and families' harmonious attendance. Often criticized as extravagant by economists and often leading to debt, such large feasts and often continuing interest-free mutual debts are what villagers see as constituting the column [G] row 2a goal of community "coherence" (*dharma*), made up of what the table's column [H] row 4b calls "matching" interactions. Feasts are thus felt by many people to be of great goodness.

These complex but usually smooth and wordless rankings by castes resemble behaviors that some nonhuman species do by scent, color, sound, or gesture and what some animal behaviorists call "marking." I borrowed that term in 1990 for what also goes on silently in Hindu intercaste feeding and working (Marriott 1976). One takes an invisible but noted and remembered "mark" signifying one's and one's whole caste being of equal or lower rank by accepting water, food cooked by, or work done for someone of another caste. One gives an invisible "mark"—a sign of one's own equal or higher caste rank—by giving water or food to, or getting work done by someone of a lower caste (Marriott 1968). One thinks before entering into any such possibly marking action and remembers it once taken, since it is likely also to define one's own caste's particular *dharma*—its vertical relations to all other castes.

Note the reverse "giving back" of the most desirable food and work in the worship of deities (who are space-constituted) as described just above under "Interactions of Worship."

Such marked (ranked) relations are not immutable. The most prosperous Parhil caste group, now known as "*Baghele Thakurs,*" some of whom were remembered by elders of 1951 as having been landless goatherds, rose in wealth by purchasing a piece of Parhil land served by a small private pipe-irrigation project. This plus their industry enriched them. Their present name implies identity with the *Vaghelya Rajputs*, a famous medieval aristocracy of distant Gujarat—a claim that no one today could prove or disprove, but that seemed to be supported by their bringing in a *Sanādhya* priest from another village to make marriages with rising groups elsewhere in U.P. who were making the same claim. *Bagheles* then may have used their economic power to persuade other castes just above them to yield a rank or two higher than the rank they previously held in Parhil feasting. This is an example of the common kind of Hindu upward mobility that anthropologist M. N. Srinivas called "sanskritization," that the table's column [H], row 4b calls "matching," and that its row 3a calls "merging." One sees such tendencies also in the similar Kshatriya-like "*Thakur*" titles held in reserve for possible future wealth by many western U.P. castes—titles which I have usually omitted here, identifying each other's castes simply as villagers do, by their occupational names.

Avoiding downward mobility is also a constant concern of highly ranked groups. Even the reputation of a high local caste group like Parhil's dominant *Sanādhya* Brahmans might fall by allowing one of its male members to take as a bride a woman whose parentage is not provably Brahman, violating his caste's rule of endogamy. The man pictured by Marriott (1955, opp. p. 216) is thus in danger of being "outcasted"—an example of what the table's column [H], row 4a calls "unmatching."

Unwittingly, I myself became a threat to the high rank of *Sanādhya*s everywhere by attempting in 1951 to employ their lordly barber-messenger to wash my aluminum plates, which would have raised me but lowered the *Sanādhyas* to my alien, previously beef-eating rank; they were alarmed, and to maintain peace I withdrew my offer as described in the next section. But by 1985, I had demonstrated in Parhil so many years of vegetarian eating that I was invited by a conservative *Sanādhya* family to eat dinner at their domestic hearth—that is, if I didn't mind washing their brass plate myself!

A House for the Anthropologist?

For my initial year's use on the less-favored north side of the dwelling area with my cook and language helper I was offered a one-room, windowless mudbrick "bridegroom house" with a foreyard bounded by the usual seven-foot mud wall. Its rupee rent, equivalent then to US$1.50 per month, seemed a princely fortune to its barber owner who had recently had the house built for the usual three-day sheltering of his daughter's husband during their wedding rituals in Paḍīl.

Living in it for a year would give me an experience of village housekeeping with attendant services by relevant castes such as repairing mud walls by the potter caste of builders and door lock by the blacksmith. There would be the making of cowdung cakes for a year's cooking, the daily sweeping of the house and "cleaning" of its cooking area (sprinkling with a fragrant solution of cowdung ash by its owner's brother's wife), preparing coals for hookah smokers, making reed screens from the hottest season's sun by the hunter living in the nearby patch of forest, painting of the exterior with white lime for many holidays, and listening to children singing songs at houses, door to door, to welcome the tiny flowerings of the many different field crops.

Living there would also give me a dozen neighbors of both Muslim and Hindu families, all sharing one large well for our drinking water, slightly muddy because it had not yet been given baked brick rim walls. I could have its water boiled by my cook and pleasantly cooled by ensievement and evaporation through a large clay pot thoughtfully left unglazed by our potter.

I had not long to feel pleased with this prospect, for my wish to reside at all in Paḍīl was on the next day fiercely opposed by the spokesman for a faction within the *Sanādhya* caste who were said to have maintained for centuries a purely vegetarian diet here and in many other chicken-less villages around Aligarh city where people of his caste were dominant. The spokesman predicted that I with my urban, egg-eating *Panjābi Brāhman* Hindī language helper and my cook (self-described as "casteless" [= a prostitute's son?]) would soon be throwing chicken bones and eggshells on the pile of household trash that must be spread on the village fields as fertilizer before the next plowing. Such trash would pollute the soil from which most residents of Paḍīl were attempting to extract a pure diet, so I and my gang must not be permitted to stay either in this house or anywhere else on the village land!

Even worse, the angry *Sanādhya* spokesman had heard that I was tempting with urban cash to put on my staff *Bābu Lāl*, the talkative Barber Lord (*Nāi Thākur*) whose proper duty was the carrying of marriage-related messages among *Sanādhya* and other high-caste families here and in dozens of other villages.

I could see that their ranks were at stake for all parties in this dispute, but later recalled from the *Bhagavad Gītā* war episode in the *Mahābhāratā* epic how each party might have seen his position in the lecture in Paḍīl by the visiting preacher's examples from the as differently distinguishing Lord Kṛṣṇa's 3 qualitative rank "strands" (*guṇas*)—words recalling for me also the twisting threads of Paḍīl's textile-making past.

I had looked on *Bābu Lāl* as what anthropologists used to call "a prize informant" on local wedding customs, but given my own initially dubious rank, his working for me threatened not only to lower him and his caste out of their honorific **S** jobs locally, but also to impair the high rankings of the *Sanādhya* and other high castes for whom he and others of his barber caste elsewhere always carried marriage messages.

The doomed (about to have his landlordship income terminated) vegetarian *Jāt Thākur* Kishan Singh, landlord of my possible Paḍīl house who saw my Jeep as good for everyone's transportation, me as likely to join his faction, and was not yet ready to give up his last days of legal ("passionate" **R**) power to deny the angry *Sanādhya* faction's demand for my expulsion)—he had thought of two possible solutions for me: (1) that I promise a purely boneless, eggless diet for myself and crew, and (2) that I cancel my "dark" **T** private offer to hire the marriage messenger as an informant.

With these two suggestions from him I readily agreed along with each of the other parties in this affair who inwardly must have celebrated his own contribution to the many-valued village community's ranked "coherence" (*dharma*). For me—a new vegetarian—the house was now mine for the year!

Neighbors and Friends

At Partition in 1947 several mansions of Muslim nobility in the suburbs of Aligarh city were burned down while Muslims going to Pakistan by trains and throngs on foot had also been attacked by urban Hindus. Soldiers were stationed at the center of the city to keep the peace, and an angry crowd had gathered for two days near the Muslim University but dispersed without violence, while rural areas anywhere near or linked with Paḍīl had remained quiet. I was told that four landless Muslim laborers of Paḍīl had hiked five hundred miles to Karachi in Pakistan, hoping to get land, but finding only temporary refugee camps, hiked back to work in Paḍīl where they still had friendly Hindu employers.

Friendship between the 1 *Jāt* landlord with a harmonium and a Muslim cultivator pal with good voice, lovers of songs of both Hindu and Muslim varieties, had developed music together with a generation-long-term sharing of agricultural work in Paḍīl among their four or five families. Analogous small musical and dance groups developed among different castes of Hindu girls and women as did comparative festival wall paintings, but the fewer Muslim women and children had little similar to show (Marriott 1955b; Wadley 1975).

The mud-brick houses whose walls and external shadows are sketched on my 1952 map were only partly covered by roofs, most being largely open to the sky and thus also to the audibility of nighttime insults or alarms by aggrieved women or to local daytime news such as personal arrivals and departures carried by children playing on connecting roofs and wall-tops during the day.

A small group of *Sanādhya* men initially wanted to drive me physically out of the village, but were effectively advised not to try by the local land accountant—so some children informed me. Rooftops, especially in later afternoons, were regarded by women as special places for grooming their hair, not to be photographed. One Brahman man bragged to me of having nighttime access to another's wife by passage through loose dry mud bricks in their two families' common wall.

Food and Medicines

The simple food of all was flatbread of wheat or barley, in 1951 ground on household stone mills, baked on iron woks, served with legumes or small potatoes boiled on fires of weeds, wood scrap, and dried cowdung over baked clay floor hearths, usually by the presiding senior woman to each member of each house, working behind movable clay and plaster screens to control drafts. She also made ghee from buffalo milk for sale, its cool residue consumed by early morning workers in the fields. Meals for residents varied by personal tastes and by seasonal variations among the wind, bile, and phlegm (*vāta, pitta,* and *kapha*)—humors (*doṣas*) of the Indian "life sciences" (*āyurveda*)—plus salt, garlic, and a few other spices were needed to make foods and medicines suitable to the revolving seasons and unique personal tastes and times suitable to each adult cook and eater. A few families celebrated with many more spices, but collective family eating was rare, occurring only after the funerals of members, when red beans alone were consumed together.

Paḍīl's limited cost-free but landlord-controlled dwelling area held not only the larger homes of the *Sanādhya* and six other Hindu cultivating castes, but also a mixture (with no more than a few feet, if any, of separation) among eighteen other specialized, occupationally nicknamed, castes of blacksmiths with carpenters, *Jogi* ballad-singers, barbers, water-carriers, potters, brick-makers, cotton-carders, weavers, Muslim cultivators, oil-pressers, bangle-sellers and dancers, and Hindu washermen (figure 7.1) and women (next to a large northeastern pond) and the sweepers called "*Bhangis,*" one of whose two unrelated houses was beside a natural (later metal pipe-tapped) spring whose water was thought to cure sore eyes.

Miscellaneous agricultural labor was mostly supplied by semi-mobile landless male *Jātavs* at rates that bound a few of them endlessly to borrow for their subsistence from certain *Sanādhya* cultivator-lenders. Many of the borrowers were my evening visitors—descendants of reputedly former beef-eating leatherworkers called *Camārs,* now unemployed cotton seed-pickers, and others.

Bhangis—lowest of the low and expecting rejection—were the only caste group whose male members never ventured to join nightly after-supper gatherings for conversations, skits and songs in my house. It was they who every night used their hogs to consume the feces deposited next to the shoes routinely dropped outside their doors at night by women of the cultivator castes. Breads were baked by those women in the morning for *Bhangi* women to receive as pay in their clean baskets, sometimes with affectionate expressions between the two.

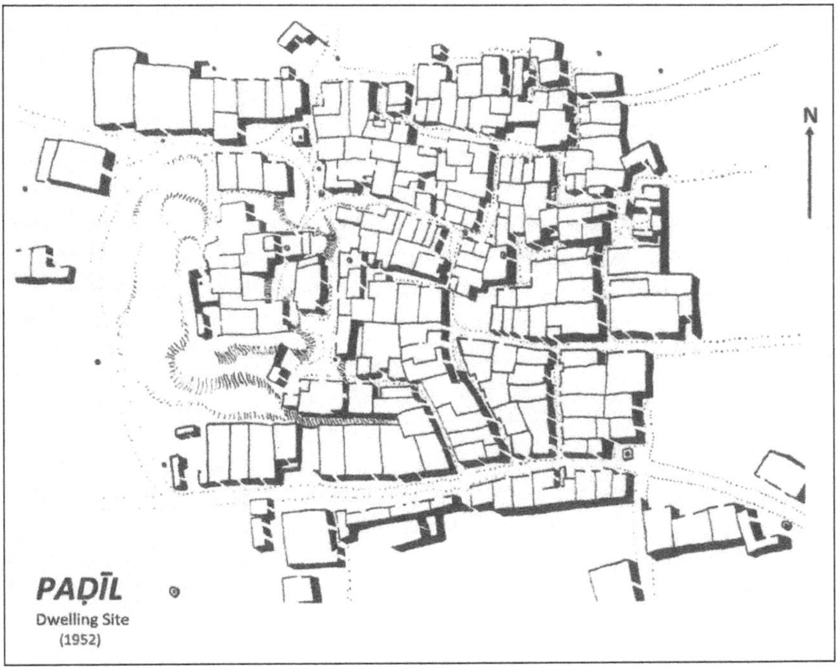

Figure 7.1. Map of Paḍīl. *Source*: Created by the author.

Changing Cross-Caste Relations

Cutting across the caste ranks displayed at feasts there had been many short-term (daily or weekly) contracts between tenants and their landless laborers of lower castes, such as *Jatavs*. Men of much lower castes or classes did not in the 1950s sit beside higher men, even on the ground; they squatted or stood, often at a distance. But by the 1970s, when land ownership had become firm, labor contracts often lengthened to a crop's whole growing season, with detailed advance understandings about inputs of labor by both, wage loans for the helper, and ultimate divisions of gains or losses. I then sometimes found men of such remote caste pairs sitting together in postures that by the table's column [H], row 3a one might call "merging."

The most frequent and lasting, one-way intercaste food transfers were those by upper-caste women who baked *roti* as payment and appreciation for their male Sweeper's early morning visits to pick up or to have his hog eat the garbage and feces left by them just outside their doorsteps, next to their shoes. (Upper-caste women did not go out at night for excretion as most lower-caste women did in groups.) High-caste women, whose pregnancies were more frequent than most of them wanted, could also be heard expressing affection for the Sweeper women who were their personal favorites as midwives. Many among the higher-caste women further judged a certain Sweeper's wife to be the most beautiful woman in the village. These gestures, too, one might call psychological "merging."

Being without effective contraceptives, pregnancy was the usual condition of most married women, leading to many birth-polluting events conducted in temporary shelters outside homes performed by *Bhangi* women as midwives. Regardless of issues of "untouchability" raised especially in the 1980s, I heard *Sanādhya* women say that they thought the most beautiful woman in Paḍīl was a long-haired, north side *Bhangin* who could sometimes be seen collecting bread as pay for her husband's filthy work in her best sari and presenting it with a full body prostration to his mother.

When one not-so-beautiful Sweeper woman and a neighboring poor Cotton-carder's daughter were groped by a young local who had ignored his respected Muslim family's cultivation work and learned insolent urban manners, a nonstatutory council of nearly two hundred village men spontaneously convened the next morning to sentence him to a disfiguring haircut, a backward donkey ride on which he suffered a bloody beating by the Sweeper woman with her shoes, and immediate exile from Parhil. His ancestral family members, shamed by their son's "unmatching" conduct, were not otherwise punished.

Postures were changing also between one ambitious Sweeper and some of his upper-caste employers in Parhil as he found employment for terms of several months in Kolkata each year on a large sewer project that paid enough cash wages to cover his rail fare and more. Parhil admirers of his enterprise sat on mounds of earth in Parhil while he stood and lectured about his hope to move with his wife and child to urban Bengal permanently. There he would not be classed as a "*Bhangi*" and might sit beside anyone who was his economic equal. The extension of sewage systems throughout Bharata is still far from realization, so the evaluation of persons as categories apart from their "untouchable" castes remains a critical issue for many Dalits. (Compare with the *Sanādhya* man above who dreaded being thrust into such a personal, casteless category thirty years earlier.)

Joining a Family

On my second long visit to Paḍīl beginning in 1969, when I had no Jeep, cook, or language helper, I was invited by the newly elected village chairman, a *Jat* cultivator named Rajendra Singh whom I addressed as "*cācā*" (my father's younger brother), to become a regular resident of his men's parlor, sleeping and eating there for my six shorter stays until 1985. His election had been due to his spectacular local success with a vastly improved government-purchased wheat seed, imitated the next year by almost every cultivator in Paḍīl and exemplifying the work of Albert Meyer's governmental administrative but also participating rural functionary elsewhere called the "Village Level Worker."

For one hundred rupees, Rajendra Singh sold me a water buffalo cow to be kept in an adjacent stall while the rest of his family—wife, three sons, two grandsons, one son's wife, and a granddaughter—grew up around me, nourished or funded partly by the cow's rich milk, yogurt, and ghee, slowly cooked by the fire of her dried dung. On my departure from his parlor he refunded me the one hundred rupees originally paid.

On my final departure from India, one of his sons asked me for a "loan" of three thousand rupees to help him purchase an adjacent field, which I gratefully did.

Rural Sciences and Worldview

When new chemicals first began appearing for agricultural use, I heard two Paḍīl cultivators discussing the nature of an artificial fertilizer of purplish color offered in a sample sack. "It must be made somehow by mixing earth with air and fire," one of them said, using words that I learned from constant weather talk were to be joined with water and sky as five "gross elements" (*mahābhūtās*) in the table's column [E]. Those element and weather words were also occasionally used to describe both human and other animal types, manners, or emotions.

Paḍīl's people had no doubt that "sky" or space (*akas*) was the highest source from whose clouds of elemental water was known to fall as rain, that the sun's fire could dry up water, that water on earth could extinguish fire, and that earth, the bottom element, could be flooded for days by water, if south winds blew strongly and thunderously enough during the monsoon. Villagers and especially cultivators often spoke of how continually and variously those five "gross elements" mixed with each other. To suggest other weather mixtures and dilutions I left blank spaces in the tentative table between the vertically listed elements. No thermometers were used or numeric temperatures were discussed.

*Im*precision appeared to be a pervasive quality of Indic understandings of nature and flexibility was a guarantee of their truth and utility (Zimmermann 1987).

When vendors of Hindu medicines visited Paḍīl in 1988 they assured me that villagers were already familiar with the "three humors" (*tridoṣa*) called "phlegm, bile, and wind," ranked terms whose bodily processes and relative temperatures were respectively homologous with those of the elements water, fire, and air, and with their local sensations respectively in the body's head and neck, stomach and bowel. Villagers used those terms routinely when they explained ailments such as headache (too hot, from too much bile), stomach ache (too cold, from too much phlegm), or constipation (from too little wind). Sanskritist colleagues of course sent me to the Indic learned books of "life science" (*āyurveda*), such as *Caraka Saṃhitā*, whose analyses are often multidimensional and more imprecise than those of Sāṃkhya: quantities of medicines or their components are never specified.

When the goals of education to be stated for students entering Paḍīl's first school building of 1969 were argued among members of its intercaste building committee—goals to be inscribed on the school's roof—some adult cultivators spoke for his personal "advantage" (*artha*), others for the larger group's "coherence" as in Manu's term "*dharma*." Apparently to avoid a divisive answer, the committee turned to the *Bhagavad Gītā* for a vaguer term on which all members could agree—"*sattva*" (goodness)—the word that also appears in row 2a at the top of the analytic table's column [A].

Holi Transformed

By March of 1970, an enterprising *Sanādhya* had imported an electric flour mill and attached its plastic-roofed building to a five-foot baked brick wall surrounding a field of half an acre on the edge of the Parhil dwelling area. His wall attracted an audience of about two hundred, including women from other villages, to sit on it and watch the formal game called "*Holi*" that his mill was sponsoring and that would be played there. Two teams had been selected—one a defending team of ten bare-headed young wives of Parhil carrying six foot sticks and surrounding a thirty-five-pound cake of village-made brown sugar (*gur*), the other attacking team a larger circle of ten hungry but weaponless young husbands.

The game began with the outer ring of husbands circling and looking for gaps in the wives' defenses through which to dart and seize the *gur* without themselves getting beaten. But there were no gaps, and every man who dared to approach felt one or more sticks on his back. Carrying the round and heavy cake was also not easy, so the first man who got hold of it immediately dropped and broke it. The pieces were grabbed in a general tussle during which one strong older wifely spectator jumped off the wall into the game space and continued to beat every man briefly within reach of her swirling stick.

Far from the community-wide participation in the riotous Parhil *Holi*s of the 1950s, its persistence only as a spectator sport focused on husbands and wives in the prosperous years following 1971 suggests that the need for playful disorder was felt only by those whose domestic lives continued in their earlier, more disciplined ways, although the needs of their later lives beyond the community may be different and greater.

Conclusion

Observed intimately in 1951–1952, Parhil's flexible, naturally ordered, Sāṃkhya-like categories with their *Holi*-qualified reversals made caste multiplicity and rank concerns, Hindu–Muslim differences and untouchability—foreign-defined social disunities typically found in mid-twentieth-century Hindu-dominated villages—look less formidable than they did at the beginning of this research. But class disparity, caste conflicts, and Hindu–Muslim differences seemed likely to persist or grow as they moved from their cohesive small community into Bharata's wider national society in the twenty-first century.

The Green Revolution and the villagers' own efforts from 1965 to 1985 quadrupled Parhil's wealth by scientific research on seeds and additives, bureaucratic reorganization, multiplying its water supply by electrical pump irrigation and more—its access to electric light and communications plus a paved road to outside jobs. Most of its cultivators joined to form a single Parhil corporation using tractors, the latest agricultural machinery, and no bullocks. Its families reacted by developing a passion for education that took the form of five elementary schools, a growing middle school, and applications to college. Commerce grew, cooking switched to petroleum, and what in 1951 had been a remote village began in 2004 to look like the struggling outpost of a new and uncertain world community.

Acknowledgments

I thank the scholars of Sanskrit who directed my field work to Sāṃkhya, namely, Margaret Trawick, J. A. B. van Buitenen, Gerald James Larson, and Alfred Collins.

References

Benedict, Ruth Fulton. 1934. *Patterns of Culture*. New York: Houghton Mifflin Company.

Buitenen, J. A. N. van. 1956–1959. "Studies in Sāṃkhya I, II, II and Akṣara." *Journal of the American Oriental Society* 76: 153–157; 77: 15–25; 79: 76–87, 188–207.

Daniel, E. Valentine. 1984. *Fluid Signs: Being a Person the Tamil Way*. Berkeley: University of California Press.

Daniel, Sheryl B. 1983. "The Tool-Box Approach of the Tamil to the Issues of Moral Responsibility and Human Destiny," in Charles F. Keyes and E. Valentine Daniel, eds. *Karma: An Anthropological Inquiry*, 27–62. Berkeley: University of California Press.

Davis, Marvin Gene. 1976. "The Politics of Family Life in Rural West Bengal." *Ethnology* 15: 189–200.

Davis, Marvin Gene. 1971. *Rank and Rivalry: The Politics of Inequality in Rural West Bengal*. Cambridge: Cambridge University Press.

Dumont, Louis. 1980. *Homo Hierarchicus*. Chicago: University of Chicago Press.

Hulin, Michel. 1978. *Le Principe de l'Ego Dans la Pensee Indienne Classique; la Notion d'Ahamkara*. Paris: College de France Institut de Civilisation Indienne. Seri In-8e, Fascicule 44.

Lamb, Sarah. 2000. *White Sarees and Sweet Mangoes; Aging, Gender, and Body in North India*. Berkeley, Los Angeles, & London: University of California Press.

Larson, Gerald James. 1969. *Classical Sāṃkhya*. Delhi: Motilal Banarsidass.

Larson, Gerald James, and Ram Shankar Bhattacharya, Editors. 1987. *Sāṃkhya, a Dualist Tradition in Indian Philosophy*. Princeton, NJ: Princeton University Press.

Marriott, McKim. 1960. *Caste Ranking and Community Structure in Five Regions of India and Pakistan*. Poona: Deccan College Postgraduate and Research Institute.

Marriott, McKim. 1955. "Little Communities in an Indigenous Civilization," in ed. McKim Marriott, *Village India*, 171–222. Chicago: University of Chicago Press.

Marriott, McKim. 1966. "The Feast of Love," in ed. Milton B. Singer, *Krishna: Myths, Rites, and Attitudes*, 200–212, 229–231. Honolulu: East-West Press. Also available in ed. Diane P. Mines and Sarah Lamb, 2002, *Everyday Life in South Asia*, 249–260. Bloomington: Indiana University Press.

Marriott, McKim. 1990. *India through Hindu Categories*. New Delhi: Sage Publications. Also available in *Contributions to Indian Studies* 23(1), 1987.

Mayer, Albert, with the assistance of McKim Marriott and Richard L. Park. 1958. Pilot Project *India: The Story of Rural Development at Etawah, Uttar Pradesh*. Berkeley & Los Angeles: University of California Press.

Mines, Diane Paull. 1990. "Hindu Periods of Death 'Impurity,'" in ed. McKim Marriott. *India through Hindu Categories*, 103–130. New Delhi: Sage Publications.

Mines, Diane Paull. 2005. *Fierce Gods*. Bloomington: University of Indiana Press.

Nevill H. R. 1926. *Aligarh: A Gazetteer*. Lucknow: Government Branch Press.
Raheja, Gloria Goodwin. 1988. *The Poison in the Gift; Ritual, Prestation, and the Dominant Caste in a North Indian Village*. Chicago: University of Chicago Press.
Smith, Brian K. 1994. *Classifying the Universe: The Ancient Indian Varna System and the Origin of Caste*. New York: Oxford University Press.
Srinivas, M. N. 1998. *Village, Caste, Gender and Method*. Delhi: Oxford University Press.
Trawick, Margaret. 2017. *Death, Beauty, Struggle: Untouchable Women Create the World*. Foreword by Ann Grodzins Gold. Philadelphia: University of Pennsylvania Press.
Wadley, Susan Snow. 1975. *Shakti: Power in the Conceptual Structure of Karimpur Religion*. Chicago: University of Chicago, Department of Anthropology.
Zimmermann, Francis B. 1987. *The Jungle and the Aroma of Meats*. Berkeley: University of California Press.

Chapter 8

Sāṃkhya / Yoga as Culture and Release

ALFRED COLLINS[1]

Introduction

The ultimate aim of the school of inquiry called Sāṃkhya and the meditative practices named Yoga is to liberate the self, which is posited as pure, objectless consciousness, with freedom from the suffering (*duḥkha*) that forms the basic or "default" state of existence in the world. Sāṃkhya proceeds by analyzing natural (principally human) existence, finding at the root of life an implicit urge to satisfy desires, which it understands to mean bringing them to a close. It aims to show that quenching of desire (*bhukti*) is similar, or even equivalent, to releasing consciousness from its apparent imprisonment in material experience (*mokṣa, kaivalya*). This connection of *bhukti* and *mokṣa* anticipates a similar unity central to Tantric philosophy that developed centuries later. Yoga lays out a moral-ascetic and meditative practice that it claims will move the human mind–body entity in the direction of a less fragmented, ignorant, overly active, and unfree state (all aspects of *duḥkha*). This practice allows one to follow and realize the argument of Sāṃkhya's ontological analysis (*jñāna*).

Religion, for Yoga, is meditation in service of a salvific insight or gnosis. Culture, which cannot be separated from religion, properly enacts and celebrates this insight (Collins 2006). While commentators on Sāṃkhya / Yoga[2] from Buddhist and other Hindu perspectives (Vedānta, etc.), as well as many Western interpreters, view it as ascetic and life-denying, a more worldly, life-affirming view of Yoga[3] has begun to appear in recent years (Chapple 2003; Whicher 1998, 2003). Lloyd Pfleuger, who is partially aligned with this trend, sees Yoga and Sāṃkhya as walking the razor's edge between a desired release (final insight into the radical difference between Puruṣa and Prakṛti, i.e., *jñāna*) and an unfulfilled reality. One perpetually approaches the goal of liberation yet remains unable to fully reach it. The never-quite-achieved *jñāna* or *mokṣa* is often glorified by the meditative practice of Yoga. "The real work is the work of treading the path to liberation. In an unexpected sense, the path can be seen as a goal in itself" (Pfleuger 2003, 79).

The basic texts of both Sāṃkhya[4] and Yoga[5] are difficult, terse, and elliptical; they have been construed in many incompatible ways. Furthermore, their traditions of teacher–disciple transmission (*paramparā*) seem to have died out centuries ago.[6] Even so, there is general agreement that both schools are of fundamental importance to contemporary Indian culture and thought. Yoga is intimately connected to the origins and early history of Buddhism, and later contributed to the pan-Asian Tantric techniques of manipulating psychobiological energy in search of enlightenment and immortality. Perhaps most of later Hinduism and Buddhism is to some degree Tantric. Sāṃkhya's legacy may be even more widespread, as its categories (for example the *guṇas* or "qualities" of *sattva* [satisfaction], *rajas* [desire], and *tamas* [frustration]) have been identified among the basic principles in many Indian sciences, social arrangements, medicine, art, music, cooking, family kinship structure, and more (Marriott 1989).

The World of the Self

I will begin by describing the person and his world as understood by Sāṃkhya / Yoga, emphasizing that the word "his" is not intended to name persons in general. This is a gendered philosophy concerned primarily with the male self. This male self, however, is caught in an ineluctable relationship with the female environment. We will then apply this understanding of man's nature to a few religious and cultural examples. As Gerald Larson (1968) accurately describes it, Sāṃkhya is an "eccentric dualism," in which one of the two fundamental principles, Prakṛti, represents almost everything and the other, Puruṣa, almost nothing. Prakṛti is psychomaterial substance of which body and mind both consist, differing only in subtlety or degree of density. Everything "from Brahma to a blade of grass" (SK 54) consists of Prakṛti, which is always implicitly personified as female. Puruṣa, literally a male person, is in Sāṃkhya the name of bare awareness, pure consciousness free from intentionality (in the sense of being about something, specifically, Prakṛti).[7] This is a fundamental fact for Sāmkhya/Yoga that explains its "eccentricity": Prakṛti is "about" Puruṣa (this is what *puruṣārtha* means), but Puruṣa is not about Prakṛti.[8] In her higher or earlier, undifferentiated state, Prakṛti is called *avyakta, mūlaprakṛti,* and *pradhāna.*[9] She evolves through a process called *pravṛtti* (development) or *pariṇāma* (devolution), falling into successively lower states of being in an emanational [d]evolutionary course in which the effect is always implicit in its earlier states or cause (*satkārya*). This is essentially the same process in Buddhism called "conditioned origination" (*pratītyasamutpada*). This process also underlies the devolution of the world process in the later Hindu imagination of a succession of "ages" (*yugas*) from the perfect past (*Kṛta,* the Golden Age) to the demonic present (*Kali yuga*). On the other hand, Prakṛti is inherently teleological, acting for the sake of Puruṣa (*puruṣārtha = Puruṣa + artha*). I emphasize the word "act" (Sanskrit root *kṛ*), for Prakṛti is impelled only by what Aristotle would understand as material, formal, and final causes, and is never subject to efficient or purely mechanical causation. Whatever happens in the world is always an *act,* never mindless reaction, despite the fact that action in the present is already infused by what we could call character, the sediment or residue of past acts (*karma, vāsana, saṃskāra,* etc.) that partially or mainly motivates new action.

As noted above, there are two sides of *puruṣārtha,* the action of Prakṛti for Puruṣa's sake. First, there is the wish or impulsion to give Puruṣa enjoyment, understood by Freud as the cessation of a desire. Second, there is the aim of liberating Puruṣa from bondage in the threefold suffering (*duḥkhatraya,* SK 1) of the human condition. The *Sāṃkhya Kārika* claims that these two, apparently quite different, aims are intrinsically similar or even identical.

> As (in) the world (a man) engages in actions
> for the sake of the cessation of a desire;

so also does the Prakṛti function
for the sake of the release of the Puruṣa.
(*Sāṃkhya Kārikā* 58, G. Larson's translation, 1968, 273)[10]

Suffering, the distance from happiness named by the word "desire" (*audsukya,* from *ud* + *suka,* literally "away from pleasure"), is found by both Sāṃkhya and Yoga to arise from a certain kind of selfhood, called *ahaṃkāra* in Sāṃkhya and *asmitā* in Yoga. This sort of self asserts itself (*ahaṁkāra*) and its "I am-ness" (*asmitā*) in a way that can and often does lead in the direction of the demonic. One of the clearest classical examples of this is the career of the demon Rāvaṇa in epic texts. Grandson of the god Brahmā, Rāvaṇa refuses to accept his place in the proper order (*dharma*) of the world and inflates his ego (*ahaṁkāra*) through ascetic practices, aiming to become lord of the whole cosmos. This leads him to cause maximum suffering to himself and others. Suffering and the cravings of egoity can be overcome through insight (*buddhi, prajñā*) that realizes the fundamental difference between our unrolling karmic process (*pariṇāma, pravṛtti*). One comes to understand the principal role of pure consciousness (Puruṣa) as it witnesses Prakṛti's evolution. Suffering is thus correlated with ignorance, and true insight comes with release from ego. We can put together these two sides of life, ignorance of Prakṛti's true nature and awareness of it, in diagrammatic form.

In figure 8.1, moments of life come into being successively, as earlier actions provide a strong basis or predisposition for later

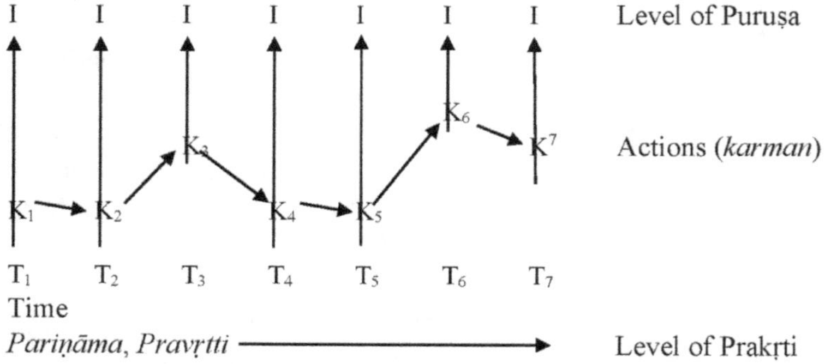

Figure 8.1. Diagram of the Relationship between Puruṣa and Prakṛti. I = Moment of Conscious Awareness; K: Karmic Transaction; T: Event in Time. *Source*: Created by the author.

ones that, however, each still constitute somewhat new and free moments of agency. The freedom in the system arises from the fact that, at each moment, constant or repeated reference is made to Puruṣa which serves as an underlying aim (*artha*) for the action that would otherwise be completely determined by the *pariṇāma* process of unfolding from within Prakṛti's nature (*satkārya*). The height of each action ($K_{n)}$ in the diagram corresponds to its degree of conscious orientation toward its Puruṣa, which is equivalent to its degree of understanding of its inherent *puruṣārtha*-hood.[11]

The insight that Puruṣa is referenced at every instant, at least implicitly, corresponds at the level of devotional religion (*bhakti*) to the *rāsa-līlā* (love play) between Lord Kṛṣṇa and the cowgirls (*gopīs*) at Vṛndāvan, shown in figure 8.2.

Figure 8.2. Love Play (Rasa-Līlā) between Krishna and the Gopīs. *Source*: Courtesy of Graham Schweig.

The story from the *Bhāgavata Purāṇa* tells that each of the young women has her own Kṛṣṇa, who is fully with and attentive to her, and who is the focus of her entire attention. Understanding Kṛṣṇa as the equivalent of Puruṣa, each Gopī is consciously oriented toward Puruṣa in the form of Kṛṣṇa, her main purpose (*puruṣārtha*). Life in the mythical world of Kṛṣṇa-līlā ("Kṛṣṇa play") imagines a culture in which human life is devoted to its innate goal of giving pleasure and enlightenment to the self which is Consciousness.

Yogic practice has two aspects: meditation and insight. These correspond to the two aims of Prakṛti. Meditation (*dhyāna*) moves the person closer to the undifferentiated (*avyakta*)[12] state of Prakṛti. In the above diagram, this process within the emanational structure moves one higher. Insight (*buddhi, jñāna, vijñāna*) cuts through the world of Prakṛti to reveal her difference from and orientation toward Puruṣa. In the diagram, this would be to glimpse the "I" (Consciousness) above each karmic action. While all of life is oriented around Puruṣa, it is possible to distinguish, to a degree, between the inner workings of Prakṛti alone and her interactions with Puruṣa. In these terms, meditation lies within the domain of Prakṛti herself. Meditation attempts to move her to an earlier and purified state, while insight helps her realize her relationship to—that is, orientation toward but distinction from—Puruṣa.

Ordinary life is lived almost entirely at the level of Prakṛti, although implicitly there is the constant reference to Puruṣa. Sāṃkhya focuses most of its attention on the worldly levels, which it treats in terms of two somewhat different schemes, the *guṇas* (qualities of psychomaterial substance) and the *bhāvas* (qualities of experience). While the *guṇa* scheme falls entirely within Prakṛti, the *bhāva* scenario includes in addition a reference to the Prakṛti–Puruṣa relationship that actually entails knowing the distinction between the two through the *bhāva* of *jnana*. We will lay the schemas out in detail, and then apply them to the religion and anthropology of Indian society and culture.

The Theories of the Guṇas and Bhāvas

Sāṃkhya, and the many aspects of life organized in terms of it, are mainly thought of in terms of *sattva, rajas,* and *tamas,* the three *guṇas* or "strands" of psychomateriality. McKim Marriott (1989) and his students have interpreted much of Hindu (and other Indian) life and culture in these terms. There is, however, a second grid of categories that maps the same territory but goes beyond describing the psychomaterial realm (Prakṛti) to treat the epistemological or soteriological question of how and why to discriminate Prakṛti from Puruṣa (Consciousness). This is the structure of the *bhāvas*, which Larson defines as "dispositions" or "fundamental strivings in the innermost core of man's nature" (1968, 192). There are eight of them rather than three. Six *bhāvas*, however, correspond (in sets of two) to the three *guṇas*, while the other two refer to our access to the Prakṛti–Puruṣa distinction. Changing the order to correspond to that of *guṇas* as traditionally arranged, they are:

> Group 1: *aiśvarya* (lordship or agency) and *anaiśvarya* (absence of lordship, non-agency) [relating to *sattva* and what is not *sattva*]
>
> Group 2: *virāga* (dispassion) *and rāga* (passion) [corresponding to *rajas* and its privation]
>
> Group 3: *adharma* (being disconnected or out of place) and *dharma* (lawful or in one's proper place) [expressing the dimension of *tamas* and its opposite]

The final group refers to the ability or lack of ability to discriminate between Puruṣa and Prakṛti:

> Group 4 *ajñāna* (ignorance), and *jñāna* (insightfulness)

This assessment aggregates much of the material given in the earlier chapters by Funes Maderey, Chapple, and Ramaswami.

Marriott understands the *guṇas* as a way of expressing dimension or aspect rather than an essence. They comprise both halves of the process of "marking," which includes both "marking" *stictu sensu* and the other side of the relationship, being "marked." The marking dimension involves a transfer of substance/code from a higher to a lower person or other entity. The *sattva* side of the transfer becomes less marked, while the *tamas* side becomes more marked. This sometimes means removing impurities from a higher "partner" and transferring them to a lower, as from a Brahman to a sweeper who removes garbage.[13] The sweeper takes on or even becomes the Brahman's "bad" (impure, *apa* filled) side. There is a sharing of nature or selfhood between the two partners in the transaction. This brings about a sort of "field" of lived relationship for both. Rather than a single, fixed meaning for the concepts of "Brahman" and "Sweeper," we have what has been called "range semantics" by Van Binsbergen (2009–2010). His idea, similar to observations made by others about the Latin term *sacer,* which can mean both "sacred" and "accursed," is that at a certain "pre-Socratic" phase of culture the dominant logic did not think in terms of binary oppositions but rather in broad categories that included both sides of what we would think of as contrary ideas. The idea is not particularly foreign even today; for example, a well-known IQ test includes several questions requiring the subject to think of an opposition in terms of an underlying "range." For example, one item asks how a friend and an enemy are similar. The "right" answer is that both are people who are significant to one, but a somewhat deeper similarity is that both occupy extreme positions on a scale of "love–hate," understood as a dimension. If we look at marking in these terms, a Brahman and a sweeper are similar because both transact marked-/unmarked-ness (sometimes purity/pollution), and this "range" is more basic than the position either category of person has within the range or spectrum. In other terms, the Brahman and the sweeper share a single nature or selfhood which embodies the dimension of unmarked (pure)/marked (polluted).

To see that *aiśvarya* and *anaiśvarya* belong on the *sattva*/non-*sattva* dimension, it is enough to recall that *sattva* characterizes the realm of the gods who lack nothing, enjoying themselves in a blissful heaven where all is perfect and suffering is absent. Most of all, the Lord of the Universe, the King of the Gods (Brahmā often occupies this position), possesses all good qualities; it is from him that all other beings in the universe receive their natures. He marks them and thus unmarks, and also thereby completes, himself. On earth, the possessors of maximal *aiśvarya* are Brahmans, kings, and the heads of families who are seen as "actors" (*kartās*) whose subordinate partial selves (wives, sons, retainers, etc.) complete them but also relieve them of their isolation and excessive self-boundedness.[14]

Rajas, the second *guṇa*, is the clearest of the three. It simply means "activity" or "heat." As the quality most natural to human existence, it refers to the restlessness and urge within humans for satisfaction. It is what makes an aim (*artha*) possible. For Marriott, *rajas* is the principle of "heat" and desire. It falls on a continuum with cold, which is quietude and dispassion. The *bhāvas* of *rāga* (passion) and *virāga* (dispassion) obviously belong with *rajas* (although the words come from different Indo-European roots, this was not recognized by the Indian grammarians).

Tamas, the principle of decay and disintegration, connotes a number of qualities that are unevenly emphasized in different contexts. Often understood as "lethargy" or dullness, the *bhāva* structure shows it as *adharma*, the absence of true or proper nature (*dharma*), called by Marriott an "inborn code for conduct." When such a code fails, as naturally in old age or disease or ethically in demons and those in the grip of evil (*pāpman*), it leads to a state of being "unmatched" and incohesive. The continuum for this strand thus includes the range from perfect form (e.g., Rilke's idealized statue of Apollo) to the disintegration identified by the Buddha in old age, sickness, and death. The early or primordial state of Prakṛti, variously called *pradhāna*, *avyakta*, and *mūlaprakṛti*, is more dharmic and less fragmentary than later states of greater differentiation (*vyakta*).

Classical Yoga is more concerned with moving the person upward on the dharmic continuum, but also toward a state of more potential (*aiśvarya* or agency), and less active frenzy and hunger for satisfaction (i.e., toward less *rāga*). The practice of Yoga aims to reverse the flow of time in the diagram presented earlier, to move *pratiprasava* (YS 4.34) or against the flow of *pariṇāma* and *pravṛtti*. In this, Yoga approaches or evokes vedic and purāṇic myths of the primordial cosmic waters. Water imagery is found explicitly in the final stage of yogic *samādhi* in the image or metaphor of the *dharma-megha-samādhi* or "rain cloud of inner code unity." In this image, the fractured, powerless, and frazzled condition of ordinary life is overcome in the unity of a gentle, sustained, drawing back into a liquid and airy source.[15]

But there is another, equally essential, aspect of the goal state in Sāṃkhya/Yoga. In addition to moving backward and achieving cool, agentic perfection, Prakṛti must realize (via her highest faculty of "insight," *buddhi*, rendered by Chapple as the platform of human impulse) that she is not the consciousness that she intuits more and more clearly. She approaches this awareness asymptotically in higher states of *samādhi* (YS 3.35). Living *puruṣārtha* in its fullness, in the end Prakṛti recognizes her own emptiness. The central verse of the *Sāṃkhya Kārika* (64) proclaims: "Thus, from the practice of the principles, there arises the pure, unmixed knowledge free from error that 'I am not (Puruṣa), I own nothing, and there is no "I" [here].' "[16] Prakṛti's knowledge of her own emptiness is a shining apophasis, a revelation through naysaying of the evolved self (*ahaṁkāra*) that she has reached her own sort of ultimate. Called *kaivalya* ("aloneness," "freedom," or "uniqueness") in Yoga, this ultimate has two aspects.

> Freedom (*kaivalya*) is the flowing backwards of the *guṇas* which have emptied themselves for the sake of Puruṣa. Kaivalya is also the power of consciousness in its innate reality (YS 4.34).[17]

Both verses describe a new way of life for the psychomaterial self (the *ahaṁkāra*-based *liṅga*) which has reversed its natural orientation and no longer seeks to assert its "I" but rather to live in emptiness, Through this released insight, the fullness of the consciousness principle that witnesses its nullity is revealed.

The philosophical systems of Sāṃkhya and Yoga have many reflections in Indian religion and culture. I will discuss three of these in the remainder of this chapter: the theme of the "demon devotee," the aesthetic theory of *dhvani* (suggestion), and the spring Holi festival as described by McKim Marriott and Sunthar Visuvalingam. The ideas explicated above from the philosophical systems are implicit in all three cases.

The Demon Devotee

A very common sculptural theme, and one found as frequently in both Sanskritic and vernacular literary mythology and ritual, is that of a demon being destroyed by a god or goddess, but at the moment of death turning to the god (or being turned by the god into a devotee). An illustration of this "demon devotee" theme (figure 8.3) is that of the demon Apasmāra ("Forgetfulness" or "Ignorance") under the feet of dancing Śiva.

A close-up of Apasmāra is seen in figure 8.4.

Figure 8.3. Śiva Nataraj, Lord of the Dance. *Source*: Photo of sculpture courtesy of Sthaneshwar Timalsina.

Figure 8.4. Śiva dancing on the demon Apasmāra. *Source*: Photo courtesy of Sthaneshwar Timalsina.

This image (*mūrti*), like all of Śaivism, shows Prakṛti and Puruṣa fused together in a single, complex figure. Their energy and excitement come from finding a way to achieve this integration. I suggest that here, as in many other forms in which Śiva is imagined, the god encompasses both Puruṣa and Prakṛti elements within one body.[18] His calm face suggests the ultimate state of Puruṣa in *kaivalya*, while the rest of his dancing body and the flames that surround him are Prakṛti. The dwarf demon Apasmāra is the part of Prakṛti that the human worshippers embody. Through identification with this figure of misunderstanding devotees make contact with the Puruṣa/Prakṛti complex that is Śiva. The demonic in us always seeks to move us illegitimately higher on the great chain (like Binsbergen's "range") that Ronald Inden (1990) has called the "scale of forms," a sort of fractal structure of embedded persons (a sort of lineage in the family/clan (*kula*) in Tantra) that organizes a dharmic universe (Collins 2010). It is precisely this wrongful attempt to rise that causes us to fall lower, into *adharma* (fragmentation), frenzy (*rajas* or mixing), and powerlessness (gross markedness), the qualities that characterize demons like Apasmāra and, on a larger screen, Rāvaṇa. Yoga, especially in its discriminative aspect (*prajñā*), is a way to overcome this demonic ego.

The paradoxical thesis of the last paragraph requires elucidation. The difficulty is that yoga, as we have seen, moves the embodied being (*liṅga*) upward or backward, via *pratiprasava* or *nivṛtti*, into successively more unified (and therefore, as Sāṃkhya says, "uncreated," *avikṛti*) states of *samādhi*. Yet we have just found that demons routinely do the same thing. To understand this, it will be helpful to visit the vexed topic of "powers" (*siddhis*). Power, of course, is precisely what demons want, and in terms of the *bhāva* theory of the *Sāṃkhya Kārikā*, this means *aiśvarya*, "lordship," which we found to be a part of the *sattva guṇa*. The *siddhis* listed in Book three of the *Yoga Sūtra* include making oneself larger or smaller, invisible, knowing the past and future, controlling or taking the experience of another, knowing one's previous births and time of death in this one, etc. All *siddhis* are the result of suppressing the *rajas* and *tamas guṇas* and expressing only the *sattva*.[19] More specifically, the *siddhi* possessor resides in the unmarked, *aiśvarya* aspect of *sattva*.[20] As this is manifest in the mental realm, it is called *buddhisattva*, or "sattvic insight." It is as if one moved one's position to the left of the temporal sequence in figure 8.1, viewing the whole process of *pariṇāma* synchronically in a single glance. The basic fact of *satkārya* (the inherence of the effect in the cause) makes this more intelligible, as all the stages of temporal unfolding (*pariṇāma*) are included within a single psychomaterial being, the *pradhāna* form of Prakṛti. Because further differentiation has not occurred, all possibilities remain open and one can select the outcome which one desires, as it were creating an alternative present reality by going back in time (to a stage when all times were unified) and choosing a different future.

This process of going back, *pratiprasava*,[21] attains the stage of the gods' heaven (YS 3.51) including the sphere of some gods who meditate on pure I-am-ness (*asmītā*, Vyāsa on YS 3.26). Here, far beyond or long before the present moment of the yogin's practice, there can arise a temptation, precisely like that of the demon, to indulge oneself in the pleasure of power (Vyāsa on 3.51). The specific temptations (sexual enjoyment, the avoidance of old age and death) are similar to those offered the Buddha by Māra on the night before he attained enlightenment, and apparently for the same reason: finishing yogic practice will dissolve the structure of Prakṛti's world and in particular the gods' (like Marā's) position. The possibility of getting caught in the trap of perfect pleasure shows the demon devotee theme in reverse: not only can a demon become a devotee, but the devotee (i.e., a yogin) can become a demon. This possibility, in fact, was routinely activated: as David White (2009) has exhaustively shown, yogis throughout much of Indian tradition have been seen as frightening, power-hungry manipulators who use their siddhis for personal gain and control of others exactly like demons such as Rāvaṇa. Which is it to be: Kṛṣṇa's Vṛṇḍāvan, or Rāvaṇa's iron fortress in Lanka? Everything depends on the *buddhi*'s choice, or ability to discriminate (is there a difference?) between two utterly different but almost indistinguishable things (that become more and more indistinguishable the more refined the *buddhi* becomes): Prakṛti (in her most sattvic form) and Puruṣa (never seen, always reflected in the crystal of the *buddhi*'s eye).[22] To choose heaven is to reap hell, while to realize and practice nihilation is to be plunged into blissful *samādhi*.

Dhvani

It is evident that the demonic yogi is a figure of art, as is the demon devotee who travels the same path but chooses (or for whom it is chosen) an opposite fork in the road. To understand them properly, we must look more deeply into the language of art and its relationship to *samādhi* and *jñāna*. In particular, we will explore the fundamental aesthetic concepts of *dhvani*, "suggestion" and what it suggests, *rasa*, a term difficult to translate but that I will call "deep flavor." The aim will be to show that art, like Yoga, moves us back along the emanative pathway in the direction of origins and higher level, less marked experience.

Obviously, Indian aesthetics are an enormous area of thought, even when filtered through its Western, Indological interpretations. I will be guided by Abhinavagupta, the tenth- to eleventh-century Kashmiri tantric philosopher whose aesthetic theory is generally considered the epitome of Indian thinking on the subject, and David Shulman (2001, 2012), a present-day author whose diachronic contextualization of Indian theories on imagination allows a more nuanced understanding of the field. *Dhvani*, originally a word for "sound," came to mean the suggestive as opposed to the literal, denotative, function of language. It rose to become, for a while, the central idea in aesthetics, and the term is found in the title of one of the basic aesthetic texts, Ānandavardhana's *Dhvanyāloka* ("Light on Dhvani"). Our questions will be: How does suggestion (*dhvani*) work? What does it do? To anticipate, we will find that its action in some ways parallels that of Sāṃkhyan discrimination and Yogic *samādhi*; that is, *dhvani* involves a "return to the source" or *pratiprasava* flow, moving in the opposite direction from the surface denotation of a text.

A good place to begin any discussion of Sanskrit poetics is where the tradition of poetry, *kāvya*, is supposed to have begun, with the first *śloka* (32-syllable metrical stanza) recorded in Book 1 of the Rāmāyaṇa.

> *mā niṣāda pratiṣṭhāṁ tvam agamaḥ śāśvatīḥ samāḥ/*
> *yat krauñcamithunād ekam avadhīḥ kāmamohitam//*

> You shall never again know peace, O hunter,
> since you slew one of this pair of Krauñca birds
> as it was overcome with passion.
> (translation by David Shulman 2001, 31)

As Shulman notes, the author (or transcriber) of the Rāmāyaṇa, Vālmīki, upon viewing a hunter killing a bird, fell into an altered state of consciousness whereupon these verses came to him, a state that is later in the Ramāyāṇa called "meditation" (*dhyāna*). That state persists as he composes (or channels) the remainder of the text, including parts describing events that had not yet happened.[23] It is revealed that this first *śloka* was dictated to Vālmiki by the creator god Brahmā, which tells us that its origin, in Sāṃkhya/Yoga terms, was in the heavenly realm of pure sattvic buddhi. This is confirmed by the compression of time, within the framing of the text, into one single cohesive story spanning past, (narrative) present, and future. The whole Ramāyāṇa is suggested by a single *śloka*. Clearly this capability is a siddhi attained by Vālmīki, whose mind (*buddhi*) had been transported by the mood of compassion (*karuṇa*) into which he was thrown by seeing the slaughter of the male Krauñca bird (and the action from being high on Brahmā, who seems to have "possessed" Vālmīki's thought process [cf Smith 2012]).

The essence of Sanskrit poetics, at least after the rasa theory was elaborated by Abhinavagupta and his predecessors in the tenth and eleventh centuries CE, has been the power of art to move a qualified audience (the *sahṛdaya*, persons whose heart is "one with" the work) toward a recognition of deep selfhood similar to the recognition in yogic meditation or insight of Puruṣa by the highest form of Prakṛti, the *sattvikā buddhi*. It does this in eight ways, through the extremely subtle and universalized (*sādhāraṇī-karaṇa*) moods that are evoked by touching latent, generally past life, memories (*vāsanās, saṁskāras*) in the mind of the audience. Again, we see the *satkārya* theory implied, as the past flows into the present and the present into the future, forming a whole that can be held open for a moment or two[24] in the vision of great art. It leads the mind back into the wholeness and essentiality of *rasa* that lies on the edge of art experience like the primordial (*avyakta* or *pradhāna*) form of Prakṛti, attained otherwise only in *samādhi* after deep meditation.

Art, like meditation, flows backward (*pratiprasava*) into the origins (past lives, karma, primordial sources) of our being, aiming at an "enhanced, . . . densely continuous consciousness" (Shulman

2012, 70) closely resembling *samādhi*. One of the ways it can do this is expressed in the concept of *dhvani*, "suggestion." The idea grew in the art theoretical literature that came in the wake of earlier grammatical traditions (*vyākāraṇa*). Analysis of the Veda (Mīmāṃsā) aimed to specify the true or literal meaning of the text. This was designated *abhidhā*. Secondary indication (*lakṣana*) had long been recognized by Mīmāṃsās and grammarians (e.g., the sentence "The Punjabi is an ox" does not indicate a literal identification of man and animal but rather asserts that the man has a common property with the beast, i.e., stupidity). Beyond *lakṣana*, other, higher or more refined senses were identified by later writers in Kashmir, particularly Anandavardhana and Abhinavagupta. In what was to prove a seminal work, the *Dhvanyāloka*, Anandavardhana argued for the importance of a power of "suggestion" or "revelation" (*vyañjana* or *dhvani*).

Interpreted in light of Sāṃkhya / Yoga, *dhvani* is a kind of aesthetic *samādhi* where the experience of art causes the life process to flow backward, thereby moving the *sahṛdaya* up the sattva dimension toward the *avyakta/mūla* stage or state of Prakṛti. This move brings "universalization" (*sadhāraṇikāraṇa*) of emotion, which, as we saw in discussing the *siddhis*, increases the power (in Sāṃkhyan language, *aiśvarya*) of the art work. In discussing "imagination" (*bhāvana*) in different strata of Indian thought from Paṇinian grammar to classical Nyāya and Mīmāṃsā to classical and Kashmiri Saiva poetics to sixteenth-century Telugu poetry, David Shulman (2012) explores this power of the imaginative function to attain and create reality. We will reflect on just a few of his many insights.

At the most basic level of language, the function of the verb is based on its power to unify and "subordinate moments of subsidiary actions coming one after another" in a single, "constructed totality" (Shulman 2012, 20). To speak at all, we are obliged to employ a power essentially like Yoga, and to move back and forth, up and down, the semantic "range" from differentiated ordinary reality to the higher power of the linguistic function that resides in what Sāṃkhya / Yoga would call the *avyakta* level where the flowing moments of time are[25] held within their single source. In literary art, too, the same power of imagination is fundamental in creating the (fictional) reality of the world pictured in the work. Shulman follows Heesterman in understanding the artistic process as analogous to a Vedic sacrifice where the sacrificer (*yajamāna*) (the man for whose sake the sacrifice is performed) moves within the rite to a higher state ("from the unreal to the real," for example) and brings about a state of affairs to which he can return later (e.g., after death) to experience its benefits (Shulman 2012, 44).

Shulman identifies a central and universal paradox at work in the Indian materials both on the sacrifice and in art: "The paradox of continuous identity echoes the paradox of memory-infused temporality itself, at once frozen in autotelic wholeness and spinning out of control in a devolutionary trajectory . . . as if the very notion of personal continuity were vitiated at every moment by the experience each person has of himself or herself in a world driven by devolving time" (Shulman 2012, 45). This well describes the world of *duḥkha* addressed by the Sāṃkhya/Yoga texts but relegates their notion of Puruṣa to a fantasy of "autotelic wholeness." Shulman's understanding is very much the same as that of the Buddhists who think "continuous identity" an impossible self-contradiction, but who find the way beyond devolving time in another way, via the idea of *nirvāṇa*, "the only unconditioned Existent" (Collins 2010, 54). Without going into the vexed (and deep) issue of the relationship of *nirvāṇa* to Puruṣa, even if Shulman opts for the former, he still (like they) must recognize that art requires a source in a deep principle that makes it possible. As Collins points out, were there not *nirvāṇa*, there would be no possibility of escaping the rounds of *pratītyasamutpada* (Shulman's "devolving time"). Collins sees *nirvāṇa* as part of a Buddhist "imaginaire," and quotes with approval Jacques Le Goff 's definition of an imaginaire as "a non-material, imaginative world constituted by texts, especially works of art and literature." Within that imaginative (or, as Henry Corbin would have it, "imaginal"[26]) world, *nirvāṇa* functions as "an imagined cessation that conquers, discursively at least, the suffering and death intrinsic to all life" (28). It is what makes an imaginaire, a world of strong imagination—a culture worth living for—possible.

Dhvani, then, like Yoga and Buddhist meditational practice, posits—or reveals—a level of reality on which it depends for its action. It is a revelation that reveals both itself and what it rests on. Similarly, *nirvāṇa*, as *experienced* by the Buddha and others after him, also reveals the reality of *nirvāṇa* as a *principle* (*tattva*) of fundamental reality, *present in some way before the Buddha attained it. Dhvani*, as it experientially manifests the deep taste (*rasa*) of art experience, shows that art is made possible by that deep flavor which previously passed unnoticed. Imagination leads to the artistic analogue or equivalent of *nirvāṇa* or *samādhi* (*rasa*), but is itself empowered by that same "deepest place" (Shulman 2012, 134). All this can be named, as we saw before in Sāṃkhya, *puruṣārtha*, "for Puruṣa's sake." Prakṛti is unconsciously motivated by the urge to give pleasure to Puruṣa and to liberate him. The poet, like other artists, also aims to give pleasure, but this is only possible by also giving a taste of Shulman's "deepest place," which for art means the underlying *rasa*.

In terms of Marriott's categories, and the Sāṃkhyan *guṇas* that they translate, *dhvani* "suggests" a move upstream, *pratiprasava*, toward the unmanifest, unmarked, *avyakta* Prakṛti. By "returning to the source," *dhvani* makes possible a new reality here below, in the art work as it manifests in "gross" (*sthāla*) form as a production on the stage or text on palm leaf. Art, that is, remarks the world through a move back into the primordial state of the unmarked.

Holī

The spring festival, carnival, or bacchanal called Holī in North India and Kāmadahanam ("burning of the Love God") or Pooram in the South, falls roughly into the category of antinomian or transgressive rites that dissolve social institutions in order to reform them in a fresh, purified form. Interest in such rituals in the West has been enormous, with figures such as Victor Turner (1967, 1969) and Michael Bakhtin (1968) placing them near the center of their thought. Visuvalingam has interpreted much of late-Vedic and classical Hinduism in this light, and even has attempted a close reading of the classic Sanskrit drama *Mṛcchakaṭṭikam* as a spring ritual of death and rebirth. In his classic description of Holī in North India, Marriott (1966) records that the festival began with the ritual holocaust of the demoness Holikā, daughter of King Harnikas (= the demon Hiraṇyakāśipu), which he understood to represent her "final spiritual liberation." This would clearly place Holī within the orbit of the "demon devotee" theme homologous to Śiva and Apasmāra, and suggest that it, too, represents a "return to the source" and so can be understood in terms of the Sāṃkhya/Yoga ideas discussed earlier.

Marriott memorably describes the two successive Holīs in which he participated. The first year, intoxicated by a massive dose of marijuana, he understood little after the bonfire of Holikā, which he notes became the occasion and source for rekindling the household fires of the village which had been extinguished in order to be renewed in this way. Preparing for the festival's return the next year, he reflected on the purpose of rituals as theorized by eminent anthropologists including Durkheim and Radcliffe-Brown, looking for the "fundamental social values" that Holī might support. At the next Holī, on the full moon of March, Marriott found that this "Festival of Love," unlike the other twelve festivals of the year, did not directly support social values but rather overturned and renewed them. In a sort of Nietzschean "transvaluation of all values," he discovered that normally submissive women became bold and aggressive toward higher-status men, tightly controlled sexuality became free and even licentious, and specialists in purification heaped "mud and dust on all the leading citizens." In summary, he writes, "Each riotous act at Holī implied some opposite, positive rule or fact of everyday social organization in the village" (Marriott 1966, 210). But beyond its transfiguration of social values and structure, Marriott found Holī to be an intensely personal, internal matter. "The dramatic balancing of Holī—the world destruction and world renewal, the world pollution followed by world purification—occurs . . . in the person of each participant . . . [who] plays and for the moment may experience the role of his opposite" (212). In keeping with the truth this passage asserts, Marriott himself understood Holī by twice living (or "playing") it himself, a respected anthropologist and "sahib" whom the festival "made to dance in the streets, fluting like Lord Krishna, with a garland of old shoes around his neck."

Holī, in North India, has been associated with the child and adolescent Lord Kṛṣṇa of the *Bhāgavata Purāṇa* for the past few hundred years. Rather than Holikā, the bonfire that commences the festival formerly cremated Putāna, the demonic wet nurse who tried to kill baby Kṛṣṇa with her poisoned breasts. As Marriott notes, the ritual recalls the childhood of the god, and it is significant that elements of it are repeated at weddings, and when a bride from the village returns home for her yearly monsoon visit. What is remembered (and enacted) is the time prior to marriage, an earlier (imaginatively reconstructed?) epoch before the fatal moment when the young girl is brutally separated from her family and natal village and sent off to live with a strange husband and unkind in-laws. This is exactly the moment celebrated in the Rasa Līlā dance cited at the beginning of this chapter, as each Gopī dances with her own, particular Kṛṣṇa. It is also the moment when Indian anthropology, in the body/mind of McKim Marriott's *liṅga śarīra,* returns to the beginning in order to reconstitute its understanding on explicitly ethnosociological lines drawn from the early stages of Sāṃkhyan evolution, a time close to the *avyakta* moment when the world could be seen to be organized according to the categories of *sattva, rajas,* and *tamas.*

In South India, the homologue of Holī, called Kāmadahana (the burning of Kāma), is associated with a well-known Śaiva myth rather than with Śrī Kṛṣṇa. Briefly, Śiva, when aroused sexually toward Pārvatī by the love god Kāma, opens his third eye and burns Kāma, thus causing the latter's wife Rati to weep and lament. The Lord relents, and Kāma is reborn. As Visuvalingam has pointed out, this story tells of a victory of consciousness (*Puruṣa, Atman,* which Visuvalingam rightly associates with the bonfire present also in the South) over sexual (and by implication, all) enjoyment (*bhukti*). As in the North Indian Holī, the Southern Spring festival celebrates the victory of world-destroying energies, but also leads to the rebirth of our world, as Kāma, and the previous social order, return at the ritual's end. Bacchanal, for example in Mardi Gras which marks the beginning of the austerities of Lent, associates the end of desire with its uncontrolled eruption. The order of events is different in India and Europe, as Carnival puts license before austerity while Holī/Kāmadahana reverses the sequence.

A feature of the Kāmadahana in parts of South India (where it goes mostly by the name of Pooram) is Marathukkali, "a performing art in which intellectual activity is given prominence. It is a competitive play in which intellectual discussion takes place on Hindu mythologies. It can also be described as a process of parochialization in which sanskritic ideas and concepts flow to the little traditions. In this play, intellectual discussions at a very high level are held by the players on competitive basis which are judged by experts in Indology, Sanskrit, and Philosophy" (Nagaraj Paturi 2014). Apparently, this is an example of Sanskrit traditions understood as paradigmatic, and therefore higher on the scale of forms than the everyday life into which they erupt at the time of Pooram. Part of the recreation of the dissolved, old world is the introduction of Sanskrit mythology, understood to constitute a paradigm of the world, into the "little tradition." In this way, everyday life in Indian villages is re-marked to correspond with the stories of the epics and purāṇas.

Visuvalingam has pointed out that this ritual process of renewal, which is also a burning of degraded, everyday life in the fire of consciousness, is explicitly understood in the Hindu tradition to be periodic. Although celebrated yearly, it also happens in the recasting of tradition as it moves into new cultural zones. For instance, the ancient spring festival in North India became assimilated to the cult of Kṛṣṇa. More recently, the Northern India Holī has found its way to South India (Chennai) and even Chicago, where Visuvalingam reported for a local Indian newspaper the filming of Prashant Bhargava's "Radhe Radhe," an interpretation of Holī referencing Stravinsky's "Rite of Spring" (Visuvalingam).

Conclusion and Reflections

The nature of the relationship between *mokṣa* and *bhukti* in Sāṃkhya/Yoga is clarified by the mythology of Holī/Kāmadahana, the figure of the demon-devotee, and *rasa/dhvani* aesthetics, all of which profit in turn by being viewed from this earlier perspective. The relationship can be summarized in this way: Enjoyment is both the road to consciousness and the latter's effect. In 1912, a neglected but essential figure in the history of Jungian and Freudian psychoanalysis, Sabina Spielrein, wrote a paper that recognized the second half of this relationship, the "destructive" (read *mokṣa*) origins of "coming to be" (*bhukti*). Her paper, which Freud acknowledged to have been influential in his later formulation of the "death instinct," reflects on our ambivalence toward sex, which she interprets as an unconscious recognition that sexual union implies our individual destruction. It leads to the production of a new generation that will supplant us. We are both attracted to sex and repelled by it for this reason. But, as Freud realized, ambivalence is not the final response; we recognize, at some level, that destruction of our limited, ego selves is needful for the coming to life, not only of the next generation, but of our potential for what he called "death in our own fashion" and a full life before that final quietus. Although he never makes the connection explicit, Freud suggests here that death involves union with our split-off other half, and that it is deeply connected to what he called "primal narcissism," or the "oceanic feeling" of oneness with the universe that he found in the writing of his friend Romain Rolland and believed to be the experience of every baby at the breast of a good enough mother. Freud disclaimed mystical experience of his own, but in discussing the oceanic feeling he could not disguise his deep longing for it and at least the intimation that to die in *his* own fashion (i.e., to die authentically), he would have to taste it again.

The implication is that a return to beginnings is the proper way to end, and to live in the time leading up to that end. Translating Freud into the terms of Sāṃkhya/Yoga, we are guided in our pleasure seeking by *puruṣārtha,* a desire for release (*mokṣa*) that is also a yearning for the deep enjoyment of new culture, of art that reworks the world and rituals that bring spring back again. This is reminiscent of the frogs in the Ṛg Vedic hymn[27] whose song brings the spring rains that dissolve the old year and usher in the new. Again and again, moments of awareness (Puruṣa) return.

Notes

1. Just prior to the printing of this book we received the sad news that Al passed away after a short illness. Dr. Collins made significant contributions to multiple fields, including psychotherapy, India studies, and philosophy. A clinical psychologist, he completed a second PhD in Indic Studies at the University of Texas, Austin. He studied as a Fulbright Scholar at Madras University with V. Raghavan and T. M. P. Mahadevan. He taught at Pacific Graduate Institute and the California Institute of Integral Studies. He often presented insightful research at the annual meetings of the Dharma Academy of North America.

2. The extent to which Sāṃkhya and Yoga form parts of what is essentially one position is disputed. Larson (1968, 1976) and Pflueger (2003) are among those who have argued that Patañjali's *Yogasūtra* belongs to a

school or subschool of Sāṃkhya. Others have tried to show that Yoga is different from Sāṃkhya in important ways. This chapter is persuaded that Larson and Pfleuger are basically correct, at least in their conclusion that Patañjali's Yoga agrees with the fundamental thesis of the *Sāṃkhya Kārika* that Prakṛti acts solely for the sake of pleasing and releasing Puruṣa, and that her increasing knowledge of her difference from Puruṣa paradoxically moves her closer to him and is salvific for her as well.

3. In order to view Yoga as a way of life in the world, Whicher and Chapple are forced to separate it from Sāṃkhya more than I find justified.

4. The *Sāṃkhya Kārikā* of Īśvarakṛṣṇa.

5. Patāñjali's *Yoga Sūtra.*

6. David White *The Yoga Sutra: A Biography*

7. Here I disagree to some extent with Gerald Larson, who argues that "consciousness [Puruṣa] is always consciousness *of* something. To be conscious of something is to be aware of that something." (Larson 1969, 175). The disagreement is not over whether Puruṣa is conscious but of the force of the preposition "of." It seems to imply that consciousness is somehow affected by what it sees, but Sāṃkhya generally denies this. Larson supports his argument by citing SK 50, which reads in part *jaramāraṇam duḥkham* prāpnoti cetanaḥ *Puruṣa,* "Puruṣa, i.e., consciousness, attains the suffering of old age and death." The latter part of the verse shows that this is due to the ongoing devolution of the *liṅga* (its failure to move from *pravṛtti* to *nivṛtti*). The question of whether Puruṣa suffers is in a way the converse of the question of whether Puruṣa experiences pleasure. See Collins (2013) for a discussion of the latter issue.

8. For a discussion of this eccentricity in feminist terms, see Collins (2000). In the language of (recent) twenty-somethings, Puruṣa is "not into" Prakṛti as she is "into" him.

9. And *mūlaprakṛti* and *avyakta.*

10. *autsukyanivṛttyartham yathā*
kriyāsu pravartate lokaḥ,
puruṣasya vimokṣārtham
pravartate tadvad avyaktam (SK 58)

11. Demonic life could be pictured in terms of this diagram as actions completely determined by their inherence in preceding states (*satkārya*) and totally ignorant of or disregarding the "I" hovering above the world of action.

12. "Unmanifest" (*avyakta*) or "root" (*mūla*) Prakṛti is "uncreated" or "undifferentiated" (*avikṛti,* SK 3).

13. See Collins (1991) for a fuller discussion of this process.

14. Loneliness and the need for a second (son or wife) is the dark side of being overly integrated or self-sufficient. Brian K. Smith (1989)

has discussed this issue in terms of the vedic words *jāmi* (overly close, insufficiently differentiated) and *pṛthak* (too fragmented or separated).

15. For the idea that Yoga aims at a return to the source see Whicher (2003, 55).

16. *evaṁ tattvābhyāsān nā'smi*
na me nā'ham ity apariśam
aviparyayād viśuddham
kevalam utpadyate jñānam (SK 64)

17. *puruṣārtha-śūnyānam guṇānām pratiprasavaḥ kaivalyam*
svarūpa-pratiṣṭhā vā citiśaktir iti. (YS 4.34).

18. Probably the clearest example of the Puruṣa–Prakṛti fusion is the common image of Śiva as *ardhanārīśvara*, "half woman."

19. Perhaps more accurately, one holds the *rajas* dimension (mixing-not mixing) at the extreme of quietude and the *tamas* dimension (unmatching-matching) at the extreme of dharmic completeness of form.

20. YS 3.49 refers to this lordship as *adhiṣthātṛtva*, "the quality of being in a position of authority."

21. Ian Wicher translates *pratiprasava* as "return to the origin" (2003, 55).

22. The image of a flower refracted in rock crystal is one of the classic figures for the relationship between Puruṣa (the crystal) and Prakṛti (the flower) ("Śaṁkara"'s *Vivaraṇa on Yogasūtra* II, 16–17; see Larson and Bhattacharya 2008, 253).

23. In our verse, the verb *mā agamas* is in the aorist imperative, and essentially amounts to a curse; it is not that the hunter simply will not achieve a balanced life (*pratiṣṭhā*) but that he is being forbidden to have one. Here, again, the *siddhi* power is at work.

24. Or even for nights on end, as in the Kerala Muttiyettu dance drama experienced and reported by David Shulman.

25. The use of the word "were" is equally accurate, but *pradhāna* is beyond time. Perhaps time itself should be viewed in this context in terms of Van Binsbergen's "range semantics."

26. Henry Corbin's term.

27. I discussed this hymn in my dissertation (Collins 1976, 66–67).

References

Bakhtin, Mikhail M. 1968. *Rabelais and His World*. Trans. Hélène Iswolsky. Cambridge, MA: MIT Press.

Chapple, Christopher Key. 2003. "Yoga and the Luminous," in Ian Whicher and David Carpenter (eds.), *Yoga: The Indian Tradition*. London & New York: Routledge Curzon.

Collins, Alfred. 1976. "The Origins of the Brahman–King Relationship in Indian Social Thought." PhD dissertation, University of Texas at Austin.

Collins, Alfred. 2000. "Dancing with Prakriti: The Sankhyan Goddess as Pativrata and Guru," in Alf Hiltebeitel and Kathleen M. Erndl (eds.), *Is the Goddess a Feminist? The Politics of South Asian Goddesses*. New York: NYU Press.

Collins, Alfred. 2006. "Dharmamegha Samadhi and the Two Sides of Kaivalya: Toward a Yogic Theory of Culture," in C. Chapple (ed.) *Yoga and Ecology: Dharma for the Earth*.

Collins, Alfred. 2009. "Lee Bontecou's Eye," paper given at the University of Alaska conference on complexity.

Collins, Alfred. 2010. *Foucault among the Demons: Power and the Self in Indian Thought and Western Postmodernism*, Dharma Association of North America, 2010.

Collins, Alfred. 2013. *Puruṣa's Pleasure: Imagining the Joy and Release of Consciousness in Samkhya-Yoga*, American Academy of Religion Annual Meeting 2013.

Inden, Ronald. 1990. *Imagining India*. Oxford: Basil Blackwell.

Larson, Gerald. 1968. *Classical Sāṃkhya*. Delhi: Motilal Banarsidass.

Larson, Gerald, and Ram Shankar Bhattacharya. 2008. *Samkhya: A Dualist Tradition in Indian Philosophy*. Volume 4 of Karl Potter (ed.) *Encyclopedia of Indian Philosophies*. Princeton, NJ: Princeton University Press.

Marriott, M. 1955. *Village India*. Chicago: University of Chicago Press.

Marriott, M. 1966. "The Feast of Love." Hawai'i: East–West Center Press.

Marriott, M. 1989. "Constructing an Indian Ethnosociology." *Contributions to Indian Sociology* 23(1): 1–39.

Paturi, Nagaraj, 2014. Pan-Indian "spring festival of love." Post #7514 in the Abhinavagupta listserv. https://groups.yahoo.com/neo/groups/abhinavagupta/conversations/messages/7514

Pfleuger, Lloyd. 2003. "Dueling with Dualism: Revisioning the Paradox of Puruṣa and Prakṛti," in Ian Whicher and David Carpenter (eds.), *Yoga: The Indian Tradition*. London & New York: Routledge Curzon.

Shulman, David. 2001. *The Wisdom of Poets. Studies in Tamil, Telugu, and Sanskrit*. New Delhi: Oxford University Press.

Shulman, David. 2012. More *than Real. A History of the Imagination in South India*. Chicago: University of Chicago Press.

Smith, Brian K. 1998. *Reflections on Resemblance, Ritual and Religion*. Delhi: Motilal Banarsidass.

Smith, Frederick. 2012. *The Self Possessed: Deity and Spirit Possession in South Asian Literature and Civilization*. New York: Columbia University Press.

Turner, Victor. 1974. *Dramas, Fields and Metaphors*. Ithaca, NY: Cornell University Press.

Turner, Victor. 1967. *The Forest of Symbols*. Ithaca, NY: Cornell University Press.

Turner, Victor. 1969. *The Ritual Process*. Ithaca, NY: Cornell University Press.

Van Binsbergen, Wim M. J. 2009–2010. "Before the Pre-Socratics." *Quest: An African Journal of Philosophy/Revue Africaine de Philosophie* 23–24(1–2).

Whicher, Ian. 1998. *The Integrity of the Yoga Darśana. A Reconsideration of Classical Yoga*. Albany, NY: SUNY Press.

Whicher, Ian. 2003. "The Integration of Spirit (*Puruṣa*) and Matter (*Prakṛti*) in the *Yoga Sūtra*," in Ian Whicher and David Carpenter (eds), *Yoga: The Indian Tradition*. London & New York: Routledge Curzon.

Appendix

Sāṃkhya Kārikā Grammatical Analysis

ROBERT ZABEL

1. Release from Threefold Suffering

दुःखत्रयाभिघाताज्जिज्ञासा तदभिघातके हेतौ ।
दृष्टे साऽपार्था चेन्नैकान्तात्यन्ततोऽभावात् ॥१॥

duḥkha-trayābhighātāj jijñāsā tad abhighātake hetau
dṛṣṭe sā'pārthā cennaikāntātyantato'bhāvāt //1//

What is the cause of the torment of the threefold suffering?
Would you like to know?
The apparent ways of dealing with it do not work.
They are insufficient.

duḥkha, suffering
traya, triad, group of three
abhighātāt (m. abl. sg.), torment
(*duḥkha-traya-abhighātāt*, m. abl. sg., from the torment of the threefold suffering)
jijñāsā (f. nom. sg., desiderative; from √*jñā*, knowing), desirous of knowing, examinining, anxious to know, wishing to know
tad (n. nom. sg.), this, that, then
abhighātake (m. loc. sg.), counteracting, removing
hetau (m. loc. sg.), in the cause

dṛṣṭe, (m. loc. sg., p. pass. participle; from √*dṛś,* seeing) in the seen
sā (f. nom. sg.), that
apārthā (f. nom. sg.), without any object, useless
ced, if
na, not
ekānta, (m.) singular end, only aim
atyantatas, (adv.) perpetual
(*ekānta-atyantatas,* adv. perpetual singular aim)
abhāvāt (m. abl. sg.) from non-existence

2. Traditional Rituals Are Not Effective

दृष्टवदानुश्रविकः स ह्यविशुद्धिक्षयातिशययुक्तः ।
तद्विपरीतः श्रेयान् व्यक्ताव्यक्तज्ञविज्ञानात् ॥२॥

dṛṣṭavadānuśravikaḥ sa hy aviśuddhi-kṣayātiśaya-yuktaḥ
tad viparītaḥ śreyān vyakta-avyakta-jña-vijñānāt //2//

Vedic rituals are impure, destructive, and excessive.
They are wrong.
The better way arises from the discernment of
the manifest, the unmanifest, and the knower.

dṛṣṭavat, (m. abl. sg) having seen or beheld
ānuśravikas, (m. nom. sg.) according to tradition
sas, (m. nom. sg.) he, this
hi, indeed
aviśuddhi, impurity
kṣaya, loss, destruction
atiśaya, excess
yuktas (m. nom. sg., p. pass. participle), joined, connected
(*aviśuddhi-kṣayātiśaya-yuktaḥ,* m. nom. sg., connected to impurity, destruction, and excess)
tad, (n. nom. sg.) this, that, then
viparītas, (m. nom. sg.), against, contrary
śreyān, (m. nom. sg., comparative), better, superior, preferable
vyakta, manifest. *vi* + √*añj,* to make distinct, clear) the manifest
avyakta, unmanifest
jña, the knower
vijñānāt (n. abl. sg), from knowing

(*vyakta-avyakta-jña-vijñānāt*, n. abl. sg., from discernment of the manifest, unmanifest, and the knower)

3. Prakṛti: Creative but Not Created

मूलप्रकृतिरविकृतिर्महदाद्याः प्रकृतिविकृतयः सप्त ।
षोडशाकस्तु विकारो न प्रकृतिर्न विकृतिः पुरुषः ॥३॥

mūla-prakṛtir avikṛtir mahadādyāḥ prakṛti-vikṛtayaḥ sapta
ṣoḍaśākas tu vikāro na prakṛtir na vikṛtiḥ Puruṣaḥ //3//

***Mūlaprakṛti* is not derivative.**
Seven aspects derive from *Prakṛti*,
starting with the *Mahat*
[and the *ahaṃkāra* and earth, water, fire, air, space].
Sixteen aspects further emerge
[mind, sense organs, action organs, rudimentary elements].
The *Puruṣa* is neither *Prakṛti* nor a derivative of *Prakṛti*.

mūla, (n.) root.
prakṛtis, (f. nom. sg.) nature.
(*mūla-prakṛtis*, f. nom. sg., root-nature)
avikṛtis, (f. nom. sg.) the inanimate, unchangeable
mahat, (m.) the intellect, *buddhi*
ādyās, (m. nom. pl.) beginning with, et cetera
(*mahad-ādyās*, m. nom. pl., beginning with the intellect)
prakṛti, (f.) nature
vikṛtayas, (f. nom. pl.) the animate, changeable
(*prakṛti-vikṛtayas*, f. nom. pl., nature and change)
sapta, seven
ṣoḍaśākas, (m. nom. sg.) the sixteen (the *manas*, *buddīndriyāni*, *karmendriyāni*, and *mahābhūtāni*)
tu, but
vikāras, (m. nom. sg.) change of form, product
na, not
prakṛtis, (f. nom. sg.) nature
na, not
vikṛtis, (f. nom. sg.) change, variation
puruṣas, (m. nom. sg.) the Self

4. Pathways to Knowledge

दृष्टमनुमानमाप्तवचनं च, सर्वप्रमाणसिद्धत्वात् ।
त्रिविधं प्रमाणमिष्टं, प्रमेयसिद्धिः प्रमाणाद्धि ॥४॥

dṛṣṭam anumānam āpta-vacanaṃ ca, sarvapramāṇasiddhatvāt
trividhaṃ pramāṇam iṣṭaṃ, prameya-siddhiḥ pramāṇāddhi //4//

Indeed, from the perfection of all means of knowledge,
it can be agreed that they are threefold:
that which is apparent, inferred, or declared authoritatively.
Success in obtaining knowledge arises from inference.

dṛṣṭam, (n. acc. sg., p. pass. participle; see verse one) perception
anumānam, (n. nom. sg.) inference
āpta, complete, full, respected
vacanam, (n. nom. sg.) speaking, saying
(*āpta-vacanam*, n. nom. sg., valid testimony)
ca, and
sarva, (m.) all
pramāṇa, (n.) correct means of knowledge
siddhatvāt, (n. abl. sg.) from the quality of perfection
(*sarva-pramāṇa-siddhatvāt*, n. abl. sg., from the perfection of all correct means of knowledge)
trividham, (n. nom. sg.) threefold
pramāṇam, (n. nom. sg.) correct means of knowledge
iṣṭam, (n. nom. sg., p. pass. participle) desired
prameya, (n.) to be measured, ascertained, or proven
siddhis, (f. nom. sg.) perfection, accomplishment
(*prameya-siddhis*, f. nom. sg., success in obtaining knowledge)
pramāṇāt, (n. abl. sg.) from correct means of knowledge
hi, indeed

प्रतिविषयाध्यवसायो दृष्टं, त्रिविधमनुमानमाख्यातम् ।
तल्लिङ्गलिङ्गिपूर्वकं, आप्तश्रुतिराप्तवचनं च* ॥५॥
*तु

prativiṣayād hy avasāyo dṛṣṭaṃ, trividham anumānam ākhyātam
tal liṅga-liṅgi-pūrvakaṃ, āpta śrutir āpta vacanaṃ ca //5//

The apparent is the apprehension of sense objects.
Inference is declared to be threefold:

From a clear mark (*tal liṅga*),
from a prior mark (*liṅga-pūrvakaṃ*),
and from reliable authority.
Authoritative declaration arises from an authoritative source.

prativiṣayāt, (m. abl. sg.) from the various objects of the senses
hi, indeed
avasāyas, (m. nom. sg.) determination, ascertainment
dṛṣṭam, (n. acc. sg., p. pass. participle; see verse one) perception
trividham, (n. nom. sg.) threefold, three aspects
anumānam, (n. nom. sg.)
ākhyātam, (n. nom. sg., p. pass. participle) described, gave an account of
tad, (n. nom. sg.) this, that, then
liṅga, (n.) characteristic, sign, mark
liṅgi, (n.) that which bears a mark
pūrvakam, (n.) earlier, previous
(*liṅga-liṅgi-pūrvakam,* a clear mark and a prior mark)
āpta, complete, full, respected
śrutis, hearing, oral tradition
(*āpta-śrutis,* f. nom. sg., a credible tradition)
āpta, complete, full, respected
vacanam, (n. nom. sg.) speaking, saying
(*āpta-vacanam,* n. nom. sg., valid testimony)
ca, and

5. The Importance of Inference

सामान्यतस्तु दृष्टादतीन्द्रियाणां प्रसिद्धिरनुमानात्* ।
तस्मादपि चासिद्धं परोक्षमाप्तागमात् सिद्धम् ॥६॥
*प्रतीतिरनुमानात्

sāmānyatas tu dṛṣṭād atīndriyāṇāṃ prasiddhir anumānāt
tasmād api cāsiddhaṃ parokṣamāptāgamāt siddham //6//

From appearance one can know what is common to all.
From inference one can know what is beyond the reach of the senses.
From authoritative declarations, one can establish successfully something that cannot be established otherwise.

sāmānyatas, (m. nom. sg.) equally, generally
tu, but

dṛṣṭāt, (n. abl. sg.) from appearance
atīndriyāṇām, (m. gen. pl.) beyond the senses, the Self
prasiddhis, (f. nom. sg.) accomplishment, success
anumānāt, (n. abl. sg.) from inference
tasmāt, (n. abl. sg.) from which, therefore
api, even
ca, and
asiddham, (n. nom. sg., p. pass. participle.) not established, not accomplished
paras, (m. nom. sg.) beyond, away
akṣam, (n. nom. sg.) sight, the eye
āpta, complete, full, respected
āgamāt, (m. abl. sg.) testimony
(*āpta-āgamāt*, m. abl. sg. reliable testimony)
siddham, (n. nom. sg., p. pass. participle.) established, accomplished

अतिदूरात् सामीप्यादिन्द्रियघातान्मनोऽनवस्थानात् ।
सौक्ष्म्याद् व्यवधानादभिभवात् समानाभिहाराच्च ॥७॥

atidūrāt sāmīpyād indriya-ghātān mano'navasthānāt
saukṣmyād vyavadhānād abhibhavāt samānābhihārāc ca //7//

[Why are we not able to see the unmanifest and the knower, *Prakṛti* and *Puruṣa*? Why we must rely upon inference to gain knowledge?]
(1) Some things are too far away.
(2) Some things are too close.
(3) Sometimes our faculties fail.
(4) The mind can be unstable.
(5) Some things are too subtle.
(6) Obstructions arise.
(7) [The evidence] can be overpowered.
(8) Intermixture of similar qualities [can obscure distintions].

atidūrāt, (n. abl. sg.) from far away
sāmīpyāt, (n. abl. sg.) from nearby
indriya, (n) sense, faculty
ghātāt, (m. abl sg.) from injury, impairment
(*indriya-ghātāt*, m. abl sg. from impaired faculties)
manas, (n. nom. sg.) mind
anavasthānāt, (n. abl. sg.) from instability
saukṣmyāt, (n. abl. sg.) from subtlety, minuteness

vyavadhānāt, (n. abl. sg.) from obstruction, interruption
abhibhavāt, (m. abl. sg.) from overpowering
samāna, similar, alike
abhihārāt, (m. abl. sg.) from bringing near, intermixing
(*samāna-abhihārāt*, m. abl. sg.) the intermixture of similar items
ca, and

6. Prakṛti, though Subtle, Is Real

सौक्ष्म्यात्तदनुपलब्धिर्नाभावात्, कार्यतस्तदुपलब्धिः ।
महदादि तच्च कार्यं, प्रकृतिविरूपं सरूपं च ॥८॥

saukṣmyāt tad anupalabdhir nābhavāt, kāryatas tad upalabdhiḥ
mahadādi tac ca kāryaṃ, prakṛti-virūpaṃ sarūpaṃ ca //8//

Due to her subtlety, she cannot be apprehended.
This does not mean she does not exist.
She is apprehended through her effects.
These effects begin with the *Mahat*.
They are similar to and different from *Prakṛti*.

saukṣmyāt, (n. abl. sg.) from subtlety, minuteness
tad, (n. nom. sg.) this, that, then
anupalabdhis, (f. nom. sg.) non-perceptible
na, not
abhavāt, (m. abl. sg.) from non-existence
kāryatas, (adv.) by effect, product
tad, (n. nom. sg.) this, that, then
upalabdhis, (f. nom. sg.) apprehend, see
mahat, (m.) the intellect, *buddhi*
ādi, (m. nom. sg.) beginning with, *et cetera*
(*mahat-ādi*, m. nom. sg., beginning with the intellect)
tad, (n. nom. sg.) this, that, then
ca, and
kāryam, (n. nom. sg., f. pass. participle) to be done
prakṛti, (f.) nature
virūpam, (n. nom. sg.) variegated, manifold
(*prakṛti-virūpam*, n. nom. sg., different in form from *prakṛti*)
sarūpam, (n. nom. sg.) the same in form, shape
ca, and

असदकरणादुपादानग्रहणात्, सर्वसम्भवाभावात् ।
शक्तस्य शक्यकरणात्, कारणभावाच्च, सत्कार्यम् ॥९॥

asad-akaraṇād upādāna-grahaṇāt, sarva-sambhāva-abhāvāt
śaktasya śakya-karaṇāt, kāraṇa-bhāvāc ca, satkāryam //9//

(1) No action arises from non-existence.
(2) Anything that can be grasped arises from perception.
(3) There is no existence that arises from all things.
(4) The efficacy of an action arises from its power.
(5) Existence arises from a material cause.
Hence, each occurrence (*karaṇa*) is real.

asat, (n.) non-existent
akaraṇāt, (n. abl. sg.) from inactivity
(*asat-akaraṇāt,* n. abl. sg., nonexistence from inactivity)
upādāna, (n.) grasping, perceiving
grahaṇāt, (n. abl. sg.) from perceiving, grasping
(*upādāna-grahaṇāt,* n. abl. sg., perception from grasping)
sarva, all
sambhāva, together
abhāvāt, (n. abl. sg.) from non-becoming
(*sarva-sambhāva-abhāvāt,* all things from non-becoming)
śaktasya, (m. gen. sg.) of power
śakya, able, possible
karaṇāt, (m. abl. sg.) from the cause
(*śakya-karaṇāt,* from the ability)
kāraṇa, (n.) cause
bhāvāt, from the existent
(*kāraṇa-bhāvāt,* existence because of a cause)
ca, and
satkāryam, (n. nom. sg.) pre-existent effect of the cause

7. Qualities of the Manifest and the Unmanifest

हेतुमदनित्यमव्यापि सक्रियमनेकमाश्रितं लिङ्गम् ।
सावयवं परतन्त्रं व्यक्तं विपरीतमव्यक्तम् ॥१०॥

hetumad anityam avyāpi sakriyam anekam āśritaṃ liṅgam
sāvayavaṃ paratantraṃ vyaktaṃ viparītam avyaktam //10//

The manifest is
(1) caused
(2) finite
(3) non-pervasive
(4) active
(5) multiple
(6) supported
(7) marked with personality (*liṅgam*)
(8) composed of parts
(9) dependent on another.
The unmanifest is the opposite.

hetumat, (n. nom. sg.) having a cause, caused
anityam, (n. nom. sg.) not eternal, finite
avyāpi, (n. nom. sg.) non-pervasive, limited
sakriyam, (n. nom. sg.) active
anekam, (n. nom. sg.) not singular, multiple
āśritam, (n. nom. sg., p. pass. participle) supported
liṅgam, (n. nom. sg.) marked
sāvayavam, (n. nom. sg.) composed of parts
paratantram, (n. nom. sg.) dependent on another, subordinate
vyaktam, (n. nom. sg., *vi* + *√añj,* to make distinct, clear) the manifest
viparītam, (n. nom. sg.) the opposite
avyaktam, (n. nom. sg.) the unmanifest

त्रिगुणमविवेकि विषयः सामान्यमचेतनं प्रसवधर्मि ।
व्यक्तं तथा प्रधानं, तद्विपरीतस्तथा च पुमान् ॥११॥

triguṇam aviveki viṣayaḥ sāmānyam acetanaṃ prasavadharmi
vyaktaṃ tathā pradhānam, tad viparītas tathā ca pumān //11//

An object is discerned due to the three *guṇas*.
It is held in common and is not conscious.
It proceeds according to its constitution (*dharma*).
The manifest is therefore linked to the *pradhāna*.
The *pumān* (*Puruṣa*) stands apart from it.

triguṇam, (n. nom. sg.) the three *guṇas*
aviveki, (n. nom. sg.) undiscerned.
viṣayas, (m. nom. sg.) an object of the senses
sāmānyam, (n. nom. sg.) after the same manner as, held in common

acetanam, (n. nom. sg.) unconscious, unthinking, inanimate
prasava, proceeds
dharmi, (n. nom. sg.) true to *dharma*
(*prasava-dharmi,* n. nom. sg., proceed according to *dharma*)
vyaktam, (n. nom. sg., see verse 10) the manifest
tathā, therefore
pradhānam, (n. nom. sg.) the cause of the manifest, *mūla-prakṛti*
tad, (n. nom. sg.) this, that, then
viparītas, (m. nom. sg.) the opposite
tathā, thus, also
ca, and
pumān, (m. nom. sg.) *Puruṣa,* the Self

8. The *Guṇas*

प्रीत्यप्रीतिविषादात्मकाः प्रकाशप्रवृत्तिनियमार्थाः ।
अन्योऽन्याभिभवाश्रयजननमिथुनवृत्तयश्च गुणाः ॥१२॥

prīty-aprīti-viṣād-ātmakāḥ prakāśa-pravṛtti-niyama-arthāḥ
anyo'nya-abhibhava-āśraya-janana-mithuna-vṛttayaś ca guṇāḥ
//12//

In regard to the guṇas, their nature is delight, disgust, and despair.
Their purpose is luminosity, activity, and restraint.
Their fluctuations combine so one overpowers the others.
One predominates while the others support.

prīti, (f.) delight
aprīti, (f.) disgust
viṣāda, (m.) despair
ātmakās, (m. nom. pl) having the nature of
(*prīty-aprīti-viṣād-ātmakās,* m. nom. pl., having the nature of delight, disgust, and despair)
prakāśa, (m.) luminosity
pravṛtti, (f.) activity
niyama, (m.) restraint
arthās, (m. nom. pl.) purpose
(*prakāśa-pravṛtti-niyama-arthās,* m. nom. pl. having the purpose of luminosity, activity, and restraint)
anyo'nya, one another

abhibhava, (m.) overpowering, overcoming
āśraya, (m.) supporting
janana, (n.) producing
mithuna, (n.) combining
vṛttayas, (m. nom. pl.) fluctuations
(*anyo'nya-abhibhava-āśraya-janana-mithuna-vṛttayas,* m. nom. pl., fluctuations combine producing an overpowering by one [and] the support of the others)
ca, and
guṇās, (m. nom. pl) the *guṇas*

सत्त्वं लघु प्रकाशकमिष्टमुपष्टम्भकं चलं च रजः ।
गुरु वरणकमेव तमः प्रदीपवच्चार्थतो वृत्तिः ॥१३॥

sattvaṃ laghu-prakāśakam iṣṭam upaṣṭambhakaṃ calaṃ ca rajaḥ
guru-varaṇakam eva tamaḥ pradīpavac cārthato vṛttiḥ //13//

***Sattva* is light and luminous.**
***Rajas* stimulates and moves.**
***Tamas* is heavy and concealing.**
A fluctuation is like a lamp.
Its purpose is to make a thing apparent.

sattvam, (n. nom. sg.) *sattva*
laghu, light
prakāśakam, (n. nom. sg.) luminous
laghu-prakāśakam, n. nom. sg., light and luminous)
iṣṭam, (n. nom. sg.) desire (not in translation?)
upaṣṭambhakam, (n. nom. sg.) stimulation
calam, (n. nom. sg.) moving, shaking
ca, and
rajas, (n. nom. sg.) *rajas*
guru, heavy.
varaṇakam, (n. nom. sg.) concealing, enveloping
(*guru-varaṇakam,* n. nom. sg., heavy and concealing)
eva, indeed (used as a rythmic filler)
tamas, (n. nom. sg.) *tamas*
pradīpavat, like a lamp
ca, and
arthatas, (adv.) for the purpose of
vṛttis, (f. nom. sg.) a fluctuation

अविवेक्यादिः सिद्धः त्रैगुण्यात्तद्विपर्ययाभावात्* ।
कारणगुणात्मकत्वात् कार्यस्याव्यक्तमपि सिद्धम् ॥१४॥
*अविवेक्यादेस्सिद्धिस्त्रैगुण्यात्तद्विपर्ययाभावात् or
अविवेक्यादि हि सिद्धं त्रैगुण्यात्तद्विपर्ययाभावात्

aviveky-ādiḥ siddhaḥ traiguṇyāt tad viparyayābhāvāt
kāraṇa-guṇa-atmakatvāt kāryasyāvyaktam api siddham //14//

The humble jumble of nondiscernment arises from the three *guṇas*.
The absence of that results in the contrary (the *pumān*).
The material cause be found in the nature of the *guṇas*.
The unmanifest is thus established in the effect.

aviveki, (n. nom. sg.) non-discernment
ādis, (m. nom. sg.) *et cetera*
(*aviveki-ādis,* (m. nom. sg.) non-discernment, *et cetera*)
siddhas, (m. nom. sg., p. pass. participle) is achieved, is accomplished
traiguṇyāt, (n. abl. sg.) by the three *guṇas*
tad, (n. nom. sg.) this, that, then
viparyaya, (m.) the contrary
abhāvāt, (m. abl. sg.) non-existence, absence
(*viparyaya-abhāvāt,* m. abl. sg., the opposite from the absence)
kāraṇa, (n.) cause
guṇa, (m.) *guṇa*
atmakatvāt, (m. abl. sg.) from the quality of being composed of
(*kāraṇa-guṇa-atmakatvāt,* (m. abl. sg.) from the quality of being composed of the cause of the *guṇas*)
kāryasya, (n. gen. sg. f. pass. participle) of that which is to be done
avyaktam, (n. nom. sg., see verse 10) the unmanifest
api, even
siddham, (n. nom. sg., p. pass. participle.) established

9. Prakṛti: The Cause

भेदानां परिमाणात्, समन्वयात्, शक्तितः प्रवृत्तेश्च ।
कारणकार्यविभागात्, अविभागाद्वैश्वरूप्यस्य ॥१५॥
कारणमस्त्यव्यक्तं प्रवर्तते त्रिगुणतः समुदयाच्च ।
परिणामतः सलिलवत् प्रतिप्रतिगुणाश्रयविशेषात् ॥१६॥

bhedānāṃ parimāṇāt, samanvayāt, śaktitaḥ pravṛtteśca
kāraṇa-kārya-vibhāgāt, avibhāgād vaiśva-rūpyasya //15//
kāraṇam asty avyaktaṃ pravartate triguṇataḥ samudayāc ca
pariṇāmataḥ salilavat pratiprati-guṇāśraya-viśeṣāt //16//

The unmanifest is the cause
(1) Because of the number of distinctions.
(2) Because all things hold a common origin.
(3) Because activity follows its own power.
(4) Because there is a distinction between cause and effect.
(5) Because all distinctions disappear back into a universal form.
(6) All things arise from the three *guṇas*
like the emergence of water as steam, liquid, and ice.
(7) All specificity relies upon the particularity of the *guṇas*.

bhedānām, (m. gen. pl.) of distinctions
parimāṇāt, (n. abl. sg.) from measuring, meting out
samanvayāt, (m. abl. sg.) from the regular succession
śaktitas, (adv.) according to its own power
pravṛttes, (f. abl. sg.) from activity
ca, and
kāraṇa, (n.) cause
kārya, (n.) effect
vibhāgāt, (m. abl. sg.) from the distinction
(*kāraṇa-kārya-vibhāgāt,* m. abl. sg., because of the distinction between cause and effect)
avibhāgāt, (m. abl. sg.) from the non-distinction
vaiśva, (m. *vṛddhi* derivative of *viśva*)
rūpyasya, (m. gen. sg. gerund √*rūp*) formed
(*vaiśva-rūpyasya,* m. gen. sg., universal form, multiplicity, manifoldness)
kāraṇam, (n. nom. sg.) the cause
asti, (third-person singular, present active; from √*as,* to be) is
avyaktam, (n. nom. sg., see verse 10) the unmanifest
pravartate, (third-person singular, present middle; from *pra+*√*vṛt,* being, existing) arises, occurs
triguṇatas, (adv.) by the three *guṇas*
samudayāt, (m. abl. sg.) from the union, coming together, aggregation
ca, and
pariṇāmatas, (adv.) by changing, emerging as
salilavat, (n. nom. sg.) having or related to water

pratiprati, specificity, being a counterpart
guṇa, (m.) the *guṇas*
āśraya, (m.) supporting
viśeṣāt, (m. abl. sg.) from the particularity, specificity of
(*pratiprati-guṇa-āśraya-viśeṣāt,* m. abl. sg., from specificity the particularity of the *guṇas*)

10. Puruṣa

संघातपरार्थत्वात्* त्रिगुणादिविपर्ययादधिष्ठानात् ।
पुरुषोऽस्ति भोक्तृभावात् कैवल्यार्थं प्रवृत्तेश्च ॥१७॥
*संङ्गातपरार्थत्वात्

saṃghāta-parārthatvāt triguṇādi-viparyayād-adhiṣṭhānāt
puruṣo'sti bhoktṛ bhāvāt kaivalya-arthaṃ pravṛtteś ca //17//

Puruṣa exists
(1) Because combinations exist for the sake of another.
(2) Because there must be something distinct from the *guṇas*.
(3) Because there must be a superintendent.
(4) Because there must be an enjoyer.
(5) Because both activity and freedom exist for its sake.

saṃghāta, (m.) combinations
parārthatvāt, (m. abl. sg.) from another's advantage
(*saṃghāta-parārthatvāt,* m. abl. sg., because combinations [exist] for the sake of another)
triguṇa, (m.) the three *guṇas*
ādi, (m.) *et cetera*
viparyayāt, (m. abl. sg.) from the opposite
(*triguṇa-ādi-viparyayāt,* from the opposite of the three *guṇas,* etc.)
adhiṣṭhānāt, (n. abl. sg.) from the superintendent
puruṣas, (m. nom. sg.) the Self
asti, (third-person singular, present active; see verse 16) is
bhoktṛ, (m.) the enjoyer
bhāvāt, (m. abl. sg.) from the existent of
(*bhoktṛ-bhāvāt,* because of the existence of an enjoyer)
kaivalya, (n.) freedom, independence, isolation, unity
artham, (n. nom. sg.) goal
(*kaivalya-artham,* n. nom. sg., the goal of freedom)

pravṛttes, (f. abl. sg.) from activity
ca, and

जननमरणकरणानां प्रतिनियमादयुगपत्प्रवृत्तेश्च ।
पुरुषबहुत्वं सिद्धं त्रैगुण्यविपर्ययाच्चैव ॥१८॥

janana-maraṇa-karaṇānāṃ pratiniyamād ayugapat-pravṛtteś ca
puruṣa-bahutvaṃ siddhaṃ traiguṇya-viparyayāc caiva //18//

It is established that there are many *Puruṣas.*
(1) Because of the diversity of births, deaths and faculties.
(2) Because activities take place at different times.
(3) Because the distinctions of the proportions of the three *guṇas* vary.

janana, (n.) birth, being born
maraṇa, (n.) dying, death
karaṇānām, (n. gen. pl.) of the actions
(*janana-maraṇa-karaṇānām,* n. gen. pl., of the actions of births and deaths)
pratiniyamāt, (m. abl. sg.) from a general rule, from a separate allotment
ayugapad, (ind.) not all at once, at separate times
pravṛttes, (f. abl. sg.) from activity
ca, and
puruṣa, (m.) *Puruṣa*
bahutvam, (n. nom. sg.) abundance, multitude
(*puruṣa-bahutvam,* multitude of *puruṣas*)
siddham, (n. nom. sg., p. pass. participle.) established, accomplished
traiguṇya, (n.) the three *guṇas*
viparyayāt, (m. abl. sg.) from the opposite, distinction
(*traiguṇya-viparyayāt,* m. abl. sg., the distinctions of the three *guṇas*)
ca, and
eva, indeed (used as a rythmic filler)

तस्माच्च विपर्यासात् सिद्धं साक्षित्वमस्य पुरुषस्य ।
कैवल्यं माध्यस्थ्यं द्रष्टृत्वमकर्तृभावश्च ॥१९॥

tasmāc ca viparyāsāt siddhaṃ sākṣitvamasya puruṣasya
kaivalyaṃ mādhyasthyaṃ draṣṭṛtvam akartṛ-bhāvaś ca //19//

The *Puruṣa* is the opposite of the three *guṇas.*
It is the witness. It is solitary (*kaivalyaṃ*), neutral (*madhyastha*).
It is the seer. It does nothing.

tasmāt, (m. abl. sg.) from this, therefore
ca, and
viparyāsāt, (m. abl. sg.) from the opposite
siddham, (n. nom. sg., p. pass. participle.) established, accomplished
sākṣitvam, (n. nom. sg.) the quality of witnessing
asya, (m. gen. sg.) its
puruṣasya, (m. gen. sg.) of the Self
kaivalyam, (n. nom. sg.) freedom, independence, isolation, unity
mādhyasthyam, (n. nom. sg.) neutral, indifferent
draṣṭṛtvam, (n. nom. sg.) the seer
akartṛ, (m.) non-actor, one who does nothing
bhāvas, (m. nom. sg.) being
(*akartṛ-bhāvas,* m. nom. sg., being one who does nothing)
ca, and

11. Compresence (*Saṃyoga*): Confusing Prakṛti for Puruṣa

तस्मात्तत्संयोगादचेतनं चेतनावदिव लिङ्गम् ।
गुणकर्तृत्वे च तथा कर्तेव भवत्युदासीनः ॥२०॥

tasmāt tat saṃyogād acetanaṃ cetanāvad iva liṅgam
guṇa-kartṛtve ca tathā karteva bhavati udāsīnaḥ //20//

Furthermore, due to compresence (*saṃyoga*),
the unconscious personality appears as if it were conscious.
Because of the fluctuations of the *guṇas*,
the indifferent one appears as if active.

tasmāt, (m. abl. sg.) from this, furthermore
tad, (n. nom. sg.) this, that, then
saṃyogāt, (m. abl. sg.) from compresence, conflation, conjunction
acetanam, (n. nom. sg.) unconscious, unthinking, inanimate
cetanāvat, (n. nom. sg.) conscious, having consciousness
iva, like, as
liṅgam, (n. nom. sg.) mark, sign
guṇa, (m.) the *guṇas*
kartṛtve, (m. loc. sg.) in the state of action, in being active
(*guṇa-kartṛtve,* m. loc. sg., in the activity of the *guṇas*)
ca, and
tathā, therefore

kartā, (m. nom. sg.) the doer
iva, like, as
bhavati, (third-person singular, present active; from √*bhū,* becoming, gaining, reflecting) is, becomes, appears
udāsīnas, (m. nom. sg.) the indifferent one (*Puruṣa*)

12. Reciprocity between Puruṣa and Prakṛti

पुरुषस्य दर्शनार्थं कैवल्यार्थं तथा प्रधानस्य ।
पङ्ग्वन्धवदुभयोरपि संयोगस्तत्कृतः सर्गः ॥२१॥

puruṣasya darśanārthaṃ kaivalyārthaṃ tathā pradhānasya
paṅgv-andhavad-ubhayor api saṃyogas tat kṛtaḥ sargaḥ //21//

The *pradhāna* provides the twin purposes
of experience and freedom for the *Puruṣa,*
like a blind person who teams up with a lame person.
Creation occurs due to compresence (*saṃyoga*).
***Puruṣa* needs *pradhāna* for experience and freedom.**
***Pradhāna* needs *Puruṣa* in order to see. When the two connect, the creation emerges.**

puruṣasya, (m. gen. sg.) of the Self
darśana, (n.) experience
artham, (n. nom. sg.) purpose, goal
(*darśana-artham,* n. nom. sg., the purpose of experience)
kaivalya, (n.) freedom, independence, isolation, unity
artham, (n. nom. sg.) purpose, goal
(*kaivalya-artham,* the purpose of freedom)
tathā, therefore
pradhānasya, (n. gen. sg.) the cause of the manifest, *mūla-prakṛti*
paṅgu, (m.) one who is lame, crippled
andhavat, (m.) one who is blind
ubhayos, (m. gen. du.) of both
(*paṅgv-andhavat-ubhayos,* m. gen. du., of both a blind person and a lame person together)
api, even
saṃyogas, (m. nom. sg.) compresence, conflation, conjunction
tad, (n. nom. sg.) this, that, then
kṛtas, (m. nom. sg., p. pass. participle; √*kṛ,* doing) done, created
sargas, (m. nom. sg.) creation, emission

13. Emergence

प्रकृतेर्महान्, ततोऽहङ्कारः तस्माद्गणश्च षोडशकः ।
तस्मादपि षोडशकात् पञ्चभ्यः पञ्च भूतानि ॥२२॥

prakṛter mahān, tato'haṅkāraḥ tasmād guṇaś ca ṣoḍaśakaḥ
tasmād api ṣoḍaśakāt pañcabhyaḥ pañca bhūtāni //22//

From *Prakṛti* come the *Mahat* and then the *ahaṃkāra*.
Then the group of sixteen arises (see verse three).
Then, from the midst of the sixteen,
one group of five (the rudiments or *tanmātras*) produces the five elements.

prakṛtes, (f. abl. sg.) from *Prakṛti*, nature
mahān, (m. nom. sg.) the intellect, *buddhi*
tatas, hence, there
ahaṅkāras, (m. nom. sg.) the ego
tasmāt, (m. abl. sg.) from this, therefore
gaṇas, (m. nom. sg.) a group
ca, and
ṣoḍaśakas, (m. nom. sg.) the sixteen (the *manas*, *buddīndriyāni*, *karmendriyāni*, and *mahābhūtāni*)
tasmāt, (m. abl. sg.) from this, therefore
api, even
ṣoḍaśakāt, (m. abl. sg.) from the sixteen (the *manas*, *buddīndriyāni*, *karmendriyāni*, and *mahābhūtāni*)
pañcabhyas, (m. abl. sg.) from the five (*tanmatra*)
pañca, five
bhūtāni, (n. nom. pl.) elements
(*pañca-bhūtāni*, n. nom. pl., the five elements)

14. The Eight *Bhāvas*

अध्यवसायो बुद्धिर्धर्मो ज्ञानं विराग ऐश्वर्यम् ।
सात्त्विकमेतद्रूपं तामसमस्माद्विपर्यस्तम् ॥२३॥

adhyavasāyo buddhir dharmo jñānaṃ virāgāiśvaryam
sāttvikam etad rūpaṃ tāmasam asmād viparyastam //23//

Mental effort in its elevated state (*sāttvika*)
leads to *dharma*, knowledge, freedom from attachment, and power.
From *tamas*, the reverse arises.

adhyavasāyas, (m. nom. sg.) mental effort
buddhis, (f. nom. sg.) *buddhi,* intellect
dharmas, (m. nom. sg.; from √*dhṛ,* holding) *dharma,* virtue, righteousness
jñānam, (n. nom. sg.; from √*jñā,* to know) knowledge, understanding
virāgas, (m. nom. sg.; from √*rañj,* to be reddened, attracted) dispassion, freedom from attachment
aiśvaryam, (n. nom. sg.; from √īś, command, rule; √*vṛ,* choose) power, dominion
sāttvikam, (n. nom. sg.) *sattvic;* in the mode of clarity, goodness, purity
etad, this
rūpam, (n. nom. sg.) form
tāmasam, (n. nom. sg.) related to *tamas,* ignorance, darkness
asmāt, (n. abl. sg.) from which
viparyastam, (n. nom. sg.) the reverse, opposite

15. Creation and the Body

अभिमानोऽहङ्कारस्तस्माद्* द्विविधः प्रवर्तते सर्गः ।
एकादशकश्च गणस्तन्मात्रः पञ्चकश्चैव ॥२४॥

*words separated to avoid ligature issue

abhimāno'haṅkāras tasmād dvividhaḥ pravartate sargaḥ
ekādaśakaś ca gaṇas tanmātraḥ pañcakaś caiva //24//

Pride characterizes ego and yields a two-fold creation:
the eleven (mind, sense organs, and action organs)
and the battalion of the five rudiments (the *tanmātras*).

abhimānas, (m. nom. sg.) pride, conceit
ahaṅkāras, (m. nom. sg.) the ego
tasmāt, (m. abl. sg.) from this, therefore
dvividhas, (m. nom. sg.) two-fold
pravartate, (third-person singular, present middle; see verse 16) arises, occurs

sargas, (m. nom. sg.) creation, emission
ekādaśakas, (m. nom. sg.) the eleven (*manas, indriyāni,* and *karmendriyāni*)
ca, and
gaṇas, (m. nom. sg.) group, battalion
tanmātras, (m. nom. sg.) subtle elements, rudiments
pañcakas, (m. nom. sg.) the five.
ca, and
eva, indeed (used as a rythmic filler)

सात्त्विक एकादशकः* प्रवर्तते वैकृतादहङ्कारात् ।
भूतादेस्तन्मात्रः स तामसः, तैजसादुभयम् ॥२५॥

sāttvika ekādaśakaḥ pravartate vaikṛtād ahaṅkārāt
bhūtādes tanmātraḥ sa tāmasaḥ, taijasād ubhayam //25//

From the energization of the ego
arises the illuminating (*sattvika*) eleven (the mind and the ten organs)
and the heavier (*tamasika*) elements, rudimentary and gross.
Both are suffused with *tejas* (*rajasika*).

sāttvika, (m.) *sattvic;* in the mode of clarity, goodness, purity
ekādaśakas, (m. nom. sg.) the eleven
(*sāttvika-ekādaśakas,* m. nom. sg., the illuminating eleven)
pravartate, (third-person singular, present middle; see verse 16) arises, occurs
vaikṛtāt, (n. abl. sg.) from the *sattvic* evolutes of ego
ahaṅkārāt, (m. abl. sg.) from ego
bhūtādes, (m. abl. sg.) from the *tamasic* evolutes of ego
tanmātras, (m. nom. sg.) subtle elements, rudiments
sa, (ind.), with
tāmasas, (m. nom. sg.) related to *tamas,* ignorance, darkness
taijasāt, (n. abl. sg.) from the *rajasic* evolutes of ego
ubhayam, (n. nom. sg.) both

बुद्धीन्द्रियाणि चक्षुःश्रोत्रघ्राणरसनस्पर्शनकानि ।
वाक्पाणिपादपायूपस्थान्* कर्मेन्द्रियाण्याहुः ॥२६॥

*two or three *variæ lectiones* found: *sparśanakāni* vs *tvagākhyāni* in the first line, *upasthān* vs *upasthāḥ* & *vākrapāṇi* vs *vākpāṇi* in the second line

buddhīndriyāni cakṣuḥ-śrotra-ghrāṇa-rasana-sparśanakāni
vāk-pāṇi-pāda-pāyūpasthān karmendriyāṇy āhuḥ //26//

The sense organs are eyes, ears, nose, taste buds, and skin.
The action organs are speech, hands, feet, anus, and genitals.

buddhi, (f.) the intellect
indriyāni, (n. nom. pl.) the senses
(*buddhi-indriyāni,* n. nom. pl., the sense organs)
cakṣus, (n.) eyes
śrotra, (n.) ears
ghrāṇa, (n.) nose
rasana, (n.) taste buds, tongue
sparśanakāni, (n. acc. pl.) skin
(*cakṣuḥ-śrotra-ghrāṇa-rasana-sparśanakāni,* n. acc. pl., eyes, ears, nose, taste buds, and skin)
vāc, (f.) speech
pāṇi, (m.) the hand
pāda, (m.) foot
pāyu, (m.) anus
upasthān, (n. acc. pl.)
(*vāk-paṇi-pāda-pāyu-upasthān,* speech, hands, feet, anus, and genitals)
karma, (n.) action
indriyāni, (n. nom. pl.) the senses
(*karma-indriyāṇi,* n. nom. pl., the organs of action)
āhus, (third-person plural, present perfect; from √*ah,* saying, speaking) it is said

उभयात्मकमत्र मनः संकल्पकमिन्द्रियं च साधर्म्यात् ।
गुणपरिणामविशेषान्नानात्वं बाह्यभेदाश्च ॥२७॥

ubhayātmakam atra manaḥ saṃkalpakam indriyaṃ ca sādharmyāt
guṇa-pariṇāma-viśeṣān nānātvaṃ bāhya-bhedāc ca //27//

The mind is of the nature of both (the sense organs and action organs).
The organs follow its intention.
From the distinctions of its constitutive guṇas,
the various aspects of the external world arise correspondingly.

ubhaya, (n.) both
ātmakam, (n. nom. pl) having the nature of

(*ubhaya-ātmakam*, n. nom. pl, having the nature of both)
atra, here, in this place, in this respect
manas, (n. nom. sg.) mind
saṃkalpakam, (m. acc. sg.) intention
indriyam, the organs (of sense and action)
ca, and
sādharmyāt, (n. abl. sg.) identity of nature, assimilation to, homogeneousness
guṇa, (m.) the *guṇas*
pariṇāma, (m.) change, transformation
viśeṣāt, (m. abl. sg.) distinctions
(*guṇa-pariṇāma-viśeṣāt*, m. abl. sg., from the transformations of the *guṇas*)
nānātvam, (n. nom. sg.) variety, difference
bāhya, (n.) external
bhedāt, (n. abl. sg.) from the divisions, aspects
(*bāhya-bhedāt*, from the different aspects of the external)
ca, and

शब्दादिषु* पञ्चानामालोचनमात्रमिष्यते वृत्तिः ।
वचनादानविहरणोत्सर्गानन्दाश्च पञ्चानाम् ॥२८॥
*रूपादिषु

śabdādiṣu pañcānām ālocana-mātram iṣyate vṛttiḥ
vacanādāna-viharaṇotsargānandaś ca pañcānām //28//

A fluctuation correlates to the awareness-only
of the five (rudimentary elements) starting with sound
or the five operations
of speaking, holding, walking, excreting, or sexual pleasure.

śabda, (m.) sound
ādiṣu, (m. loc. pl.) beginning with, *et cetera*
(*śabda-ādiṣu*, in sound, *etc*)
pañcānām, (m. gen. pl.) of the five
ālocana, (n.) awareness, perception
mātram, (n. nom. sg.) only, merely
(*alocana-mātram*, n. nom. sg. awareness-only)
iṣyate, (third-person singular, present passive; from √*iṣ*, causing) is said, becomes possible
vṛttis, (f. nom. sg.) a fluctuation
vacana, (m.) speaking

adāna, (m.) holding
viharaṇa, (m.) walking
utsarga, (m.) excreting
ānandas, (m. nom. sg.) bliss, sexual pleasure
(*vacana-adāna-viharaṇa-utsarga-ānandas*, speaking, holding, walking, excreting, or sexual pleasure)
ca, and
pañcānām, (m. gen. pl.) of the five

16. *Guṇas* and Breath Present in All Operations

स्वालक्षण्यं वृत्तिस्त्रयस्य सैषाभवत्यसामान्या ।
सामान्यकरणवृत्तिः प्राणाद्या वायवः पञ्च ॥२९॥

svālakṣaṇyaṃ vṛttis trayasya saiṣā bhavaty asāmānyā
sāmānya-karaṇa-vṛttiḥ prāṇādyā vāyavaḥ pañca //29//

A fluctuation has the three characteristics (*guṇas*).
No (fluctuation) is held in common.
The five winds, expressed through the breath,
form a fluctuation that is common in every operation.

svālakṣaṇyam, (n. nom. sg.) identifying quality or characteristic
vṛttis, (f. nom. sg.) fluctuation
trayasya, (n. gen. sg.) of the three
sā, (f. nom. sg.) that
eṣā, (f. nom. sg.) this
bhavati, (third-person singular, present active; see verse 20) is, becomes
asāmānyā, (f. nom. sg.) not common; not shared
sāmānya, (f.) common, shared
karaṇa, (n.) action, operation
vṛttis, (f. nom. sg.) a fluctuation
(*sāmānya-karaṇa-vṛttis*, f. nom. sg., a fluctuation common in every operation)
prāṇa, (m.) *prāṇa*, the first of the five winds with *apāna, samāna, vyāna,* and, *udāna*
ādyās, (m. nom. pl.) beginning with, *et cetera*
(*prāṇa-ādyās*, m. nom. pl., beginning with *prāṇa*)
vāyavas, (m. nom. pl.) winds
pañca, (m. nom. sg.) five

युगपच्चतुष्टयस्य तु वृत्तिः क्रमशश्च तस्य निर्दिष्टा ।
दृष्टे तथाऽप्यदृष्टे त्रयस्य तत्पूर्विका वृत्तिः ॥३०॥

yugapac catuṣṭayasya tu vṛttiḥ kramaśaś ca tasya nirdiṣṭā
dṛṣṭe tathā'py adṛṣṭe trayasya tatpūrvikā vṛttiḥ //30//

A fluctuation, it is said, arises in steps and simultaneously
due to four (functions) [of *buddhi, ahaṃkāra, manas,* and an *indriya*].
Furthermore, it can be seen that every action
has an unseen precedent [governed] by the three (*guṇas*).

yugapad, (ind.) all at once, simultaneously
catuṣṭayasya, (n. gen. sg.) of the four (*buddhi, ahaṃkāra, manas, and an indriya*)
tu, and, or, but
vṛttis, (f. nom. sg.) a fluctuation
kramaśas, (ind.) in steps, gradually
ca, and
tasya, (n. gen. sg.) of it
nirdiṣṭā, (f. nom. sg., p. pass. participle) governed
dṛṣṭe, (m. loc. sg., p. pass. participle; see verse one) in the seen
tathā, therefore
api, even
adṛṣṭe, (m. loc. sg., p. pass. participle; see verse one) in the unseen
trayasya, (n. nom. sg.) of the three (*guṇas*)
tad, (n. nom. sg.) this, that, then
pūrvikā, (f. nom. sg.) precedent
vṛttis, (f. nom. sg.) a fluctuation

17. All Things Have Puruṣa as Their Purpose

स्वां स्वां प्रतिपद्यन्ते परस्पराकूतहेतुकां वृत्तिम् ।
पुरुषार्थ एव हेतुर्न केनचित्कार्यते करणम् ॥३१॥

svāṃ svāṃ pratipadyante parasparākūta-hetukāṃ vṛttim
puruṣārtha eva hetur na kenacit kāryate karaṇam //31//

Each fluctuation arises
due to its mutuality of cause and resulting condition.

Each occurrence (*karaṇa*) is created
for nothing other than for the purpose of *Puruṣa*.

svām svām, (fem. acc. sg.) each its own
pratipadyante, (third-person plural, present passive; from *prati* + √*pad,* going moving) arises, begins
paraspara, (n.) mutuality
ākūta, (n.) intention, purpose
hetukām, (m. abl. pl.) cause
(*paraspara-ākūta-hetukām,* m. abl. pl., mutuality of cause and resulting condition)
vṛttim, (f. acc. sg.) fluctuation
puruṣa, (m.) *Puruṣa*
arthas, (m. nom. sg.) goal, aim, purpose
(*puruṣa-arthas,* m. nom. sg., the purpose of *Puruṣa*)
eva, only
hetus, (m. nom. sg.) cause
na, not
kenacit, (n. ins. sg.) by anyone
kāryate, (third-person singular, present passive causative; from √*kṛ,* doing) is caused to act
karaṇam, (n. nom. sg.) action, operation

करणं त्रयोदशविधं तदाहरणधारणप्रकाशकरम् ।
कार्यं च तस्य दशधाऽऽहार्यं धार्यं* प्रकाश्यं च ॥३२॥
**varia lectio* धार्य्यं

karaṇaṃ trayodaśa-vidhaṃ tad āharaṇa-dhāraṇa-prakāśa-karam
kāryaṃ ca tasya daśadhā''hāryaṃ dhāryaṃ prakāśyaṃ ca //32//

Occurrences happen through a thirteen-fold process
resulting in holding, sustaining, and revealing.
The result of this is tenfold,
allowing all that is to be held, sustained, and revealed
[through the ten sensory and action organs].

karaṇam, (n. nom. sg.) action, operation
trayodaśavidham, (n. nom. sg.) thirteen-fold
tad, (n. nom. sg.) that
āharaṇa, (n.) holding
dhāraṇa, (n.) sustaining

prakāśa, (m.) revealing
karam, (n. nom. sg., *in fine compositi*) causing, resulting in
(*āharaṇa-dhāraṇa-prakāśa-karam,* n. nom. sg., resulting in holding, sustaining, and revealing)
kāryam, (n. nom. sg., f. pass. participle) to be done
ca, and
tasya, (n. gen. sg.) of this
daśadhā, (ind.) ten-fold
hāryam, (n. nom. sg., f. pass. participle) to be held
dhāryam, (n. nom. sg., f. pass. participle) to be sustained
prakāśyam, (n. nom. sg., f. pass. participle) to be revealed
ca, and

18. Inner and Outer Worlds

अन्तःकरणं त्रिविधं दशाधा बाह्यं त्रयस्य विषयाख्यम् ।
साम्प्रतकालं बाह्यं त्रिकालमाभ्यन्तरं करणम् ॥३३॥

antaḥ-karaṇaṃ trividhaṃ daśādhā bāhyaṃ trayasya viṣayākhyam
sāmprata-kālaṃ bāhyam trikālam ābhyantaraṃ karaṇam //33//

The inner occurrence is threefold [*buddhi, ahaṃkāra, manas*]
The external is tenfold [involving sense and action organs].
The context for experiencing an object is predicated by the three (*guṇas*).
The external always exists in the present.
The internal occurrence (*karaṇam*) resides in all three times (past, present, future).

antaḥkaraṇam, (n. nom. sg.) the inner occurence, the internal organ (*buddhi, ahaṃkāra,* and *manas*)
trividham, (n. nom. sg.) threefold
daśādhā, (ind.) tenfold.
bāhyam, (n. nom. sg.) the external
trayasya, (m. nom. sg.) of the three (*guṇas*)
viṣaya, (m.) an object of the senses
ākhyam, (m. acc. sg., *in fine compositi*) called, known as
(*viṣaya-ākhyam,* m. acc. sg., that which is known to the senses)
sāmprata, (n.) present
kālam, (n. nom. sg.) time

(*sāmprata-kālam*, n. nom. sg., the present time)
bāhyam, (n. nom. sg.) the external
trikālam, (n. nom. sg.) the three times (past, present, and future)
ābhyantaram, (n. nom. sg.) the internal
karaṇam, (n. nom. sg.) action, operation

बुद्धीन्द्रियणि तेषां पञ्च विशेषाविशेषविषयाणि ।
वाग्भवति शब्दविषया शेषाणि तु पञ्चविषयाणि ॥३४॥

buddhīndriyāni teṣāṃ pañca viśeṣāviśeṣa-viṣayāṇi
vāg bhavati śabda-viṣayā śeṣāṇi tu pañca-viṣayāṇi //34//

The sense organs take five forms.
Their objects can be distinct (*mahābhūtas*) or indistinct (*tanmātras*).
Speech (an action organ) finds its object in sound.
The remaining (action organs) include all five objects.
[holding, walking, passing of water, and moving of the bowels entail all five elements, with degrees of breath, heat, water, and earth involved in each occurrence]

buddhi, (f.) the intellect
indriyāni, (n. nom. pl.) the senses
(*buddhi-indriyāni*, n. nom. pl., the sense organs)
teṣām, (n. gen. pl.) of which
pañca, (n. nom. pl.) five
viśeṣa, (m.) distinct
aviśeṣa, (m.) indistinct
viṣayāṇi, (n. nom. pl.) objects of the senses
(*viśeṣa-aviśeṣa-viṣayāṇi*, n. nom. pl., distinct and indistinct objects of the senses)
vāk, (f. nom. sg.) speech
bhavati, (third-person singular, present active; see verse 20) is, becomes
śabda, (m.) sound
viṣayā, (f. nom. sg.) object of the senses
(*śabda-viṣayā*, f. nom. sg., sound as its object)
śeṣāṇi, (n. nom. pl.) the rest, the remainder
tu, and, or, but
pañca, (n. nom. pl.) five
viṣayāṇi, (n. nom. pl.) objects of the senses

19. Buddhi: Platform for Human Impulse

सान्तःकरणा बुद्धिः सर्वं विषयमवगाहते यस्मात ।
तस्मात् त्रिविधं करणं द्वारि द्वाराणि शेषाणि ॥३५॥

sāntaḥkaraṇā buddhiḥ sarvaṃ viṣayam avagāhate yasmāt
tasmāt trividhaṃ karaṇaṃ dvāri dvārāṇi śeṣāṇi //35//

Because the *buddhi*, as part of the inner occurrence,
comprehends all objects,
therefore, the threefold occurrence [*buddhi, ahaṃkāra, manas*]
holds the door for all remaining doors.

sa, with
antaḥkaraṇās, (m. nom. pl.) inner occurence, inner organ
buddhis, (f. nom. sg.) *buddhi*, intellect
sarvam, (n. nom. sg.) all
viṣayam, (m. acc sg.) an object of the senses
avagāhate, (third-person singular, present middle; from *ava* + √*gāh*, shaking, stirring) plunges, enters, possesses
yasmāt, (n. abl. sg.) because, from which
tasmāt, (m. abl. sg.) therefore, from this
trividham, (n. nom. sg.) threefold
karaṇam, (n. nom. sg.) occurence, the *antaḥkarana*)
dvāri, (f. loc. sg.) in the door
dvārāṇi, (n. nom. pl.) doors
śeṣāṇi, (n. nom. pl.) the rest, the remainder

एते प्रदीपकल्पाः परस्परविलक्षणा गुणविशेषाः ।
कृत्स्नं पुरुषस्यार्थं प्रकाश्य बुद्धौ प्रयच्छन्ति* ॥३६॥
*प्रयच्छति

ete pradīpa-kalpāḥ paraspara-vilakṣaṇā guṇa-viśeṣāḥ
kṛtsnaṃ puruṣasyārthaṃ prakāśya buddhau prayacchanti //36//

These (experiences), like a lamp, are distinct,
one from another, determined by the *guṇas*.
They are brought to light in the *buddhi*,
utterly for the purpose of *Puruṣa*.

ete, these

pradīpa, (m.) a lamp
kalpās, (m. nom. pl., *in fine compositi*) having the manner or form of, resembling
(*pradīpa-kalpās,* m. nom. pl., like a lamp)
paraspara, (n.) one another
vilakṣaṇās, (m. nom. pl.) distinct
(*paraspara-vilakṣaṇās,* m. nom. pl., distinct from one another)
guṇa, (m.) the *guṇas*
viśeṣās, (m. nom. pl.) distinguished, determined
(*guṇa-viśeṣās,* m. nom. pl., determined by the *guṇas*)
kṛtsnam, (n. nom. sg.) all, completely, utterly
puruṣasya, (m. gen. sg.) of the Self
artham, (n. nom. sg.) purpose, goal
prakāśya, (n.) to be illuminated
buddhau, (m. loc. sg) in the *buddhi*
(*prakāśya-buddhau,* m. loc. sg., illuminated in the *buddhi*
prayacchanti, (third-person plural, present active; from *pra* + √*yam,* moving around, presenting) bring out, present

सर्वं प्रत्युपभोगं यस्मात् पुरुषस्य साधयति बुद्धिः ।
सैव च विशिनष्टि पुनः प्रधानपुरुषान्तरं सूक्ष्मम् ॥३७॥

sarvaṃ praty upabhogaṃ yasmāt puruṣasya sādhayati buddhiḥ
saiva ca viśinaṣṭi punaḥ pradhāna-puruṣāntaraṃ sūkṣmam //37//

Therefore, the *buddhi* delivers all experience to the *Puruṣa*.
Furthermore, it alone distinguishes
the subtle boundary between the *pradhāna* and *Puruṣa*.

sarvam, (n. nom. sg.) all
prati, (ind.) upon, towards, to
upabhogam, (m. acc. sg.) enjoyment, experience, sensory gratification
yasmāt, (n. abl. sg.) therefore
puruṣasya, (m. gen. sg.) of the Self
sādhayati, (third-person singular, present active causative; from √*sidh,* going, driving) causes to go, delivers
buddhis, (f. nom. sg.) *buddhi,* intellect
sas, (m. nom. sg.) he, this, (the *buddhi*)
eva, alone
ca, and
viśinaṣṭi, (third-person singular, present active; from *vi* + √*śiṣ,* distinguishing, discriminating from others) distinguishes, discerns
punar, (ind.) again, furthermore

pradhānam, (n.) the cause of the manifest, *mūla Prakṛti*
puruṣa, (m.) the *Puruṣa*
antaram, (n. acc. sg.) end, boundary, interior, within
(*pradhāna-puruṣa-antaram,* (n. acc. sg., the boundary between the *pradhāna* and *Puruṣa* OR the [subtle] *Puruṣa* within *pradhānam*)
sūkṣmam, (n. acc. sg.) subtle

तन्मात्राण्यविशेषाः तेभ्यो भूतानि पञ्च पञ्चभ्यः ।
एते स्मृता विशेषाः शान्ता घोराश्च मूढाश्च ॥३८॥

tanmātrāṇy aviśeṣāḥ tebhyo bhūtāni pañca pañcabhyaḥ
ete smṛtā viśeṣāḥ śāntā ghorāś ca mūḍhāś ca //38//

The rudimentary elements are indistinct.
From them the five gross elements arise.
These are seen to be distinct:
peaceful, turbulent, and stultified.

tanmātrāṇi, (n. nom. pl.) subtle elements, rudiments
aviśeṣās, (m. nom. pl.) indistinct
tebhyas, (n. abl. pl) from them, from these
bhūtāni, (n. acc. pl.) the gross elements
pañca, five
pañcabhyas, (abl. pl.) from the five
ete, (m. nom. pl.) those
smṛtās, (m. nom. pl., p. pass. participle; from √*smṛ,* to remember) are seen as, described to be
viśeṣās, (m. nom. pl.) distinct
śāntās, (m. nom. pl., p. pass. participle; from √*śam,* being tranquil) peaceful, calm
ghorās, (m. nom. pl.) turbulent, terrible
ca, and
mūḍhās, (m. nom. pl., p. pass. participle; from √*muh,* fainting, becoming senseless) stultified
ca, and

20. The Threefold Origin of the Body

सूक्ष्मा* मातापितृजाः सह प्रभूतैस्त्रिधा विशेषाः स्युः ।
सूक्ष्मास्तेषां नियता मातापितृजा निवर्तन्ते ॥३९॥
*सूक्ष्माः

sūkṣmā mātā-pitṛ-jāḥ saha prabhūtais tridhā viśeṣāḥ syuḥ
sūkṣmās teṣāṃ niyatā mātā-pitṛ-jā nirvartante //39//

Three distinct factors can be postulated (in regard to the human):
(1) the subtle [factors],
(2) (the body) born of a mother and father,
(3) and acts of will.
The subtle influences and restraints endure (from life to life)
while those (bodies) born of mother and father pass away.

sūkṣmās, (m. nom. sg.) the subtle
mātā, (f.) mother
pitṛ, (m.) father
jās, (m. nom. sg.) born of
(*mātā-pitṛ-jās,* m. nom. sg, born of a mother and father)
saha, with
prabhūtais, (m. ins. pl.) with the elements
tridhās, (m. nom. pl.) threefold, three factors
viśeṣās, (m. nom. pl.) distinct
syus, (third-person plural, optative active; from √*as,* to be) be they, should they be
sūkṣmās, (m. nom. sg.) subtle
teṣām, (n. gen. pl.) of them
niyatās, (m. nom. pl.) restraints
mātā, (f.) mother
pitṛ, (m.) father
jās, (m. nom. sg.) born of
(*mātā-pitṛ-jās,* m. nom. sg, born of a mother and father)
nirvartante, (third-person plural, present active; from *nir* + √*vṛt,* being, existing) cease, pass away

21. Personality: The *Liṅgam*

पूर्वोत्पन्नमसक्तं नियतं महदादिसूक्ष्मपर्यन्तम् ।
संसरति निरुपभोगं भावैरधिवासितं लिङ्गम् ॥४०॥

pūrvotpannam asaktaṃ nityaṃ mahadādi-sūkṣma-paryantam
saṃsarati nirūpa-bhogaṃ bhāvair adhivāsitaṃ liṅgam //40//

The personality, which is cloaked with the *bhāvas,*
has already arisen, but is not yet connected.

It endures within the *Mahat* to the edge of the subtle.
Because it has not experienced enjoyment, it transmigrates.

pūrva, (n.) before
utpannam, (n. acc. sg., p. pass. participle; from √*pad,* going, moving) arisen
(*pūrva-utpannam,* n. acc. sg., p. pass. participle, already arisen
asaktam, (n. nom. sg., p. pass. participle; from √*sañj,* sticking to) unconnected, unattached
nityam, (ind.) always, eternal
mahat, (m.) the intellect, *buddhi*
ādi, (m.) beginning with, *et cetera*
sūkṣma, (m.) subtle
paryantam, (n. nom. sg.) ending with, altogether
(*mahat-ādi-sūkṣma-paryantam,* n. nom. sg., from the *mahat* down to the subtle)
saṃsarati, (third-person singular, present active; from *sam* + √*sṛ,* flowing) flows together, transmigrates
nirupabhogam, (n. nom. sg.) not enjoying
bhāvais, (n. ins. pl.) by the *bhāvas*
adhivāsitam, (n. nom. sg., p. pass. participle; from √*vas,* wearing, putting on) cloaked with, steeped in
liṅgam, (n. nom. sg.) the personality

चित्रं यथाश्रयमृते स्थाण्वादिभ्यो यथा विना* छाया ।
तद्वद्विनाऽविशेषैः न तिष्ठति निराश्रयं लिङ्गम् ॥४१॥
*order reversed: विना यथा

citraṃ yathāśrayam ṛte sthāṇv-ādibhyo yathā vinā chāyā
tadvad vinā'viśeṣaiḥ na tiṣṭhati nirāśrayaṃ liṅgam //41//

Just as art requires color,
just as without pillars there can be no shadow,
similarly, the personality cannot exist without the specifics (of the *bhāvas*).

citram, (m. acc. sg.) color, variation
yathā, just as
āśrayam, (m. acc. sg.) support; dependance
ṛte, (ind.) without, unless
sthāṇu, (m.) a stump, trunk, post, pillar
ādibhyas, (m. abl. pl.) beginning with, *et cetera*
(*sthāṇu-ādibhyas,* m. abl. pl., from a pillar, *et cetera*)

yathā, just as
vinā, (ind.) without
chāyā, (f. nom. sg.) shadow, shade
tadvat, (ind.) likewise, just as
vinā, (ind.) without
aviśeṣais, (m. ins. sg.) without specifics, lacking distinction
na, not
tiṣṭhati, (third-person singular, present active; from √*sthā,* resorting, stopping, being restrained) exists
nirāśrayam, (m. acc. sg.) without support
liṅgam, (n. nom. sg.) the personality

पुरुषार्थहेतुकमिदं निमित्तनैमित्तिकप्रसङ्गेन ।
प्रकृतेर्विभुत्वयोगात् नटवद्व्यवतिष्ठते लिङ्गम् ॥४२॥

puruṣārtha-hetukam nimitta-naimittika-prasaṅgena
prakṛter vibhutva-yogāt naṭavad vyavatiṣṭhate liṅgam //42//

The personality performs like an actor
due to its connection (*yoga*) with the allurement of *Prakṛti*.
This is the cause of human exertion:
yearning for both the secular (*nimitta*, experience)
and the transcendent (*naimittika*, freedom).

puruṣa, (m.) the self, *Puruṣa*
artha, (m.) goal, aim, purpose
hetukam, (n. nom. sg.) cause
(*puruṣa-artha-hetukam,* n. nom. sg., the cause of human exertion)
nimitta, (n.) secular
naimittika, (n.) transcendent
prasaṅgena, (m. ins. sg.) by attachment
(*nimitta-naimittika-prasaṅgena,* m. ins. sg., by yearning for the secular and transcedent)
prakṛtes, (f. abl./gen. sg.) from nature, *Prakṛti*
vibhutva, (n.) omnipresence, allure
yogāt, (m. abl. sg.) due to connection
(*vibhutva-yogāt,* m. abl. sg., due to connection with allure)
naṭavat, (n. nom. sg.) an actor, a dancer
vyavatiṣṭhate, (third-person singular, present middle; from *vi* + *ava* + √*sthā,* resorting, stopping, being restrained)
liṅgam, (n. nom. sg.) the personality

22. The *Bhāvas*

सांसिद्धिकाश्च भावाः प्राकृतिका वैकृतिकाश्च धर्माद्याः ।
दृष्टाः करणाश्रयिणः कार्याश्रयिणश्च कललाद्याः ॥४३॥

sāṃsiddhikāś ca bhāvāḥ prākṛtikā vaikṛtikāś ca dharmādyāḥ
dṛṣāḥ karaṇāśrayiṇaḥ kāryāśrayiṇaś ca kalalādyāḥ //43//

The *bhāvas*, including *dharma* and the others, are primary.
They are seen in the way life occurrences unfold
and in the unfolding growth of an embryo.

sāṃsiddhikās, (m. nom. pl.) natural, innate
ca, and
bhāvās, (m. nom. sg.) the *bhāvas*
prākṛtikās, (m. nom. sg.) natural, primary, related to *Prakṛti*
vaikṛtikās, (m. nom. sg.) derivative, secondary
ca, and
dharma, (m.) *dharma,* virtue, righteousness
ādyās, (m. nom. pl.) beginning with, *et cetera*
(*dharma-ādyās,* m. nom. pl., beginning with *dharma*)
dṛṣās, (m. nom. pl, p. pass. participle) are seen
karaṇa, (n.) cause, *buddhi* (Mainkar says buddhi, Larson says it's the 13)
āśrayiṇas, (m. gen./abl. sg.) from the attached
(*karaṇa-āśrayiṇas,* m. abl. sg., from the connected cause)
kārya, (n.) effect, the body
āśrayiṇas, (m. gen./abl. sg.) from the attached
(*kārya-āśrayiṇas,* m. nom. sg., from the connected effects/qualities)
ca, and
kalala, (n.) embryo
ādyās, (m. nom. pl.) beginning with, *et cetera*
(*kalala-ādyās,* m. nom. pl., an embryo, *et cetera*)

धर्मेण गमनमूर्ध्वं गमनमधस्ताद् भवत्यधर्मेण ।
ज्ञानेन चापवर्गो विपर्ययादिष्यते बन्धः ॥४४॥

dharmeṇa gamanam ūrdhvaṃ gamanam adhastād bhavaty adharmeṇa
jñānena cāpavargo viparyayādiṣyate bandhaḥ //43//

With *dharma* there is movement upward.
Without *dharma,* things move downward.

With knowledge freedom arises.
From its opposite, bondage.

dharmeṇa, (m. ins. sg.) with *dharma,* virtue, righteousness
gamanam, (n. nom. sg.) going
ūrdhvam, (n. nom. sg.) upwards
gamanam, (n. nom. sg.) going
adhastāt, (n. abl. sg. or ind.) downward
bhavati, (third-person singular present active; see verse 20) is, becomes
adharmeṇa, (m. ins. sg.) without *dharma*
jñānena, (n. ins. sg.) with knowledge
ca, and
apavargas, (m. nom. sg.) freedom, emancipation, completion
viparyayāt, (m. abl. sg.) from the opposite
iṣyate, (third-person singular, passive present; see verse 28) causes
bandhas, (m. nom. sg.) bondage

वैराग्यात् प्रकृतिलयः संसारो भवति राजसाद्रागात् ।
ऐश्वर्यादविघातो विपर्ययात् तद्विपर्यासः ॥४५॥

vairāgyāt prakṛti-layaḥ saṃsāro bhavati rājasādrāgāt
aiśvaryād avighāto viparyayāt tad viparyāsaḥ //45//

From nonattachment, things resolve themselves back into *Prakṛti.*
From passionate attachment, *saṃsāra* arises.
From power, obstacles dissolve.
From its opposite, they persist.

vairāgyāt, (n. abl. sg.) from nonattachment
prakṛti, (f.) *Prakṛti*
layas, (m. nom. sg.) dissolution, absorption
(*prakṛti-layas,* m. nom. sg., resolve back into *Prakṛti*)
saṃsāras, (m. nom. sg.) *saṃsāra,* transmigration
bhavati, (third-person singular present active; see verse 20) arises
rājasāt, (n. abl. sg.) from that related to passion, *rajas*
rāgāt, (n. abl. sg.) from attachment
aiśvaryāt, (n. abl. sg.) from power
avighātas, (m. nom. pl.) unimpeded
viparyayāt, (m. abl. sg.) from the opposite
tad, (n. nom. sg.) this, that, then
viparyāsas, (m. nom. sg.) opposite

एष प्रत्ययसर्गो विपर्ययाशक्तितुष्टिसिद्ध्याख्यः ।
गुणवैषम्यविमर्द्देन तस्य* भेदास्तु पञ्चाशत् ॥४६॥
*गुणवैषम्यविमर्द्दात्तस्य च

eṣa pratyaya-sargo viparyayāśakti-tuṣṭi-siddhyākhyaḥ
guṇa-vaiṣamya-vimarddena tasya bhedās tu pañcāśat //46//

The mental drama can also be described
in terms of ignorance, incapacity, complacency, and perfection.
Due to the diversity of disturbances of the *guṇas*,
there are fifty varieties.

eṣa, (m. nom. sg.) this
pratyaya, (m.) consciousness, the *buddhi*
sargas, (m. nom. sg.) creation, emission
(*pratyaya-sargas,* m. nom. sg., the emission of consciousness, the mental drama)
viparyaya, (m.) ignorance, obstruction
aśakti, (f.) weakness, incapacity
tuṣṭi, (f.) complacency
siddhi, (f.) perfection
ākhyas, (m. nom. sg., *in fine compositi*) called, known as
(*viparyaya-aśakti-tuṣṭi-siddhi-ākhyas,* described in terms of ignorance, incapacity, complacency, and perfection)
guṇa, (m.) the *guṇas*
vaiṣamya, (m.) unevenness
vimarddena, (m. ins. sg.) with the disturbance
(*guṇa-vaiṣamya-vimarddena,* m. ins. sg., with the diversity of the disturbances of the *guṇas*)
tasya, (n. gen. sg.) of it
bhedās, (m. nom. pl.) varieties
tu, and, or, but
pañcāśat, (f. nom. sg.) fifty

पञ्च विपर्ययभेदा भवन्त्यशक्तिश्च करणवैकल्यात् ।
अष्टाविंशतिभेदा तुष्टिर्नवधाऽष्टधा सिद्धिः ॥४७॥

pañca viparyaya-bhedā bhavanty aśaktiś ca karaṇa-vaikalyāt
aṣṭāviṃśati-bhedā tuṣṭir navadhā'ṣṭadhā siddhiḥ //47//

There are five varieties of ignorance.
There are 28 incapacities due to defects in occurrences (*karaṇa*), nine contentments, and eight perfections.

pañca, five
viparyaya, (m.) ignorant, perverse
bhedās, (m. nom. pl.) varieties
(*pañca-viparyaya-bhedā,* m. nom. pl., five varieties of ignorance)
bhavanti, (third-person plural, present active; see verse 20) are
aśaktis, (f. nom. sg.) incapacity
ca, and
karaṇa, (m.) occurences, the instrument, *buddhi*
vaikalyāt, (n. abl. sg.) from defects, imperfection
(*karaṇa-vaikalyāt,* n. abl. sg., defects in occurences)
aṣṭāviṃśati, twenty-eight
bhedās, (m. nom. pl.) varieties
(*aṣṭāviṃśati-bhedā,* m. nom. pl., twenty-eight varieties)
tuṣṭis, (f. nom. sg.) contentment
navadhā, (ind.) ninefold
aṣṭadhā, (ind.) eightfold
siddhis, (f. nom. sg.) perfections

भेदस्तमसोऽष्टविधो मोहस्य च, दशविधो महामोहः ।
तामिस्रोऽष्टादशधा, तथा भवत्यन्धतामिस्रः ॥४८॥

bhedas tamaso'ṣṭavidho mohasya ca, daśavidho mahāmohaḥ
tāmisro'ṣṭādaśadhā, tathā bhavaty andhatāmisraḥ //48//

There are eight varieties of darkness (*tamas*).
There are ten varieties of delusion [extending] to great delusion.
Thus there are 18 forms of darkness, [extending] into the abyss.

bhedas, variety
tamasas, (m. nom. pl.) darkness, *tamas*
aṣṭavidhas, (m. nom. sg.) eightfold
mohasya, (m. gen. sg.) of delusion
ca, and
daśavidhas, (m. nom. sg.) tenfold
mahāmohas, (m. nom. sg.) great delusion
tāmisras, (m. nom. sg.) darkness

aṣṭādaśadhā, (ind.) eighteen-fold
tathā, therefore
bhavati, (third-person singular, present active; see verse 20) is, becomes
andhatāmisras, (m. nom. sg.) complete darkness, the abyss

एकादशेन्द्रियवधाः सह बुद्धिवधैरशक्तिरुद्दिष्टा ।
सप्तदश वधा बुद्धेविपर्ययात् तुष्टिसिद्धीनाम् ॥४९॥

ekādaśendriya-vadhāḥ saha buddhi-vadhair aśaktir uddiṣṭā
saptadaśa vadhā buddhe viparyayāt tuṣṭi-siddhīnām //49//

There are eleven injuries to the senses.
There are also injuries to the *buddhi*.
The injuries to the *buddhi* are seventeen:
the opposite of the nine contentments and the eight perfections.

ekādaśa, eleven
indriya, (n.) senses
vadhās, (m. nom. pl.) injuries
(*ekādaśa-indriya-vadhās*, m. nom. pl., eleven injuries to the senses)
saha, together with
buddhi, (f.) the intellect, *buddhi*
vadhais, (m. ins. pl.) with injuries
(*buddhi-vadhais*, (m. ins. pl.) with injuries to the *buddhi*
aśaktis, (f. nom. sg.) weakness, injury
uddiṣṭās, (m. nom. pl., p. pass. participle; from √*diś*, giving) mentioned, given
saptadaśa, seventeen
vadhās, (m. nom. pl.) injuries
buddhes, (f. gen. sg.) of the *buddhi*
viparyayāt, (m. abl. sg.) from the opposite
tuṣṭi, (f.) contentments
siddhīnām, (f. gen. pl.) of the perfections
(*tuṣṭi-siddhīnām*, (f. gen. pl.) of the [nine] contentments and [eight] perfections

आध्यात्मिकाश्चतस्रः प्रकृत्युपादानकालभाग्याख्याः ।
बाह्या विषयोपरमात् पञ्च, नव तुष्टयोऽभिहिताः* ॥५०॥
*तुष्टयोऽभिमताः

ādhyātmikāś catasraḥ prakṛty-upādāna-kāla-bhagyākhyāḥ
bāhyā viṣayoparamāt pañca, nava tuṣṭayo'bhihitāḥ //50//

The contentments are imagined as nine.
There are four inherent contentments that arise:
nature (*Prakṛti*); material goods (*upādāna*); time (*kāla*); and luck (*bhāgya*).
There are five external contentments,
derived from overcoming the objects of the senses.

ādhyātmikās, (m. nom. pl.) inherent, related to the higher self
catasras, (f. nom. pl.) the four
prakṛti, (f.) *Prakṛti*
upādāna, (n.) material goods
kāla, (m.) time
bhagya, (m.) luck
ākhyās, (m. nom. pl., *in fine compositi*) called, known as
(*prakṛti-upādāna-kāla-bhagya-ākhyās,* m. nom. pl., known as nature, material goods, time, and luck
bāhyās, (m. nom. sg.) external
viṣayoparamāt, (m. abl. sg.) from overcoming the objects of the senses
pañca, five
nava, nine
tuṣṭayas, (f. nom. pl.) contenments
abhihitās, (m. nom. sg., p. pass. participle) declared, said, imagined

ऊहः शब्दोऽध्ययनं दुःखविघातास्त्रय सुहृत्प्राप्तिः ।
दानं च सिद्धयोऽष्टौ सिद्धेः पूर्वोऽङ्कुशस्त्रिविधः ॥५१॥

ūhaḥ śabdo'dhyayanaṃ duḥkha-vighātās traya suhṛt-prāptiḥ
dānaṃ ca siddhayo'ṣṭau siddheḥ pūrvo'ṅkuśas trividhaḥ //51//

Thoughtfulness, [attentiveness to] sound, introspection, overcoming the threefold suffering, obtaining the good heart, and generosity are the eight successes (*siddhis*).
From success, one tames the prior threefold (suffering).

ūhas, (m. nom. sg.) removing, changing, adding
śabdas, (m. nom. sg.) sound
adhyayanam, (n. nom. sg.) reading, studying, recitation
duḥkha, (m.) suffering
vighātās, (m. nom. pl) injuring, overcoming
(*duḥkha-vighātās,* m. nom. pl., overcoming suffering)
traya, three, threefold
suhṛd, (m.) a good heart

prāptis, (f. nom. sg.) obtaining, achieving
(*suhṛd-prāptis,* f. nom. sg., obtaining the good heart)
dānam, (n. nom. sg.) giving, generosity
ca, and
siddhayas, (f. nom. pl.) successes
aṣṭau, eight
siddhes, (f. abl. sg.) from success
pūrvas, (m. nom. sg.) prior
aṅkuśas, (m. nom. sg.) goading, taming
trividhas, threefold

न विना भावैर्लिङ्गं न लिङ्गेन भावनिर्वृत्तिः ।
लिङ्गाख्यो भावाख्यस्तस्माद् द्विविधः प्रवर्तते सर्गः ॥५२॥

na vinā bhāvair liṅgaṃ na liṅgena bhāvanir vṛttiḥ
liṅgākhyo bhāvākhyas tasmād dvividhāḥ pravartate sargaḥ //52//

Without the *bhāvas*, there is no personality.
Through the personality, there is the quelling of the *bhāvas*.
Therefore, the resultant created world (*sarga*)
emerges in a twofold manner (subtle and gross).

23. The Threefold Cosmos

अष्टविकल्पो दैवस्तैर्यग्योनश्च पञ्चधा भवति ।
मानुषश्चैकविधः* समासतोऽयं त्रिधा* सर्गः ॥५३॥
*मानुषकश्चैकविधः, *समासतो भैतिकः

aṣṭavikalpo daivas tairyagyonaś ca pañcadhā bhavati
mānuṣaś caika vidhaḥ samāsato'yaṃ tridhā sargaḥ //53//

The heavenly realm is eightfold.
Animals are fivefold.*
Humans are all of one kind.
In short, this is the threefold world (*sarga*).
***domestic, wild, birds, reptiles, plants**

aṣṭa, eight
vikalpas, (m. nom. sg.) variation
(*aṣṭa-vikalpas,* m. nom. sg., eight varieties, eightfold)

daivas, (m. nom. sg.) heavenly, related to the *devas*
tairyagyonas, (m. nom. sg.) related to animals
ca, and
pañcadhā, (ind.) fivefold
bhavati, (third-person singular, present active; see verse 20) is, becomes
mānuṣas, (m. nom. sg.) related to humans
ca, and
ekavidhas, (m. nom. sg.) of one kind
samāsatas, (adv.) in summation, in short
ayam, (m. nom. sg.) this
tridhā, (ind.) threefold
sargas, (m. nom. sg.) creation, emission

24. The *Guṇas*

ऊर्ध्वं सत्त्वविशालस्तमोविशालश्च मूलतः सर्गः ।
मध्ये रजोविशालो ब्रह्मादिस्तम्बपर्यन्तः ॥

ūrdhvaṃ sattva-viśālas tamo-viśālaś ca mūlataḥ sargaḥ
madhye rajo-viśālo brahmādi-stamba-paryantaḥ //54//

In the upper realm, there is an abundance of *sattva,*
at the lower side of creation, an abundance of *tamas,*
and in the middle, an abundance of *rajas.*
This extends from *Brahmā* to a blade of grass.

ūrdhvam, (n. nom. sg.) upper
sattva, (n.) *sattva*
viśālas, (m. nom. sg.) an abundance, predominance
(*sattva-viśālas,* m. nom. sg., an abundance of *sattva*)
tamas, (n.) *tamas*
viśālas, (m. nom. sg.) an abundance, predominance
tamas-viśālas, m. nom. sg., an abundance of *tamas*)
ca, and
mūlatas, (adv.) at the lower side
sargas, (m. nom. sg.) creation, emission
madhye, (m. loc. sg.) in the middle
rajas, (n.) *rajas*
viśālas, (m. nom. sg.) an abundance, predominance
(*rajas-viśālas,* m. nom. sg., an abundance of *rajas*)
brahma, (m.) Brahma

ādi, (m.) beginning with, *et cetera*
stamba, (m.) a blade of grass
paryantas, (m. nom. sg.) extends, including
(*brahma-ādi-stamba-paryantas,* m. nom. sg., from Brahma to a blade of grass)

25. *Duḥkhaṃ*: Suffering

तत्र जरामरणकृतं दुःखं प्राप्नोति चेतनः पुरुषः ।
लिङ्गस्याविनिवृत्तेः, तस्माद् दुःखं स्वभावेन ॥५५॥

tatra jarā-maraṇa-kṛtaṃ duḥkhaṃ prāpnoti cetanaḥ puruṣaḥ
liṅgasyāvinivṛtteḥ, tasmād duḥkhaṃ svabhāvena

Therein, the conscious *Puruṣa*
meets with the suffering of old age and death.
Due to the *svabhāvas* of the personality not being turned back, there is suffering.

tatra, there
jarā, (f.) old age
maraṇa, (n.) death, dying
kṛtam, (n. nom. sg.) doing, perfomance
(*jarā-maraṇa-kṛtam,* n. nom. sg., old age and death)
duḥkham, (n. nom. sg.) suffering
prāpnoti, (third-person singular, present active; from *pra* + √āp, obtaining) reaches, attains, meets
cetanas, (m. nom. sg.) conscious
puruṣas, (m. nom. sg.) *Puruṣa*
liṅgasya, (m. nom. gen.) of the personality
avinivṛttes, (f. abl. sg.) not turned back
tasmāt, (m. abl. sg.) from this, therefore
duḥkham, (n. nom. sg.) suffering
svabhāvena, (m. ins. sg.) with the *svabhāvas*

26. All Things Exist for Puruṣa

इत्येष प्रकृतिकृतौ* महदादिविशेषभूतपर्यन्तः ।
प्रतिपुरुषविमोक्षार्थं स्वार्थ इव परार्थ आरम्भः ॥५६॥
* प्रकृतिकृतो

ityeṣa prakṛti-kṛtau mahadādi-viśeṣabhūta-paryantaḥ
pratipuruṣa-vimokṣārthaṃ svārtha iva parārtha ārambhaḥ //56//

This is created by *Prakṛti,* from the *Mahat* down to the distinct elements.
Its purpose is to liberate each *Puruṣa.*
This is undertaken for the purpose of the other,
but as if it were for the purpose of itself.

iti, this
eṣas, (m. nom. sg.) this, that
prakṛti, (f.) *Prakṛti*
kṛtau, (f. loc. sg.) in creation. (Mainkar writes *kṛtau,* but translates *kṛtāḥ*)
(*prakṛti-kṛtau,* f. loc. sg., within the creation of *Prakṛti*)
mahat, (n.) *mahat*
ādi, (m.) beginning with, *et cetera*
viśeṣa, (m.) distinct, particular
bhūta, (n.) elements
paryantas, (m. nom. sg.) extends, including
(*mahadādi-viśeṣabhūta-paryantas,* m. nom. sg., from *mahat* down to the distinct elements)
prati, (ind.) each
puruṣa, (m.) *Puruṣa*
vimokṣa, (m.) liberation
artham, (n. nom. sg.) purpose, goal
(*prati-puruṣa-vimokṣa-artham,* n. nom. sg. for the purpose of liberating each *Puruṣa*)
sva, (n.) one's own
arthas, (m. nom. sg.) purpose
(*svārthas,* m. nom. sg., for one's own purpose
iva, like
para, (m.) the other, another
arthas, (m. nom. sg.) purpose
(*para-arthas,* m. nom. sg., for the purpose of the other)
ārambhas, (m. nom. sg.) commencement, creation

वत्सविवृद्धिनिमित्तं क्षीरस्य यथा प्रवृत्तिरज्ञस्य ।
पुरुषविमोक्षनिमित्तं तथा प्रवृत्तिः प्रधानस्य ॥५७॥

vatsa-vivṛddhi-nimittaṃ kṣīrasya yathā pravṛttir ajñasya
puruṣa-vimokṣa-nimittaṃ tathā pravṛttiḥ pradhānasya //57//

Just as milk spontaneously flows forth for the growth of the calf, the flow from the *Pradhāna* occurs for the liberation of *Puruṣa.*

vatsa, (m.) calf
vivṛddhi, (f.) growth
nimittam, (n. nom. sg.) for the sake of, in order to cause
(*vatsa-vivṛddhi-nimittam,* n. nom. sg., forth for the growth of the calf)
kṣīrasya, (n. gen. sg.) of milk
yathā, just as
pravṛttis, (f. nom. sg.) a fluctuation
ajñasya, (n. gen. sg.) of unconscious, spontaneous
puruṣa, (m.) *Puruṣa*
vimokṣa, (m.) liberation
nimittam, (n. nom. sg.) for the sake of, in order to cause
(*puruṣa-vimokṣa-nimittam,* n. nom. sg., for the liberation of *Puruṣa*)
tathā, so also
pravṛttis, (f. nom. sg.) a fluctuation
pradhānasya, (n. gen. sg.) of *pradhāna,* the cause of the manifest, *mūla Prakṛti*

औत्सुक्यनिवृत्त्यर्थं यथा क्रियासु प्रवर्तते लोकः ।
पुरुषस्य विमोक्षार्थं प्रवर्तते तद्वदव्यक्तम् ॥५८॥

autsukya-nivṛtty-arthaṃ yathā kriyāsu pravartate lokaḥ
puruṣasya vimokṣārthaṃ pravartate tadvad avyaktam //58//

Just as actions in the world proceed
for the purpose of quelling anxiety, likewise,
the *avyaktam* proceeds
for the purpose of the liberation of *Puruṣa.*

autsukya, (n.) anxiety
nivṛtti, (f.) quelling
artham, (n. nom. sg.) purpose, goal
(*autsukya-nivṛtti-artham,* n. nom. sg., for the purpose of quelling anxiety)
yathā, just as
kriyāsu, (f. loc. pl.) in actions
pravartate, (third-person singular, present middle; see verse 16) arises, occurs
lokas, (m. nom. sg.) world
puruṣasya, (m. gen. sg.) of the Self
vimokṣa, (m.) liberation

artham, (n. nom. sg.) purpose, goal
(*puruṣasya-vimokṣa-artham,* n. nom. sg., for the purpose of the liberation of *Puruṣa*)
pravartate, (third-person singular, present middle; see verse 16) arises, occurs
tadvat, (ind.) likewise, just as
avyaktam, (n. nom. sg., see verse 10) the unmanifest

27. Freedom

रङ्गस्य दर्शयित्वा निवर्तते नर्तकी तथा नृत्यात् ।
पुरुषस्य तथात्मानं प्रकाश्य विनिवर्तते प्रकृतिः ॥५९॥

raṅgasya darśayitvā nivartate nartakī tathā nṛtyāt
puruṣasya tathātmānaṃ prakāśya vinivartate prakṛtiḥ //59//

Just as a dancer stops dancing
when the charade ends,
so also, *Prakṛti* ceases
once the nature of *Puruṣa* is revealed.

raṅgasya, (m. gen. sg.)
darśayitvā, (causative gerund; from √*dṛs,* to see) having caused to see, having charaded
nivartate, (third-person singular, present middle; see verse 16) stops, desists
nartakī, (f. nom. sg.) a dancer
tathā, just as
nṛtyāt, (n. abl. sg.) from dancing
puruṣasya, (m. gen. sg.) of the Self
tathā, so also
ātmānam, (m. acc. sg.) the self, *Puruṣa*
prakāśyas, (m. nom. sg.) illumination, revelation
vinivartate, (third-person singular, present middle; see verse 16) ceases
prakṛtis, (f. nom. sg.) *Prakṛti*

नानाविधैरुपायैरुपकारिण्यनुपकारिणः पुंसः ।
गुणवत्यगुणस्य सतस्तस्यार्थमपार्थकं चरति ॥६०॥

nānāvidhair upāyair upakāriṇy anupakāriṇaḥ puṃsaḥ
guṇavaty aguṇasya satas tasyārtham apārthakaṃ carati //60//

She is helpful in various ways.
He is not helpful.
She possesses the *guṇas*.
He has no *guṇas*.
She moves for the sake of him.
He has no purpose.

nānāvidhais, (m. ins. pl.) various
upāyais, (m. ins. pl.) ways, means
upakāriṇī, (f. nom. sg.) helpful
anupakāriṇas, (m. nom. sg.) not helpful
puṃsas, (m. gen. sg.) of *Puruṣa*
guṇavatī, (f. nom. sg.) possessing the *guṇas* (*Prakṛti*)
aguṇasya, (m. gen. sg.) of no qualities, without the *guṇas* (*Puruṣa*)
satas, (ind.) equally
tasya, (m. gen. sg.) of him
artham, (n. nom. sg.) purpose, goal
apārthakam, (m. nom. sg.) without a purpose
carati, (third-person singular, present active; from √*car*, going) moves

प्रकृतेः सुकुमारतरं न किञ्चिदस्तीति मे मतिर्भवति ।
या दृष्टास्मीति पुनर्न दर्शनमुपैति पुरुषस्य ॥६१॥

prakṛteḥ sukumārataraṃ na kiñcid astīti me matir bhavati
yā dṛṣṭāsmīti punar na darśanam upaiti puruṣasya //61//

It is my thought that there is nothing more exquisite
than *Prakṛti* who exclaims "I have been seen!"
and retreats from the view of *Puruṣa*.

prakṛtes, (f. abl. sg.) from *Prakṛti*, nature
sukumārataram, (n. nom. sg.) more exquisite
na, not
kiñcit, (ind.) anything
asti, (third-person singular, present active; see verse 16) is
iti, this
me, my (the author's)
matis, (f. nom. sg.) thought, opinion
bhavati, (third-person singular, present active; see verse 20) is, becomes
yā, (f. nom. sg.)
dṛṣṭā, (f. nom. sg., p. pass. participle; see verse one) seen

asmi, (first-person singular, present active; from √*as,* to be) I am
iti, thus
punar, (ind.) again
na, not
darśanam, (n. acc. sg.) view, sight
upaiti, (third-person singular, present active; from *upa* + √*e* OR √*i,* approaching) approaches
puruṣasya, (m. gen. sg.) of the Self

तस्मान्न बध्यते नापि* मुच्यते नापि संसरति कश्चित् ।
संसरति बध्यते मुच्यते च नानाश्रया प्रकृतिः ॥६२॥
* बध्यतेऽसौ न or बध्यतेऽद्धा न

tasmānna badhyate nāpi mucyate nāpi saṃsarati kaścit
saṃsarati badhyate mucyate ca nānāśrayā prakṛtiḥ //62//

Therefore, no one is bound.
Indeed, no one is released.
It is only *Prakṛti* in her various costumes
that transmigrates, is bound, and is free.

tasmāt, (m. abl. sg.) from this, therefore
na, not
badhyate, (third-person singular, present passive; from √*bandh,* binding) bound
na, not
api, even
mucyate, (third-person singular, present passive; from √*muc,* liberating) released
na, not
api, even
saṃsarati, (third-person singular, present active; see verse forty) transmigrates
kaścit, any
saṃsarati, (third-person singular, present active; see verse forty) transmigrates
badhyate, (third-person singular, present passive; from √*bandh,* binding) bound
mucyate, (third-person singular, present passive; from √*muc,* liberating) released
ca, and
nānāśrayā, (f. nom. sg.) various costumes
prakṛtis, (f. nom. sg.) *Prakṛti*

रूपैः सप्तभिरेव तु बध्नात्यात्मानमात्मना प्रकृतिः ।
सैव च पुरुषार्थं प्रति विमोचयत्येकरूपेण ॥६३॥

rūpaiḥ saptabhir eva tu badhnāty ātmānam ātmanā prakṛtiḥ
saiva ca puruṣārthaṃ prati vimocayaty ekarūpeṇa //63//

By seven forms, Prakṛti binds herself through her own self.
She does this for the purpose of Puruṣa.
One form (*eka rūpeṇa*: *jñāna*) causes freedom.

rūpais, (n. ins. pl.) by forms
saptabhis, (n. ins. pl.) by seven
eva, indeed (used as a rythmic filler)
tu, and, or, but
badhnāti, (third-person singular, present active; from √*bandh*, binding) binds
ātmānam, (m. acc. sg.) herself
ātmanā, (m. ins. sg.) by herself
prakṛtis, (f. nom. sg.) *Prakṛti*
sas, (m. nom. sg.) he, this
eva, alone
ca, and
puruṣa, (m.) *Puruṣa*
artham, (n. nom. sg.) goal, aim, purpose
(*puruṣa-artham,* n. nom. sg., the purpose of *Puruṣa*)
prati, (ind.) upon, towards, to
vimocayati, (third-person singular, present active causative; from *vi* + √*muc*, liberating) causes freedom
eka, one
rūpeṇa, (n. ins. sg.) with form
(*eka-rūpeṇa,* n. ins. sg., with one form)

एवं तत्त्वाभ्यासान्नास्मि न मे नाहमित्यपरिशेषम् ।
अविपर्ययाद्विशुद्धं केवलमुत्पद्यते ज्ञानम ॥६४॥

evaṃ tattvābhyāsānnāsmi na me nāham ity apariśeṣam
aviparyayād viśuddhaṃ kevalam utpadyate jñānam //64//

Thus from the practice of the *tattvas*
comes the knowledge:
"I am not, nothing is mine, there is no I."
From this certainty, knowledge arises,
pure and singular, without remainder.

evam, (adv.) thus
tattva, (n.) *tattva*
abhyāsāt, (m. abl. sg.) from the practice
tattva-abhyāsāt, m. abl. sg., from the practice of the *tattvas*
na, not
asmi, (first-person singular, present active; see verse 61) I am
na, not
me, (m. gen. sg.) mine
na, not
aham, (m. nom. sg.) I
iti, thus
apariśeṣam, (n. nom. sg.) without remainder
aviparyayāt, (m. abl. sg.) not from the opposite
viśuddham, (n. nom. sg.) pure
kevalam, (n. nom. sg.) singular
utpadyate, (third-person plural, present passive; from *ut* + √*pad,* going moving) arises
jñānam, (n. nom. sg.) knowledge, understanding

तेन निवृत्तप्रसवामर्थवशात् सप्तरूपविनिवृत्ताम् ।
प्रकृतिं पश्यति पुरुषः प्रेक्षकवदवस्थितः स्वस्थः* ॥६५॥
*सुस्थः or स्वच्छः

tena nivṛtta-prasavām artha-vaśāt sapta-rūpa-vinivṛttām
prakṛtiṃ paśyati puruṣaḥ prekṣakavad-avasthitaḥ svasthaḥ //65//

Through that, *Puruṣa,* like a spectator standing established in himself, sees *Prakṛti* who, from completing her purpose, has ceased her outflows and no longer manifests the seven forms.

tena, (n. ins. sg.) through that
nivṛtta, (m.) turned back
prasavām, (f. acc. sg.) outflow
(*nivṛtta-prasavām,* f. acc. sg., ceasing outflow)
artha, (m.) aim, goal
vaśāt, (m. abl. sg.) from completion
(*artha-vaśāt,* m. abl. sg., from completing her purpose)
sapta, seven
rūpa, (n.) forms
vinivṛttām, (f. acc. sg., p. pass. participle) turned back
(*sapta-rūpa-vinivṛttām,* f. acc. sg., turned back from the seven forms)
prakṛtim, (f. acc. sg.) *Prakṛti*

paśyati, (third-person singular, present active; from √*paś,* seeing) sees
puruṣas, (m. nom. sg.) the Self
prekṣakavat, (adv.) like a spectator
avasthitas, (m. nom. sg., p. pass. participle; from *ava* + √*sthā,* stopping) established
svasthas, (m. nom. sg.) himself

रङ्गस्थ इत्युपेक्षक एको दृष्टाहमित्युपरमत्येका* ।
सति संयोगेऽपि तयोः प्रयोजनं नास्ति सर्गस्य ॥६६॥
*दृष्टाहमित्युपरमत्यन्या

raṅgastha ity upekṣaka eko dṛṣṭāham ity uparam atyekā
sati saṃyoge'pi tayoḥ prayojanaṃ nāsti sargasya //66//

He who is indifferent says, "The dancer stands still!"
She who stands still says, "I have been seen!"
The confusion of the two comes to an end,
There is no more incentive for further creation.

raṅgasthas, (m. nom. sg.) still dancer
iti, thus
upekṣakas, (m. nom. sg.) indifferent
ekas, (m. nom. sg.) the one (*Puruṣa*)
dṛṣṭā, (f. nom. sg., p. pass. participle; see verse one) seen
aham, (m. nom. sg.) I
iti, thus
uparamati, (third-person singular, present active; from √*ram,* stopping) stops
ekā, (f. nom. sg.) the one (*Prakṛti*)
sati, (m. loc. sg.) in existence
saṃyoge, (m. loc. sg.) in connection, union
api, even
tayos, (n. gen. du.) of the two
prayojanam, (n. nom. sg.) incentive
na, not
asti, (third-person singular, present active; see verse 16) is
sargasya, (m. gen. sg.) of creation, emission

28. Life Continues, like the Spinning of the Potter's Wheel

सम्यग्ज्ञानाधिगमाद्धर्मादीनामकारणप्राप्तौ ।
तिष्ठति संस्कारवशाच्चक्रभ्रमवद्धृतशरीरः ॥६७॥

samyag-jñānād hi gamād dharmādīnām akāraṇa-prāptau
tiṣṭhati saṃskāra-vaśāc cakra-bhramavad dhṛta-śarīraḥ //67//

From the advent of this perfect knowledge,
***dharma* and the six others no longer hold sway.**
Yet, due to the force of *saṃskāras*,
the body holds on, standing like a potter's spinning wheel.

samyak, (n.) perfect, correct
jñānāt, (n. abl. sg.) from knowledge
(*samyak-jñānāt,* n. abl. sg., from perfect knowledge)
hi, indeed
gamāt, (n. abl sg.) from reaching, attaining
dharma, (m.) *dharma,* virtue, righteousness
ādīnām, (m. gen. pl.) of those beginning with, *et cetera*
(*dharma-ādīnām,* m. gen. pl., of *dharma* and the others (the *bhāvas*)
akāraṇa, (n.) the absence of cause
prāptau, (f. loc. sg.) on arrival
(*akāraṇa-praptau,* f. loc. sg., upon arrival at inactivity, when there is no more cause)
tiṣṭhati, (third-person singular, present active; from √*sthā,* resorting, stopping, being restrained) remains, holds on
saṃskāra, (m.) *saṃskāras,* impressions on the mind of acts done in a former state of existence.
vaśāt, (m. abl. sg.) from the force.
(*saṃskāra-vaśāt,* m. abl. sg., due to the force of *saṃskāras*)
cakra, (n.) wheel
bhramavat, (adv.) like the turning
(*cakra-bhramavat,* adv., like the turning of a wheel)
dhṛta, (m.) holding, prolonging
śarīras, (m. nom. sg.) the body
dhṛta-śarīras, m. nom. sg., the body holds on)

29. No Return after Death

प्राप्ते शरीरभेदे चरितार्थत्वात् प्रधानविनिवृत्तौ ।
ऐकान्तिकमात्यन्तिकमुभयं कैवल्यमाप्नोति ॥६८॥

prāpte śarīra-bhede caritārthatvāt pradhāna-vinivṛttau
aikāntikam ātyantikam ubhayaṃ kaivalyam āpnoti //68//

From this purpose having been told and fulfilled,
the body is cast off and the *pradhāna* ceases.
***Kaivalyam* is attained, both enduring and singular.**

prāpte, (m. loc. sg., locative absolute, p. pass. participle; from *pra* + *√ap,* obtaining) in attaining
śarīra, (m.) the body
bhede, (m. loc. sg.) in cutting, casting off
(*śarīra-bhede,* m. loc. sg., in casting off the body)
carita, (n.) fulfilled, told
arthatvāt, (n. abl. sg.) from purpose, use
(*carita-arthatvāt,* n. abl. sg., from this purpose having been told and fulfilled)
pradhāna, (n.) the cause of the manifest, *mūla Prakṛti*
vinivṛttau, (m. loc. sg., p. pass. participle) in being turned back
(*pradhāna-vinivṛttau,* m. loc. sg., in the turning back of *pradhāna*)
aikāntikam, (n. nom. sg.) singular
ātyantikam, (n. nom. sg.) enduring
ubhayam, (n. nom. sg.) both
kaivalyam, (n. nom. sg.) freedom, independence, isolation, unity
āpnoti, (third-person singular, present active; from *√āp,* obtaining) attains

30. Conclusion

पुरुषार्थज्ञानमिदं गुह्यं परमर्षिणा समाख्यातम् ।
स्थित्युत्पत्तिप्रलयाश्चिन्त्यन्ते यत्र भूतानाम् ॥६९॥

puruṣārtha-jñānam idaṃ guhyaṃ parama-ṛṣiṇā samākhyātam
sthity-utpatti-pralayāś cintyante yatra bhūtānām //69//

This mystery, this knowledge
regarding all things serving the purpose of *Puruṣa*
has been explained by the Supreme Sage.
The origin, development, and dissolution of the elements (*bhūta*)
is thus brought to consciousness.

puruṣa, (m.) *Puruṣa*
artha, (m.) aim, goal
jñānam, (n. nom. sg.) knowledge, understanding

(*puruṣa-artha-jñānam*, n. nom. sg., knowledge regarding that which serves the purpose of *Puruṣa*)
idam, (n. nom. sg.) this
guhyam, (n. nom. sg.) secret, mystery
parama, (m.) highest, supreme
ṛṣiṇā, (m. ins. sg.) by the sage, *ṛṣi*
(*parama-ṛṣiṇā*, m. ins. sg., by the Supreme Sage)
samākhyātam, (n. nom. sg., p. pass. participle; from *sam* + *ā* + √*khyā*, telling) has been explained
sthiti, (f.) persistence, development
utpatti, (f.) origin
pralayās, (m. nom. pl.) dissolutions
(*sthiti-utpatti-pralayās*, m. nom. pl., the origin, development, and dissolution)
cintyante, (third-person plural, present passive; from √*cint*, remembering, pondering) are contemplated, brought to consciousness
yatra, (ind.) thus
bhūtānām, (n. gen. pl.) of the elements

एतत्पवित्रमग्र्यं मुनिरासुरयेऽनुकम्पया प्रददौ ।
आसुरिरपि पञ्चशिखाय तेन च बहुधा कृतं तन्त्रम् ॥७०॥

etat pavitram agryaṃ munir āsuraye'nukampayā pradadau
āsurir api pañcaśikhāya tena ca bahudhā kṛtaṃ tantram //70//

The sage imparted this excellent and pure knowledge
to Āsuri with compassion.
Āsuri in turn passed it to Pañcaśikha
who expanded it into a complete philosophy.

etad, (n. nom. sg.) this
pavitram, (n. nom. sg.) pure
agryam, (n. nom. sg.) excellent
munis, (m. nom. sg.) sage, *muni*
āsuraye, (m. dat. sg.) for Āsuri
anukampayā, (n. ins. sg.) with compassion
pradadau, (third-person singular, perfect active; from √*dā*, giving) gave
āsuris, (m. nom. sg.) Āsuri
api, even
pañcaśikhāya, (m. dat. sg.) for Pañcaśikha

tena, (m. ins. sg.) by him
ca, and
bahudhā, (adv.) in many ways, greatly, completely
kṛtam, (n. nom. sg.) making
tantram, (n. nom. sg.) a Tantra, philosophical system

शिष्यपरम्परयाऽऽगतमीश्वरकृष्णेन चैतदार्याभिः ।
संक्षिप्तमार्यमतिना सम्यग्विज्ञाय सिद्धान्तम् ॥७१॥

śiṣya-paramparayā"gatamīśvarakṛṣṇena caitad āryābhiḥ
saṃkṣiptam āryamatinā samyag-vijñāya siddhāntam //71//

Through guru-disciple transmission,
it was rendered into verse by Īśvarakṛṣṇa,
who compiled this with noble thoughts,
arguing the case for correct knowledge.

śiṣya, (m.) student
paramparayā, (f. ins. sg.) through transmission
(*śiṣya-paramparayā,* f. ins. sg., through the guru-disciple transmission)
āgatam, (n. nom. sg., p. pass. participle; from *ā* + √*gam,* going) arrived
īśvarakṛṣṇena, (m. ins. sg.) by Īśvarakṛṣṇa
ca, and
etad, (n. nom. sg.) this
āryābhis, (f. ins. pl.)
saṃkṣiptam, (m. nom. sg.,) rendered
ārya, (m.) noble
matinā, (m. ins. sg.) with mind, thought
(*ārya-matinā,* m. ins. sg., with noble thoughts)
samyak, (n.) perfect, correct
vijñāya, (n. dat. sg.) for knowledge
(*samyak-vijñāya,* n. dat. sg., for correct knowledge)
siddhāntam, (m. nom. sg.) philosophy, treatise

सप्तत्यां किल येऽर्थास्तेऽर्थाः कृत्स्नस्य षष्टितन्त्रस्य ।
आख्यायिकाविरहिताः परवादविवर्जिताश्चापि ॥७२॥

saptatyāṃ kila ye'rthāste'rthāḥ kṛtsnasya ṣaṣṭi-tantrasya
ākhyāyikā-virhitāḥ paravāda-vivarjitāś cāpi //72//

Verily, in these 70 verses are contained
all the purposes found in the complete 60-fold philosophy,

though the illustrative stories are not told,
nor the objections of others.

saptatyām, (f. loc. sg.) in seventy
kila, (ind.) verily
ye, (m. nom. pl.) those which
arthās, (m. nom. pl.) purposes, topics
te, (m. nom. pl.) those
arthās, (m. nom. pl.) purposes, topics
kṛtsnasya, (n. gen. sg.) of the complete
ṣaṣṭi-tantrasya, (n. gen. sg.) of the *Ṣaṣṭi Tantra*
ākhyāyikās, (m. nom. pl.) illustrative stories
virahitās, (m. nom. pl.) excluding, removing
paravāda, (m.) objections, the talk of others
vivarjitās, (m. nom. pl.) abandoning, excluding
(*paravāda-vivarjitās,* m. nom. pl., excluding the objections of others)
ca, and.
api, even.

तस्मात्समासदृष्टं शास्त्रमिदं नार्थतश्च परिहीनम् ।
तन्त्रस्य च बृहन्मूर्तेर्दर्पणसंक्रान्तमिव बिम्बम् ॥७३॥

tasmāt samāsa-adṛṣṭaṃ śāstram idaṃ nārthaś ca parihīnam
tantrasya ca bṛhan-mūrter darpaṇa-saṃkrāntam iva bimbam //73//

Therefore, this summary *śāstra* leaves out nothing.
The vast form of philosophy is here,
like the reflection of the moon in a mirror.

tasmāt, (m. abl. sg.) therefore
samāsa, (m.) thrown together
ādṛṣṭam, (n. nom. sg., p. pass. participle) direct examination, overview
(*samāsa-adṛṣṭam,* n. nom. sg., summary)
śāstram, (n. nom. sg.)
idam, (n. nom. sg.) this
na, not
arthatas, (adv.) in content, in truth
ca, and
parihīnam, (n. nom. sg.) deficient
tantrasya, (n. gen. sg.) of the Tantra
ca, and
bṛhat, (f.) vast, great

mūrtes, (f. gen. sg.) of form
(*bṛhat-mūrtes,* f. gen. sg., vast form)
darpaṇa, (m.) a mirror
saṃkrāntam, (n. nom. sg., p. pass. participle; from *sam* + √*kram,* stepping) reflected
(*darpaṇa-saṃkrāntam,* n. nom. sg., reflected in a mirror)
iva, like
bimbam, (m. acc. sg.) the moon, an image

Bibliography

Primary Sources

GBh *Gauḍapādabhāṣya*. 1972. *Sāṃkhyakārikā of Īśvarakṛṣṇa with the commentary of Gauḍapāda*. Trans. T. G. Mainkar. Poona: the Oriental Book Agency.

PYS *Pātañjalayogaśāstra*. Kāśinātha Śāstrī Āgāśe, ed. *Vācaspatimiśraviracitaṭīkā saṃvalitavyāsabhāṣyasametāni pātañjalayogasūtrāṇi, tathā bhojadevaviracitarājamārtaṇḍābhidhavṛttisametāni pātañjalayogasūtrāṇi. sūtrapāṭhasūtravarṇānukramasūcībhyāṃ ca sanāthīkṛtāni*. Ānandāśrama Sanskrit Series, no. 47. Pune: Ānandāśramamudraṇālaye, 1904.

SK *Sāṃkhyakārikā*. 1979. Sanskrit and English translation. In G. J. Larson, *Classical Sāṃkhya*. Delhi: Motilal Banarsidass (2nd revised ed.; 1st ed., 1969), Appendix B.

SS *Suvarṇasaptati*. 1932. *The Sāṃkhya Karikā Studied in Light of its Chinese Version*. Trans. M. Takakusu, Madras: The Diocesan Press.

TV *Tattvavaiśāradī*. 1904. *The Yoga-sūtra with Three Commentaries: Vyāsa, Vācaspatimiśra and Bhojadeva*. Kashinath Shastri Agashe (Ed.). Pune: Ananda Ashram Press.

YD *Yuktidīpikā*. 1990–1992. Two volumes. Trans. Dr. Shiv Kumar and Dr. D. N. Bhargava. Delhi.

Yuktidīpikā. 1998. *The most significant commentary on the* Sāṃkhyakārikā. Critically edited by A. Wezler and S. Motegi. Stuttgart: Franz Steiner Verlag.

Secondary and Translated Sources

Amritchandra, Shri Suri. 2012. *Purushartha Siddhyupaya: Realization of the Pure Self*. Vijay K. Jain, translated by Dehradun: Vikalp Printers.

Āraṇya, Swāmī Hariharānanda. 2000. *Yoga Philosophy of Patañjali with Bhāsvatī*, translated by P. N. Mukerji. Kolkata: Calcutta University Press.

Āraṇya, Swāmī Hariharānanda. 2001. *A Unique Travelogue. An Allegorical Exploration of Spirituality and Yoga*, translated by S. Guha. Madhupur: Kāpil Math.

Āraṇya, Swāmī Hariharānanda. 2003. *Progressive and Practical Sāṃkhya-Yoga*, edited by A. Chatterjee. Madhupur: Kāpil Math.

Āraṇya, Swāmī Hariharānanda. 2005. *Sāṃkhya Across the Millenniums*, edited by Adinath Chatterjee. Madhupur: Kāpil Math.

Āraṇya, Swāmī Hariharānanda. 2008. *The Doctrine of Karma (Karmatattva). A Philosophical and Scientific Analysis of the Theory of Karma*, translated by I. Guptā. Madhupur: Kāpil Math.

Apte, Prin. Vaman Shivaram. 1912. *The Practical Sanskrit-English Dictionary*, revised edition. Kyoto, Japan: Rinsen Book Company, 1998.

Bakhtin, Mikhail M. 1968. *Rabelais and His World*, translated by Hélène Iswolsky. Cambridge, MA: MIT Press.

Ballantyne, James R., translator. 1885. *The Sánkhya Aphorisms of Kapila, with Illustrative Extracts fromthe Commentaries*. 3rd ed. London: Trübner & Co.

Benedict, Ruth Fulton. 1934. *Patterns of Culture*. New York: Houghton Mifflin Company.

Bhāratī, Swāmī Veda, translator. 2001. *Yoga Sūtras of Patañjali with the Exposition of Vyāsa: Translation and Commentary*, Vol. 2: *Sādhana-Pāda*. Delhi: Motilal Banarsidass.

Bhattacharyya, K. C. 1956. *Studies in Philosophy*. Calcutta: Progressive Publishers.

Bodhi, Bhikku, editor. 2005. *In the Buddha's Words: An Anthology of Discourses from the Pāli Canon*. Somerville, MA: Wisdom Publications.

Braun, Whitny. 2008. "*Sallekhana*: The Ethicality and Legality of Religious Suicide by Starvation in the Jain Religious Community." *Medicine and Law* 27(4): 913–924.

Brockington, John. 2003. "Yoga in the *Mahābhārata*," in Ian Whicher and David Carpenter, eds. *Yoga: The Indian Tradition*. London: Routledge-Curzon, 13–24.

Bronkhorst, Johannes. 1997. "Sāṃkhya in the Abhidharmakośa Bhāṣya." *Journal of Indian Philosophy* 25: 393–400.

Bryant, Edwin F. 2014. "Agency in Sāṃkhya and Yoga: The Unchangeability of the Eternal," in ed. Matthew R. Dasti and Edwin F. Bryant, *Free Will, Agency, and Selfhood in Indian Philosophy* (16–41). New York: Oxford University Press.

Burke, B. David. 1988. "Transcendence in Classical Sāṃkhya," *Philosophy East and West* 38(1): 19–29.

Burley, Mikel. 2007. *Classical Sāṃkhya and Yoga: An Indian Metaphysics of Experience*. New York: Routledge.

Chapple, Christopher, editor. 1982. *Sāṃkhya-Yoga: Proceedings of the IASWR Conference, 1981*. Stony Brook, NY: IASWR, 1982.

Chapple, Christopher Key. 2008. *Yoga and the Luminous: Patañjali's Spiritual Path to Freedom*. Albany, NY: SUNY Press.

Chatterjea, T. 2003. *Knowledge and Freedom in Indian Philosophy*. Lanham, MD: Lexington Books.

Colebrooke, Henry Thomas, translator. 1837. *The Sánkhya Káriká, or Memorial Verses on the Sánkhya Philosophy, by Íswara Krishna*, trans.; *also the Bháshya or Commentary of Gaurapáda* [*sic*], translated by Horace Hayman Wilson. London: Valpy.

Collins, Alfred. 1976. "The Origins of the Brahman-King Relationship in Indian Social Thought." PhD dissertation, University of Texas at Austin.

Collins, Alfred. 2000. "Dancing with Prakṛti: The Sāṃkhyan Goddess as *pativrata* and *guru*," in ed. Alf Hiltebeitel and Kathleen M. Erndl, *Is the Goddess a Feminist? The Politics of South Asian Goddesses*. New York: New York University Press.

Collins, Alfred. 2006. "Dharmamegha Samādhi and the Two Sides of Kaivalya: Toward a Yogic Theory of Culture," in ed. C. Chapple, *Yoga and Ecology: Dharma for the Earth*. Hampden, VA: Deepak Heritage Books.

Crangle, Edward Fitzpatrick. 1994. *The Origin and Development of Early Indian Contemplative Practices*. Wiesbaden: Harrassowitz.

Daniel, E. Valentine. 1984. *Fluid Signs: Being a Person the Tamil Way*. Berkeley: University of California Press.

Daniel, Sheryl B. 1983. "The Tool-box Approach of the Tamil to the Issues of Moral Responsibility and Human Destiny," in ed. Charles F. Keyes and E. Valentine Daniel, *Karma: An Anthropological Inquiry*, 27–62. Berkeley: University of California Press.

Davies, John. 1881. *Hindū Philosophy. The Sānkhya Kārikā of Īśwara Kṛishṇa: An Exposition of the System of Kapila*. London: Trübner & Co.

Davis, Marvin Gene. 1976. "The Politics of Family Life in Rural West Bengal." *Ethnology* 15: 189–200.

Deutsch, Eliot. 1989. "Knowledge and the Tradition Text in Indian Philosophy," in ed. G. J. Larson and E. Deutsch, *Interpreting across Boundaries: New Essays in Comparative Philosophy*. Delhi: Motilal Banarsidass, 165–173.

Feuerstein, Georg. 1980. *The Philosophy of Classical Yoga*. Manchester: Manchester University Press.

Fitzgerald, James. 2015. "Saving Mokṣadhamra" in Epic "Mokṣadhamra." *International Journal of Hindu Studies* 19(1–2): 97–137.

Frauwallner, E. 1973. *History of Indian Philosophy*, Vol. 1. Delhi: Motilal Banarsidass.

Ganeri, Jonardon, editor 2002. *The Collected Essays of Bimal Krishna Matilal: Ethics and Epics*. Delhi: Oxford University Press.

Richard Garbe. 1894. *Die Sâṃkhya-Philosophie. Eine Darstellung des indischen Rationalismus nach den Quellen*. Leipzig: Haessel.

Harzer, Edeltraud. 2006. *The Yuktidīpikā. A Reconstruction of Sāṅkhya Methods of Knowing*. Aachen: Shaker Verlag.

Honda, M. 1977. "Karma-yoni." *Journal of Indian and Buddhist Studies* 26(1): 506–511.

Hulin, Michel. 1978. *Le Principe de l'Ego Dans la Pensee Indienne Classique; la Notion d'Ahamkara*. Paris: College de France Institut de Civilisation Indienne. Seri In-8e, Fascicule 44.

Hume, Robert Ernest Hume. 1931. *The Thirteen Principal Upanisads*. Oxford: Oxford University Press.

Irigaray, Luce. 2008. *Sharing the World*. New York: Continuum.

Inden, Ronald. 1990. *Imagining India*. Oxford: Basil Blackwell.

Jacobsen, Knut A. 2006. "What Similes in Sāṃkhya Do: A Comparison of the Similes in the Sāṃkhya Texts in the Mahābhārata, the Sāṃkhyakārikā and the Sāṃkhyasūtra." *Journal of Indian Philosophy* 34(6): 587–605.

Jacobsen, Knut A. 2005. "In Kapila's Cave: A Sāṁkhya-Yoga Renaissance in Bengal," in ed. Knut A. Jacobsen, *Theory and Practice of Yoga: Essays in Honour of Gerald James Larson*. Leiden: Brill, 333–349.

Jacobsen, Knut A. 2018. *Yoga in Modern Hinduism: Hariharānanda Āraṇya and Sāṁkhyayoga*, London & New York: Routledge.

Jakubczak, Marzenna. 2012. "Why Didn't Siddhartha Gautama Become a Sāṃkhya Philosopher, After All?" in ed. Irina Kuznetsova, Ganeri Jonardon, and Chakravarthi Ram-Prasad, *Hindu and Buddhist Ideas in Dialogue: Self and No-Self*. Farnham, UK: Ashgate. 29–45.

Jhâ, Gangânâtha, translator. 1896. *Tattva-Kaumudî (Sânkhya) of Vâchaspati Miśra*. Bombay: Tookaram Tatya.

Johnston, E. H., translator. 1972. *Aśvaghosa's Buddhacarita*. A complete Sanskrit text supplemented by the Tibetan version and Chinese translation, Delhi: Motilal Banarsidass (reprint of the 1936 Lahore edition).

Kakar, Sudhir. 2014. "A Jain Tradition of Liberating the Soul by Fasting Oneself" in *Death and Dying*. London: Penguin.

Kelsang, Gyatso. 1995. *The Bodhisattva Vow: A Practical Guide to Helping Others*. Ulverston: Tharpa Publications.

Kent, S. A. 1982. "Early Sāṃkhya in the *Buddhacarita*," *Philosophy East and West* 32: 259–278.

Kimball, James. 2016. "The Relationship between the "*bhāvas*" and the "*pratyayasarga*" in Classical Sāṃkhya." *Journal of Indian Philosophy* 44(3): 537–555.

Kimball, James. 2013. "The Soteriological Role of the *ṛṣi* Kapila, According to the *Yuktidīpikā*." *Journal of Indian Philosophy* 41(6): 603–614.

Krishna, D. 1996. "Is Īśvarakṛṣṇa's *Sāṁkhya-Kārikā* Really Sāṁkhyan?" in *Indian Philosophy. A Counter Perspective*. New Delhi: Oxford University Press. 144–155.

Kumar, Shiv, and D. N. Bhargava, translators. 1992. *Yuktidīpikā*, Vol. 2. Delhi: Eastern Book Linkers.

Lamb, Sarah. 2000. *White Sarees and Sweet Mangoes; Aging, Gender, and Body in North India*. Berkeley, Los Angeles, & London: University of California Press.

Larson, Gerald James. 1979. *Classical Sāṃkhya: An Interpretation of its History and Meaning*. Delhi: Motilal Banarsidass.

Larson, Gerald James. 2018. *Classical Yoga Philosophy and the Legacy of Sāṃkhya*. Delhi: Motilal Banarsidass.

Larson, Gerald James, and Bhattacharya, R. S. 1987. *Sāṃkhya: A Dualist Tradition in Indian Philosophy, Encyclopedia of Indian Philosophies*. Vol. 4. Delhi: Motilal Banarsidass.

Larson, Gerald James. 1983. "An Eccentric Ghost in the Machine: Formal and Quantitative Aspects of the Sāṃkhya-Yoga Dualism," in ed. Christopher Chapple, *Sāṃkhya-Yoga: Proceedings of the IASWR Conference, 1981*. Stony Brook, NY: The Institute for Advanced Studies of World Relgions. 1–30.

Larson, Gerald. James. 1989. "An Old Problem Revisited: The Relation Between Sāṁkhya, Yoga and Buddhism." *Studien zur Indologie und Iranistik* 15: 129–146.

Larson, Gerald. James. 1999. "Classical Yoga as Neo-Sāṃkhya," in *Asiatische Studien / études Asiatiques* 52 (Proceedings of the Conference on Sāṃkhya, Lausanne 5–8.11.1998), 723–732.

Larson, Gerald. James. 2000. "The 'Tradition Text' in Indian Philosophy for Doing History of Philosophy in India," in *The Aestethic Turn: Reading Eliot Deutsch on Comparative Philosophy*, ed. R. T. Ames. Peru, IL: Carus Publishing Company. 59–69.

Maas, Philip A. 2013. "A Concise Historiography of Classical Yoga Philosophy," in ed. Eli Franco, *Periodization and Historiography of Indian Philosophy*. De Nobili Series, 53–90. Vienna: Institute für Südasien-, Tibet- und Buddhismuskunde der Universität Wien.

Maas, Philip A. 2017. "From Theory to Poetry: The Reuse of Patañjali's *Yogaśāstra* in Māgha's *Śiśupālavadha*," in ed. Elisa Freschi and Philipp

A. Maas, *Adaptive Reuse: Aspects of Creativity in South Asian Cultural History*. Abhandlungen für di Kunde des Morgenlandes 101. Wiesbaden: Harrassowitz. 29–62.

Macdonnell, Arthur A. 1900. *A History of Sanskrit Literature*. London: Heinemann.

Maharaj, Ayon 2013. "Yogic Mindfulness: Hariharānanda Āraṇya's Quasi-Buddhistic Interpretation of *Smṛti* in Patañjali's *Yogasūtra* I.20." *Journal of Indian Philosophy* 41: 57–78.

Mahāthera, P. V. 1962. *Buddhist Meditation in Theory and Practice: A General Exposition According to the Pāli Canon of the Therevāda School*. Colombo: M. D. Gunasena.

Mainkar, T. G., translator. 1972. *Sāṁkhyakārikā of Īśvarakṛṣṇa, with the Commentary of Gauḍapāda*. 2nd ed. Poona: Oriental Book Agency.

Malinar, Angelika. 2017. "Narrating Sāṃkhya Philosophy: Bhīṣma, Janaka and Pañcaśikha at Mahābhārata 12.211–212. *Journal of Indian Philosophy* 45(4): 609–649.

Marriott, McKim. 1955. "Little Communities in an Indigenous Civilization," in ed. Marriott McKim, *Village India*. Chicago: University of Chicago Press. 171–222.

Marriott, McKim. 1966. "The Feast of Love," in ed. Milton B. Singer, *Krishna: Myths, Rites, and Attitudes*. Honolulu: East–West Press. 200–212, 229–231. Also available in Diane P. Mines and Sarah Lamb, editors. 2002. *Everyday Life in South Asia*. Bloomington: Indiana University Press. 249–260.

Marriott, McKim. 1972. *Kishan Garhi Village: A Generation of Change*. New York: The State Education Department, Foreign Area Materials Center.

Marriott, McKim. 1990. *India through Hindu Categories*. New Delhi: Sage Publications. Also available in *Contributions to Indian Studies* 23(1): 1987.

Marriott, McKim. 1955. *Village India*. Chicago: University of Chicago Press.

Marriott, McKim. 1989. "Constructing an Indian Ethnosociology." *Contributions to Indian Sociology* 23(1): 1–39.

Mayer, Albert, with the assistance of McKim Marriott and Richard L. Park. 1958. Pilot Project *India: The Story of Rural Development at Etawah, Uttar Pradesh*. Berkeley & Los Angeles: University of California Press.

Mines, Diane Paull. 1990. "Hindu Periods of Death 'Impurity,'" in ed. Marriott McKim, *India through Hindu Categories*. New Delhi: Sage Publications. 103–130.

Mines, Diane Paull. 2005. *Fierce Gods*. Bloomington: University of Indiana Press.

Monier-Williams, Sir Monier. 1899. *A Sanskrit-English Dictionary*. Oxford: Oxford University Press.

Motegi, S. 1978–1980. "Research on the Yuktidīpikā I-III." *Journal of Indian and Buddhist Studies* 28(2): 904–907.

Ñāṇamoli, Bhikkhu, and Bhikkhu Bodhi, translators. 1995. *The Middle Length Discourses of the Buddha: A New Translation of the Majjhima Nikāya*. Boston: Wisdom Publications.

Oberhammer, G. 1977. *Strukturen Yogischer Meditation*. Vienna: Verlag der Österreichischen Akademie der Wissenschaften.

Odorisio, David M. 2021. *Merton & Hinduism: The Yoga of the Heart*. Louisville, KY: Fons Vitae.

Olivelle, Patrick, translator. 2008. *Life of the Buddha by Aśvaghoṣa*. New York: New York University Press.

Ortega y Gasset, José. 1914 [1961]. *Meditations on Quixote* (*Meditaciones del Quijote*), translated by Evelyn Rugg and Diego Marin, Introduction by Julián Marías. New York: W. W. Norton.

Ortega y Gasset, José. 1932. *Obras Completas*, Vols. I–XI. Madrid: Revista de Occidente, 1965.

Osto, Douglas. 2018. "No-Self in Sāṁkhya: A Comparative Look at Classical Sāṁkhya and Theravāda Buddhism." *Philosophy East and West* 68(1): 201–222.

Parrott, Rodney J. 1985. "The Experience Called 'Reason' in Classical Sāṃkhya." *Journal of Indian Philosophy* 13(3): 235–264.

Paturi, Nagaraj. 2014. "Pan-Indian 'Spring Festival of Love.'" https://groups.yahoo.com/neo/groups/abhinavagupta/conversations/messages/7514

Pfleuger, Lloyd. 2003. "Dueling with Dualism: Revisioning the Paradox of Puruṣsa and Prakṛti," in ed. Ian Whicher and David Carpenter, *Yoga: The Indian Tradition*. London & New York: Routledge Curzon.

Podgorski, Frank R. 1984. *Ego: Revealer-Concealer, A Key to Yoga*. Lanham, MD: University Press of America.

Radhakrishnan, Sarvepalli, translator. 1953. *The Principal Upaniṣads*. London: George Allen & Unwin.

Raheja, Gloria Goodwin. 1988. *The Poison in the Gift: Ritual, Prestation, and the Dominant Caste in a North Indian Village*. Chicago: University of Chicago Press.

Ruzsa, Ferenc. 2019. "Sāṁkhya: Dualism without Substances," in ed. Joerg Tuske, *Indian Epistemology and Metaphysics*. New York: Bloomsbury Academic. 153–181.

Sen Gupta, Anima. 1969. *Classical Samkhya: A Critical Study*. Lucknow: Monoranjan Sen Gour Ashram.

Schterbatsky, Th. 1923. *The Central Conception of Buddhism and the Meaning of the Word "Dharma."* London: Royal Asiatic Society.

Sharma, Har Dutt, translator. 1933. *The Sāṁkhya-Kārikā: Iśvara Kṛṣṇa's Memorable Verses on Sāṁkhya Philosophy with the Commentary of Gauḍapādācārya*. Poona: Oriental Book Agency.

Shevchenko, Dmitry. 2017. "Natural Liberation in the *Sāṃkhyakārikā* and its Commentaries." *Journal of Indian Philosophy* 45(5): 863–892.

Shulman, David. 2001. *The Wisdom of Poets: Studies in Tamil, Telugu, and Sanskrit*. New Delhi: Oxford University Press.

Shulman, David. 2012. *More than Real: A History of the Imagination in South India*. Chicago: University of Chicago Press.

Singh, Bhagwan B. 1997. *Yoga Siddhi: Yoga Sutras of Patanjali with Commentary*. Las Vegas, NV: International Institute of American and Indian Studies.

Smith, Brian K. 1994. *Classifying the Universe: The Ancient Indian Varna System and the Origin of Caste*. New York: Oxford University Press.

Smith, Brian K. 1998. *Reflections on Resemblance, Ritual and Religion*. Delhi: Motilal Banarsidass.

Smith, Frederick. 2012. *The Self Possessed: Deity and Spirit Possession in South Asian Literature and Civilization*. New York: Columbia University Press.

Srinivas, M. N. 1998. *Village, Caste, Gender and Method*. Delhi: Oxford University Press.

Trawick, Margaret. 2017. *Death, Beauty, Struggle: Untouchable Women Create the World*. Philadelphia: University of Pennsylvania Press.

Turner, Victor. 1974. *Dramas, Fields and Metaphors*. Ithaca, NY: Cornell University Press.

Turner, Victor. 1967. *The Forest of Symbols*. Ithaca, NY: Cornell University Press.

Turner, Victor. 1969. *The Ritual Process*. Ithaca, NY: Cornell University Press.

van Binsbergen, Wim M. J. 2009–2010. "Before the Pre-Socratics." *Quest: An African Journal of Philosophy /Revue Africaine de Philosophie* 23–24(1–2).

van Buitenen, Johannes Adrianus Bernardus. 1956. "Studies in Sāṃkhya I." *Journal of the American Oriental Society* 6(3): 153–157.

van Buitenen, Johannes Adrianus Bernardus. 1957. "Studies in Sāṃkhya II." *Journal of the American Oriental Society* 7(1): 15–25.

van Buitenen, Johannes Adrianus Bernardus. 1957. "Studies in Sāṃkhya III." *Journal of the American Oriental Society* 7(2): 88–107.

van Buitenen, Johannes Adrianus Bernardus, translator. 1962. *The Maitrāyaṇīya Upaniṣad: A Critical Essay, with Text, Translation and Commentary*. Gravenhage: Mouton & Co.

von Glasenapp, Helmuth. 1942. *The Doctrine of Karman in Jain Philosophy*. Varanasi: Parshvanath Research Institute.

Wadley, Susan Snow. 1975. *Shakti: Power in the Conceptual Structure of Karimpur Religion*. Chicago, Illinois, Department of Anthropology, University of Chicago.

Weerasinghe, S. G. M. 1993. *The Sāṅkhya Philosophy: A Critical Evaluation of Its Origins and Development*. Delhi: Sri Satguru.

Wezler, Albrecht. 2001. "Zu der Frage des Strebens nach äuβerster Kürze in den Śrautasūtras." *Zeitschrift der Deutschen Morgenländischen Gesellschaft* 151: 351–366.

Wezler, Albrecht, and Shujun Motegi, editors. 1998. *Yuktidīpikā: The Most Significant Commentary on the Sāṃkhyakārikā*, Vol. 1. Stuttgart: Steiner.

Whicher, Ian. 1998. *The Integrity of the Yoga Darśana: A Reconsideration of Classical Yoga* Albany, NY: SUNY Press.

Whicher, Ian. 2003. "The Integration of Spirit (*Puruṣa*) and Matter (*Prakṛti*) in the *Yoga Sūtra*," in ed. Ian Whicher and David Carpenter, *Yoga: The Indian Tradition*. London & New York: Routledge Curzon.

Whicher, Ian, and David Carpenter, eds. 2003. *Yoga: The Indian Tradition*. London & New York: Routledge Curzon.

Yamaguchi, E. 1967. A Consideration to 'Pratyaya-Sarga. *JIBSt* 30, 1967, 972–979. www.jstage.jst.go.jp/article/ibk1952/15/2/15_2_979/_pdf/-char/ja

Contributors

Geoff Ashton is Professor of Philosophy at the University of San Francisco.

Mikel Burley is Associate Professor of Religion and Philosophy at the University of Leeds.

Christopher Key Chapple is Doshi Professor of Indic and Comparative Theology at Loyola Marymount University.

Alfred Collins was an independent scholar and psychotherapist in Fairbanks, Alaska.

Marzenna Jakubczak is Professor of Philosophy at the Jagiellonian University in Krakow, Poland.

Ana Laura Funes Maderey is Professor of Philosophy at Fairfield University.

McKim Marriott is Emeritus Professor of Anthropology at the University of Chicago.

Srivatsa Ramaswami taught Yoga teacher trainings for nearly twenty years at Loyola Marymount University.

Robert Zabel is a graduate student at the University of Chicago.

Index

Abhinavagupta, 200–202
abhiniveśa, 105, 116
abhivyakta, 48, 50
adhyātma, 117
adhyāya, 55, 58
Advaita Vedānta, 35, 52, 140
ahaṃkāra, 6–7, 11, 15–17, 27–28, 39, 47, 53, 57
artha, 33, 163, 182, 189, 191, 195
 See also Puruṣartha, 189
Aiśvarya, 53, 55, 58, 65, 97, 104, 193–195, 198, 202
 See also anaiśvarya, 57, 58, 104, 194
Andhatāmiśra, 56–58, 106, 116
aniruddha, 125–126
apāna, 47–51, 58–59, 59, 65–67, 72–73
aparokṣa, 116
Āraṇya, Dharmamegha, 129, 211
Āraṇya, Hariharānanda, 9, 127, 129
Arjuna, 6, 165, 170
aśakti, 3, 57, 58, 106, 117
asana, 128
Ascetic (practitioner), 125, 127, 133, 187–188
 Asceticism (practices of), 44–45, 126, 190
 See also Brahmacārin, 44
 See also Renounce, 104, 127
 See also Sannyāsin/Saṃnyāsin, 116, 123, 127–130, 136, 140
Aśoka, King/Emperor, 127
Aṣṭāṅga Yoga, 128, 144
āsuri, 22, 126
ātman, 52, 83, 116, 117, 135, 138
 anātman, 135, 137, 141
avidyā, 53–54, 56, 105, 116, 132
 See also *ajñāna*, 4, 56, 58, 104, 193
avyakta, 20, 38, 63, 78, 95, 102, 144, 162, 189, 192, 195, 201–202, 204, 206, 209
 See also unmanifest, 5–7, 11–13, 26, 85, 94–96
Ayurveda, 163

Bengali, 123–129, 133, 142, 156, 163
 See also Bengal (country), 9, 155, 180
Bhagavad Gītā, 4–6, 163, 165, 170, 176, 182
Bhagavata Purāṇa, 153
bhakti, 191
 See also devotion, 169, 171
Bhattacharyya, K. C., 42–44, 59–60, 70

bhāva, 7–8, 18–20, 29, 41–42, 52–59, 64, 67, 69, 92–113, 192–193, 195
Bhojarāja, 126
bhukti, 187, 206–207
Britain, 149
British colonialism, 151, 158
Body-mind complex, 2, 38, 116, 119, 187, 206
Brahmā, 19, 190, 194, 201
Brahman, 7, 66, 118, 154, 167, 170, 174, 177, 194
Brahmavihāra, 109
buddhi, 6, 15–17, 19, 27–29, 39, 47, 53, 55, 68–71, 81, 83, 88, 93, 96, 98–99, 100, 102, 190, 192, 196, 199, 201
Buddhism, 3, 7, 77, 134–147, 188–189
Buddhist (literature), 7, 127, 128, 135
Buddhist (practice), 2, 9, 71, 101, 124, 203

Caste, 127, 149, 151, 151–158, 163–167, 170–186
citta, 115–116, 132
Classical Sāṃkhya, 41, 43, 44, 52, 125, 130–133, 137, 140, 144
Compresence, 35–39, 96
See also *saṃyoga*, 5, 6, 8, 14, 25, 26, 30, 83, 85

darśana, 8, 88, 111, 116, 130, 134, 139
Darwinism, 133–134
Death, ix, 14, 20, 56, 96, 129, 143, 197–199, 203–204, 207–209
Demon, 190, 195–199, 205, 207, 209
Demoness, 152, 162, 204
Desire, 31, 34, 42–46, 48, 60, 62, 81, 83, 105–106, 138, 143, 187, 189, 195, 199
Desire for liberation/release, 45, 60, 64, 190, 208
Desire to know, 42, 61, 63–67
Deva, 7
Durgā and Lakṣmī, 169
Gangā Devī, 153, 159, 169
Śiva/Shiva, 153, 169, 197, 198, 204, 206, 210
dharma, 13, 15–16, 18, 21, 46, 53, 55, 58, 64–65, 95, 97, 103–104, 134–135, 173, 176, 182, 190
adharma, 56, 193, 195, 198
dhvani, 196, 199–204, 207
dhyāna, 46, 141, 144, 192, 201
Buddhist Meditation (general), 147, 203
Meditation, 2, 45, 67, 80, 82, 85, 87–89, 107–108, 120, 132, 140, 187
Vipassanā Meditation, 144
doṣa, 154, 161
pitta, kapha, vata (*tridoṣa*), 178
Dualism, 35, 37–38, 131
dveṣa, 105, 106, 116

Ego, 2–8, 15, 26–29, 34–36, 40, 52, 66, 69, 96–98, 100, 103, 109, 119, 138–139, 152, 160–163, 190, 198, 208
Endogamy, 153, 174

Freud, Sigmund, 189, 207–208

Ganges (river), 157–158
gopī, 191–192, 106
grahaṇa (grasp), 47
Green Revolution, 184

Gauḍapāda, 1, 80, 82, 89, 94, 97–98, 105, 112
guṇa, 4–8, 13–18, 20, 29, 38, 61, 62, 83, 86, 87, 92, 93, 94–101, 109, 112, 119, 132, 144, 204
rajas, 6–7, 13, 15, 19, 53, 57, 62–63, 65, 95, 99, 111–112, 132, 161, 165, 171, 188, 192–193, 195, 198, 206, 210n19
sattva, 6–7, 13, 19, 55, 62, 65–66, 81, 95, 99, 103, 111, 112, 120, 132, 161, 163, 165, 171, 183, 186, 192–194, 198, 202, 206
tamas, 6–7, 12, 15, 18, 19, 39, 56, 57, 62, 63, 65, 95, 97, 99, 103, 104, 105, 106, 111, 112, 116, 132, 161, 165, 171, 188, 192, 193, 195, 198, 206, 210
triguṇa, 27, 150, 160, 161, 165, 166, 188, 192, 193, 196

Haṭhayoga, 67, 73, 125–126
Heidegger, Martin, ix, 2, 26, 34, 36
Himalayas, 159, 172
Hinduism
Classical, 204
Deity, 170
Modern, 125–128
Orthodox, 134
Philosophy, 141–142, 162, 164, 166–167, 173–178, 187–189, 206–207
Priests, 154
Villagers, 149–150, 152, 157, 165
Hindu-Muslim, 149, 152, 175, 177, 184
Holi/Holī, 152–153, 159, 162, 169, 171, 183, 196, 204–207
Husserl, Edmund, ix, 28–29, 34, 40

Identity, 3, 88, 100, 111, 131, 142, 173, 203
Non-identity, 82, 88
Self-identity, 130
Impurity, 194, 215
indriya, 15–16, 39, 56, 57, 59, 69, 72, 98, 118
See also Sense Organ, 11, 15–16, 96, 103, 106, 216
Īśvara (Lord, God), 2
Īśvarakṛṣṇa, 5, 11, 22, 30, 28, 53, 74, 93–146 passim, 165–166, 209–210

Jain/Jaina, 2, 128, 143
Tradition, 7, 8, 102
jñāna, 4, 21, 42, 53, 55, 65, 86, 97, 103–104, 111, 119, 187–188, 192–193, 200, 210
vijñāna, 42, 46, 78–79, 85–86, 192
Jung, Carl, ix, 207

kaivalya, 4, 14, 21, 28, 32, 35, 37, 81, 88, 96, 116–118, 136, 187, 196, 198
Kant, Immanuel, 8, 28, 29, 34, 139
Kāpil Maṭh, 123 - 134, 140, 142, 145
Kapila, 44, 60, 79
karma, 7, 28
karmayoni, 41, 46, 59, 61, 62
karmendriya, 98, 163, 216
kleśa, 105, 116
kliṣṭa/akliṣṭa, 139
Kolkata, 127, 145, 180
Krishna/Kṛṣṇa, 6, 153, 165, 169, 191–192, 205

Larson, Gerald C., ix, x, 1, 2, 4, 8, 25–28, 35, 36, 38, 71n4, 82, 83, 88, 98, 100, 101, 124, 144n22,

Larson, Gerald C. *(continued)* 150, 160, 162, 163, 166, 171, 188, 193, 208, 209, 210n22
liṅga, 13, 30, 100, 101–102, 172, 196, 198
  liṅga-pūrvakaṃ, 11, 101
  tal liṅga, 11, 101, 218
  visuvaliṅgam, 196, 204, 206, 207

Mādhava, 126
mahābhārata, 5, 8, 10, 135, 170, 176
mahābhutā, 16, 28, 159–161
mahat, 12, 17, 20, 29, 101, 216
  mahat-buddhi, 27, 39, 96
manas, 6, 7, 15–17, 27, 39, 47, 53, 57, 69, 71, 99, 162, 216
Merton, Thomas, 111, 113
Mīmāmsā, 8, 202
moha, 56, 105, 116
mokṣa (liberation), 60, 123, 132, 139, 161, 187–188, 207–208
mūlaprakṛti, 11, 25–40, 144, 189, 195, 209, 215
Muslim, 151–157, 169, 172, 175–178, 180

Neoclassical Sāṃkhya, 124, 125, 131, 137, 141
New Delhi, 149, 181, 184
nirvāṇa, 109
niyama (observances), 128
Nyāya, 8, 77

Ortega y Gasset, José, ix, 26, 33–37, 40, 105

Parhil (Padil), 149–155, 160, 163, 165–166, 169–170, 172–174, 180, 183–184
pariṇāma (outward flow of senses), 4, 83, 120, 189–191, 195, 199
parokṣa, 116
Patañjali, 5, 47, 116, 123, 126, 142
  Patañjali *Yogasūtra*, 43, 78–79, 91, 105, 115, 117, 119, 124, 127–128, 144, 208–209
Podgorski, Frank, ix, 2, 3, 110, 111
Pradhāna, 13–14, 17, 20–21, 27, 30, 63, 95, 102, 132, 144, 189, 195, 199, 201, 210
Prakṛti, 1, 3, 7–8, 11–12, 15, 20–21, 27, 33, 38n6, 42, 44, 47, 64, 69, 70, 81–82, 84, 88, 91n34, 100, 107, 110, 111–112, 116–117, 119, 132, 189–190, 192, 196, 198–199, 204, 209–210, 216
  mūlaprakṛti, 11, 25–40, 144, 189, 195, 209, 215
  vyaktaprakṛti, 25–30, 32–33, 36–37, 39
prāṇa, 8, 41–54, 58–71, 72n7, 98, 118
pratiprasava (return to the source), 195, 198–201, 204, 210
pratyaya, 8, 54–56, 58–59, 66–67, 115–119
  pratyayasarga, 53–56, 59, 92n43
Pre-classical Sāṃkhya, 125–126
Psychology, 1, 3, 7, 54, 150
pūjā (worship), 49 135, 164, 165, 169, 171, 172, 198
Purity, 62, 66, 86, 108, 194
  Impurity, 215
Puruṣa, 1, 3, 4–8, 11, 12–14, 16, 17, 20, 21, 25, 26–40, 42, 46, 47, 52, 59, 65, 68–70, 81–86, 88, 90–93, 95, 96, 99, 100, 102, 110–112, 115, 116, 118–120, 132, 137–140, 144, 161, 170, 188–193, 196, 198, 199, 201, 203, 204, 206, 208–212, 215, 216

raga, 193, 57–58, 104–105, 116, 195

rasa (taste), 163, 200, 201, 204
Raja Yoga, 116
Ramāyāṇa, 201
Ṛg Veda, 1, 208

sādhana, 43, 116
Śākyamuni, 136
samāna, 47, 49, 58, 65–68, 221
Sāṃkhya Kārikā, 11, 25, 39, 78, 80–89, 93–94, 108–109, 112, 115, 118, 150, 160, 164–165, 213
Sāṃkhyayoga, 123–145
  Sāṃkhyayogins (practitioners of), 123
saṃsāra, 18, 44, 83, 103, 132, 135, 136
saṃskāra (past conditioning), 4, 21, 39, 52, 119–120, 132
Sanādhya Brahman, 154, 157, 174, 194
Sanskrit, 71, 90n18, 91n28, 125, 128, 133, 137, 142, 144n21, 150, 160, 165, 170–171, 174, 182, 189, 196, 200–201, 204, 207
satkārya, 189, 191, 199, 201, 209
  satkāryavāda, 25, 29, 31, 38, 60, 70, 144
Seer, one who sees, 4–6, 14, 96, 119
Self-realization, 46, 134
Sen Gupta, Anima, 110, 113n3
Siddhārtha Gautama, 137–138, 141
siddhi, 19, 53, 55, 58, 67, 108, 117, 118, 198, 199, 201, 210
Sociology, 150, 206
Suffering, 2–7, 11, 19, 20, 35, 42, 46, 53, 67, 78, 101, 102, 108, 111, 118, 119, 132, 137, 139, 187, 189, 190, 194, 203, 209, 213
Sweeper, 154, 167, 172, 178, 180, 194

tanmātras, 15, 16, 28, 39, 161, 163
Tantra, 198
tapas, 125
tattva, 6, 7 21, 27, 28, 36, 39, 46, 52, 81, 82, 96, 104, 115, 132, 161, 203
tattva-abhyāsa, 4, 78, 80, 86, 87, 88, 100
Theistic, 125, 134
tuṣṭi, 45, 53, 67, 117, 126–127

udāna, 47, 49, 58, 65, 66, 68, 244
Universalism, 131, 134, 135, 143
Upaniṣads, 7
  Bṛhadāraṇyaka Upaniṣad, 82, 90n22
  Chāndogya Upaniṣad, 166
  Maitrī Upaniṣad, 83
  Saṃnyāsa Upaniṣad, 128
  Śvetāśvatara Upaniṣad, 1, 113n2
  Taittirīya Upaniṣad, 52, 118

Vācaspati Miśra, 43, 72, 74, 80, 8xs1, 82, 126
Vaiśeṣika, 8
Vaisnava, 151, 169, 170
Vārṣagaṇya, 126, 130
Vāsana, 189
vāyu
  Breath, vital winds, 16, 67, 41, 50, 53–54, 59, 61, 64, 67, 72–73
  Wind Element, 6, 52
Vedānta (theology), 3, 7, 8, 77, 116, 119, 125, 126, 134, 188
  Advaita Vedānta, 35, 52, 140
Vegetarian, 154, 174, 175, 176
viparyaya, 105
  viparyaya pratyaya, 116
virāga, 43, 53, 55, 65, 97, 103–104, 193, 195

vṛtti, 93, 97, 98, 119
citta-vṛitti, 115, 116
pravṛtti, 30, 33, 37, 40n12, 189–190, 195, 209n7
pravṛtti dharma, 134–135
vyakta /avyakta, 78, 94, 95, 102, 105, 144, 162, 189, 192, 195, 201, 202, 204, 206, 209, 214, 215
Vyāsa (commentator), 80, 84, 199
vyāna, 47, 50, 58, 65, 67

Whicher, Ian, 80, 188, 209, 210

yajna, 135
Ritual (general), 175, 204, 205, 208
Vedic ritual, 11, 108, 214
Yama (restraint), 128
Yogācāra, 130
Yuktidīpikā, 1, 8, 41–47, 52, 54, 59, 61, 64, 71, 86, 90, 110

www.ingramcontent.com/pod-product-compliance
Lightning Source LLC
Chambersburg PA
CBHW030758090425
24824CB00001B/32
* 9 7 8 1 4 3 8 4 9 8 3 6 2 *